12—
:4B

# PRIVATIZATION

## NOMOS

# LX

**NOMOS**

# NOMOS LX

Yearbook of the American Society for Political and Legal Philosophy

# PRIVATIZATION

Edited by

**Jack Knight and Melissa Schwartzberg**

NEW YORK UNIVERSITY PRESS • *New York*

NEW YORK UNIVERSITY PRESS
New York
www.nyupress.org

References to Internet websites (URLs) were accurate at the time of writing.
Neither the author nor New York University Press is responsible for URLs that may
have expired or changed since the manuscript was prepared.

Library of Congress Cataloging-in-Publication Data
Names: Knight, Jack, 1952– editor. | Schwartzberg, Melissa, 1975– editor.
Title: Privatization / edited by Jack Knight and Melissa Schwartzberg.
Description: New York : New York University Press, 2018. | Series: Nomos ; LX |
Includes bibliographical references and index.
Identifiers: LCCN 2018012196 | ISBN 9781479842933 (cl : alk. paper)
Subjects: LCSH: Privatization.
Classification: LCC HD3850 .P7323 2018 | DDC 338.9/25–dc23
LC record available at https://lccn.loc.gov/2018012196

New York University Press books are printed on acid-free paper, and their binding
materials are chosen for strength and durability. We strive to use environmentally
responsible suppliers and materials to the greatest extent possible in publishing
our books.

Manufactured in the United States of America

10 9 8 7 6 5 4 3 2 1

Also available as an ebook

# CONTENTS

## PART II: PRIVATIZATION AND THE STATE

# PREFACE

## JACK KNIGHT AND MELISSA SCHWARTZBERG

This volume of NOMOS—the sixtieth in the series—emerged from papers and commentaries given at the annual meeting of the American Society for Political and Legal Philosophy, held in conjunction with the annual meeting of the Association for American Law Schools in New York, NY, on January 6, 2016. Our topic, "Privatization," was selected by the Society's membership.

The conference consisted of three panels: (1) "Some (Largely) Ignored Problems with Privatization"; (2) "Three Dimensions of Privatization"; and (3) "Is Rule of Law Possible Without Privatization?" This volume includes revised versions of the principal papers delivered at the conference by Debra Satz, Henry Farrell, and Gillian Hadfield and Barry Weingast. It also includes essays that developed from the commentaries on those papers by Eric MacGilvray, Laura Dickinson, Joseph Heath, Alon Harel, and Alex Gourevitch. Alexander Guerrero contributed a valuable commentary on the Hadfield-Weingast paper at the original conference, to which several papers refer. The volume also features solicited papers from Chiara Cordelli, Cécile Fabre, Jessica Flanigan, and Peter Jaworski. We are grateful to all of these authors for their excellent contributions. Thanks also to Samuel Bagg of McGill University for his valuable assistance during the editorial phase of this volume, and to Sam Boren Reast of New York University for his help during the production phase and in compiling the index.

We wish to thank the editors and production team at New York University Press, particularly Ilene Kalish and Maryam Arain. On behalf of the society, we wish to express our gratitude to the Press for its ongoing support both for the series and for the tradition of interdisciplinary scholarship that it represents. We would also like to thank Brown University, Duke University, New York University, and Stanford University for subventions in support of this and future NOMOS volumes.

Finally, we thank the members of the ASPLP council—President James Fleming, Vice-Presidents Stephen Macedo and Michelle Moody Adams, at-large members David Estlund and Deborah Hellman, former presidents Debra Satz and Nancy Rosenblum, and secretary-treasurer Andrew Valls for their guidance.

# CONTRIBUTORS

Chiara Cordelli
*Assistant Professor of Political Science, University of Chicago*

Laura A. Dickinson
*Oswald Symister Colclough Research Professor of Law, George Washington University*

Cécile Fabre
*Professor of Political Philosophy, Oxford University*

Henry Farrell
*Professor of Political Science and International Affairs, George Washington University*

Jessica Flanigan
*Associate Professor of Leadership Studies and Philosophy, Politics, Economics and Law, University of Richmond*

Alex Gourevitch
*Associate Professor of Political Science, Brown University*

Gillian K. Hadfield
*Professor of Law and Professor of Strategic Management, University of Toronto*

Alon Harel
*Phillip and Estelle Mizock Chair in Administrative and Criminal Law, Hebrew University of Jerusalem*

Joseph Heath
*Professor of Philosophy, and Public Policy and Governance, University of Toronto*

Peter Jaworski
*Assistant Teaching Professor of Business Ethics, Georgetown University*

Eric MacGilvray
*Associate Professor of Political Science, Ohio State University*

Debra Satz
*Marta Sutton Weeks Professor of Ethics in Society, Stanford University*

Barry R. Weingast
*Ward C. Krebs Family Professor of Political Science, Stanford University*

# INTRODUCTION

## MELISSA SCHWARTZBERG

This volume presents twelve interventions into debates over privatization: broadly, the transfer of state-provided or state-owned goods and services to the private sector. As we prepared to send the volume to press, President Donald Trump announced a plan to privatize the nation's air traffic controllers. A private, nonprofit corporation, governed by a board composed primarily of representatives of the major airlines, would operate and manage air traffic control, currently under the purview of the Federal Aviation Administration. Supporters of privatization argue that the current system is inefficient and antiquated. Moreover, privatization would remove air traffic control from the congressional budget process, the unpredictability of which supporters claim has hindered progress, including the adoption of valuable new technology. Opponents of privatization complain that it would shift power to the airline industry, replacing ticket taxes with user fees (and thereby privatizing the power to tax), and, further, that privatization is not a solution to the challenge of modernization.

It might seem that the theoretical approaches of a NOMOS volume could shed relatively little light on issues such as who should have responsibility for air traffic control. Yet the lines of inquiry raised in these papers help to clarify what is at stake in such a decision. The papers press us to consider whether we should evaluate the prospect of privatization instrumentally, in terms of the relative quality of outcomes, or whether public or private control reflects some non-instrumental values—equality, accountability, non-coercion—that would be imperiled by erroneous assignment of responsibility for action. In particular, the papers urge us to think beyond efficiency in evaluating decisions to privatize. They also encourage us to reflect upon whether privatization in a given domain will hinder, enable, or transform the development of the state itself: in shifting control from legislatures to private actors, do we weaken or strengthen structures of governance?

The volume is in two parts. The first part takes up the moral implications of privatization. Debra Satz argues that privatization can sometimes alter the structure of governance in ways that worsen inequality and which distort, fragment, and corrupt important public goals. Her emphasis is on instrumental reasons (though she acknowledges that privatization can fail for non-instrumental reasons, as in the case of the privatization of the criminal justice system, which she considers an inherently governmental function). Satz rejects "abstract claims for and against privatization in the overwhelming majority of cases," holding that the degree to which we should worry about inequality and the corruption of public purposes depend upon background details, existing regulations, and the range of available policy alternatives.

While Satz argues that a focus on accountability often falls short of the target, and that inequality and the distortion of public ends generate more significant concerns, scholars such as Laura Dickinson disagree. Dickinson argues that a more expansive conception of accountability, which addresses the structural transformation of governance, includes concerns about distortion and equality. Through examples of security and military privatization, Dickinson maintains that such privatization has enabled the expansion of executive power and the fragmentation and diffusion of governmental authority, threats to accountability with serious consequences for democracy.

Alon Harel challenges the instrumental approach to the assessment of privatization, which evaluates privatization strictly by reference to the agent who is most likely to make the just or correct decision, and to bring about the desired ends. Rather, Harel argues that the identity of the decision-maker, regardless of his or her probability of correctness, matters: he holds that privatization "severs the link" between citizens and decision-making processes, threatening citizens' engagement and shared responsibility. Peter Jaworski disagrees, arguing that institutions have only instrumental value, and must be evaluated—empirically—by reference to their outcomes.

Moreover, Jaworski suggests, the values of equality and fairness (for instance) that critics allege are intrinsic to state ownership are often realized as well, if not better, by privately owned enterprises; theoretical inquiries cannot prove that state-owned enterprises outperform their privately owned rivals on these dimensions.

Chiara Cordelli disputes the conception of privatization as delegation to privately owned enterprises rather than state ownership; rather, she argues that privatization is better understood as the discharging of justice-based, public responsibilities through private rather than public agents. These private agents need not be motivated by the aim of profit; nonprofits also constitute private actors on this model. Like Harel, Cordelli emphasizes the identity of the decision-maker: she holds that only public officials possess the shared institutional orientation that makes common political agency possible. Private actors, however benevolent their motives, impede the state's capacity to realize simultaneously the functions of establishing an *omnilateral* system of rules (to guarantee equal freedom), to *externalize* certain burdens (realizing value pluralism) and to *express* through institutional arrangements civil reciprocity.

Finally, Jessica Flanigan offers a non-instrumentalist defense of privatization, arguing that the moral risk associated with coercion gives rise to a presumption against government provision of services. Against Harel (separately and in his joint work with Avihay Dorfman), Flanigan argues that private actors may, for instance, legitimately inflict violence for the right reasons, and that public officials may well act for bad reasons in exercising coercion. Against Cordelli, Flanigan argues that public institutions are not necessarily superior to private associations in their representation of moral equality or instantiation of justice, or other core values. Her wider argument is that because the public provision of goods and services generally entails coercion of those who do not consent to receive or contribute to the goods in question, where possible, private actors should provide such goods. The relevant moral consideration is the permissibility of coercion in a given context; unlike public provision, privatization reflects the ideal of voluntarily providing goods and services.

The second part of the volume turns to the political consequences of privatization, or the effect that privatization has on the state itself. Henry Farrell argues that rather than constraining the state, replacing political inefficiencies with market competition, privatization has transformed the nature of state control to emphasize regulatory power. Rather than ushering in deregulation, as many anticipated, Farrell demonstrates that privatization has in fact increased states' reliance on regulation. Such reliance has in turn produced far-reaching changes in the interactions among markets, states, and international regulatory processes.

Whereas Farrell locates the inception of the current wave in the 1980s, Joseph Heath holds that the pre-history of this wave—the phase of "corporatization" of state-owned enterprises—served as the true driver of the changes Farrell identifies, such as increased reliance on contracting. Heath suggests that the reforms aimed to remove state-owned enterprises from the political sphere, as a means of redressing agency problems, but in so doing changed their governance to such a degree that they were virtually indistinguishable from the operation of private firms. Once the state-owned enterprises had become corporatized in response to these management problems, however, the argument for preserving public ownership when a privately owned firm could accomplish the same objective at lower cost became less compelling. Ultimately, Heath identifies a number of circumstantial changes which affected the distribution of transaction costs, and which undermined the case for state involvement.

Eric MacGilvray argues that the logic of a principled distinction between public and private presupposes the existence of a liberal state, and that the key value liberals have typically appealed to in drawing the boundary is that of freedom. MacGilvray insists that such freedom is complex: in analyzing liberal freedom, we aim both at identifying the conditions under which agents can properly be held responsible (termed *republican freedom*), and at defining a social space within which the requirements of responsible agency may be diminished (*market freedom*). Liberalism unifies republican and market freedom; the debate over the boundary between public and private, understood this way, is core to its project, and is unresolvable. In debating where to draw this boundary demarcating the proper allocation of responsibility for social outcomes, MacGilvray suggests that we distinguish between the *abdication* and *delegation* of public responsibility. In so doing, he also highlights differences between de facto and de jure existence of private non-responsibility, and between the question of whether a domain of conduct is a matter of public concern (a second-order question) and the first-order question of whether public or private hands should hold responsibility. These questions, however, must be resolved in the domain of republican freedom, through public contestation over tradeoffs and boundaries, and the rules governing the domains both of republican and market freedoms.

Gillian Hadfield and Barry Weingast argue against the presumptive priority of government even in the domain of law: in recent work, they have developed a framework for analyzing law in which they suggest that the main distinction between legal and other social orders is the presence of an entity capable of changing rules. But an equilibrium in which these rules generate compliance does not require a centralized enforcement authority; indeed, Hadfield and Weingast argue that fully centralized enforcement is in fact incapable of sustaining an equilibrium characterized by rule of law. Rather, the need to coordinate and incentivize voluntary participation under decentralized enforcement yields the normatively attractive legal attributes associated with the rule of law, and Hadfield and Weingast draw on classical Athens to illustrate this model. On their account, private enforcement—in the sense of social sanctions and exclusion, limited use of force, and cooperation with authorized enforcers—are essential for a legal system to achieve the rule of law.

In his response to Hadfield and Weingast, Alex Gourevitch lauds their model as a first, promising example of "Leninist game theory"—how a stateless utopia can nonetheless sustain the enforcement of the rule of law, the need for which in turn ultimately dissolves once exploitation and poverty are removed. Given the injustices of mass incarceration and racial subjection in the United States, a vision of reducing, if not eliminating, the coercive enforcement of law is attractive. Nonetheless, Gourevitch argues that the Hadfield-Weingast model actually provides a positive theory of dystopia. Rather than yielding an equilibrium of decentralized, private citizens enforcing laws that they rightly regard as commanding their obedience, Gourevitch holds that a more plausible equilibrium would provide for enforcement of the rule of law to secure dominant interests against a subject population without such enforcement powers. Insofar as Athens constitutes an example, it is as an unjust hierarchy rather than a democratic ideal: one in which rule of law prevails among citizens on the backs of slaves.

The final paper, by Cécile Fabre, examines the Hadfield-Weingast argument in the context of the international legal system. Fabre turns to the justifiability of the privatization of war, asking whether the state should allow private actors to decide whether or not to enforce international moral norms by means of war. If just enforcement of international moral norms requires adherence to the rule of law, Hadfield and Weingast's argument—which Fabre characterizes as the "radical view"—holds that decentralized and private actors must play an essential role undertaking enforcement decisions and tasks. Fabre rejects the claim that private actors are necessary, but also challenges Harel's argument (elsewhere, but relying on a similar logic to his paper in this volume) that insofar as war is intrinsically a public enterprise, as a means of defending state interests, it cannot justifiably be conducted by private agents. In contrast, Fabre develops a hybrid view, arguing that in some contexts non-state actors may wage a just war of defensive enforcement, and that insofar as just wars aim at protecting individuals' fundamental moral rights, if private actors are better able than official actors to protect those norms, there should be no moral objection to their participation.

# PART I

# THE MORALITY OF PRIVATIZATION

# 1

# SOME (LARGELY) IGNORED PROBLEMS WITH PRIVATIZATION

## DEBRA SATZ

"Privatization" has its fans and its critics. By "privatization" I mean the transfer of governmentally (i.e., state) provided resources and/or services to the private sector. Although privatization can cover a diverse set of institutional arrangements, I will focus on privatization that is accompanied by the use of some degree of market competition.[1]

A mixed reception makes sense because the case for or against privatization almost always depends critically on context-specific details; there are examples in which privatization has yielded beneficial consequences, while in other cases the results have had dubious benefit or been harmful. Consider: currently, about 50% of all US cities contract out garbage collection to private firms. Overall it is hard to argue against the efficiencies of doing so, even if it is true that not every case has worked out. Similarly, the privatization of the steel industry in Brazil generated growth and social benefit. By contrast, when Britain attempted to privatize its public transportation sector, including the railways, it was forced to renationalize the rail network after the privately owned operator collapsed amidst problems of escalating costs, poor safety, and poor service. And the results of market-based privatization in Russia could scarcely have been worse.[2]

The fact that there are a variety of outcomes suggests that abstract theories that claim—in the absence of empirical investigation—to provide support for, or criticism of, privatization in general cannot be correct. For example, economic reasoning is sometimes taken to show that private firm competition must *always* be more efficient than government provision since the latter lacks the disciplining bottom line of the market. But that is simply not the case—as economists well know, natural monopolies, externalities, imperfect information, and other forms of market failure are common phenomena. In reality, bureaucratic red tape sometimes beats out the invisible hand.

Libertarians often argue as if any privatization of a state monopoly yields greater freedom, empowering individuals and their communities over and against the state. This too is mistaken: many private entities are bastions of arbitrary power and privilege; and turning private associations into social service providers can threaten the mission of these associations. It is also important to note that privatization has often been accompanied by an *increase* in government regulations, usually in response to concerns about the accountability of the private agencies. Privatization, laissez faire, and weakened government power need not go hand in hand.[3] In actuality, freedom is challenged and sustained on both sides of the private provision/government provision divide.

While a focus on the consequences of a privatization proposal is generally justified in making an assessment of it, I believe that the class of consequences that have been considered relevant is too narrow. In brief, the literature and the debate have focused primarily (although not exclusively) on two dimensions of the privatization decision: efficiency and accountability. Proponents stress the efficiency of privatization while critics flag the lack of accountability (which sometimes leads to inefficiency). But more than efficiency and accountability are at stake in the decision to privatize many publicly provided goods or owned resources. In this paper, I want to make the case for considering two other potential consequences of privatization: inequality and the distortion/corruption of public purposes.[4] I will argue that moving a good or service out of the public sector and into the private sector can sometimes change the structure of governance in ways that worsen inequality and both distort and fragment important public goals.[5]

To begin with, however, I acknowledge and set aside a class of cases where privatization can be ruled out for reasons other than bad consequences. These are cases where privatization fails for non-instrumental reasons, where it simply cannot deliver the good or service in question. Consider criminal justice. It is necessary to the purposes of our criminal justice system that judges and other officers of the court not be motivated by financial considerations when they consider punishments. Privatization of the judging system cannot work because the private buying and selling of judicial services will always be—automatically as it were—a corruption of the process of dispensing justice.[6] We might say that criminal justice has government provision as its "irreducible core" and is an "inherently" governmental function[7] that cannot be provided by the market. Any consequence-focused account of privatization like mine must acknowledge that there is a class of inherently governmental activities.

But many of the most contentious cases of privatization are not like this. Consider the privatization of prisons or schools or even of military operations. In all of these cases, private entities (including non-profit organizations) arguably deliver the very same goods and services as the public sector does.[8] Privately managed prisons theoretically might be run more decently than state prisons typically are; private schools might deliver a high quality education; private mercenary groups—notwithstanding Machiavelli's concerns that they will not make the effort in risky situations[9]—may fight more effectively and humanely for the nation than public armies. In most of these cases, moreover, the public sector already collaborates with private entities: in schools and prisons, private companies usually provide cafeteria food and uniforms. It is also possible that privatization in these cases already yields or would yield greater efficiency—better outcomes at lower costs. Nonetheless, I will argue that privatization in such cases raises the two distinct concerns—inequality and the corruption and fragmentation of public ends—that I want to pursue here.

## I. ACCOUNTABILITY

To be sure, debates about the shifting boundaries between public and private have a long and complex history[10] and the current negative reaction to many privatization initiatives shares similarities with its predecessors. Critics have long worried that transfers to the "private" sector weaken the power of government and give increased power to unaccountable agents. A good way to understand such concerns is in terms of a principal-agent problem: when a principal and his agent are not identical, the principal can have difficulty controlling his representative. For example, a government may contract out a military operation to a private company in the hopes that this company will efficiently deliver the service it wants. Suppose that service is security. If the private agent is dishonest, this can lead to waste, fraud, and abuse.

It is not surprising then that discussions of privatization generally wind up arguing over whether the main concerns can be dealt with through systems of increased accountability that give the principal added power over its agent. In an article detailing the new partnerships between the public and the private sector, legal scholar Martha Minow has identified accountability as *the* central issue with privatization: "The urgent challenge posed by a shifting mix of public and private providers of education, welfare and prison services is how to ensure genuine and ongoing accountability to the public."[11] If we are concerned by private military contractor behavior, according to this perspective, we need a more transparent and effective system for tracking expenses and monitoring operations. We need to ensure that the contractors are really accountable to their principals.

Admittedly, we have not done well with accountability in the case of military provisioning by private contractors. Yet, while increasing accountability is undeniably important in many cases of privatization, there are three initial problems with making this the central, and often exclusive, focus of concern. In the first place, this kind of diagnosis may tacitly assume that the government isn't in a principal-agent relationship—with the broader public as well as with its own subparts. This is false. Consider that the government itself can take actions that are not transparent to the public. For example, the government may refuse to release information about its spying program, or it may bury certain actions in a complex international agreement that most of the public remains unaware of. One government agency can run afoul of the goals of another agency. Principal-agent problems are everywhere, even within a single organization. So the relevant question is always comparative: do forms of privatized service delivery raise additional accountability concerns over those already involved in government provision?

Second, a focus on accountability runs the risk of turning the central task of responding to privatization as one of controlling rogue private actors. But in the cases I am concerned with—education, the military, and prisons—serious problems can remain even when no one cheats or commits fraud. Indeed, the problems can persist even when there is no inefficiency. Below, I will also argue that there is reason to think that even a broad understanding of accountability that includes the idea of making the private actors accountable to public purposes will be an insufficient remedy to the problems that I identify. The privatization decision itself can lead, either more or less automatically or through unintended byproducts and feedback loops, to changes in public policies.

Third, in some cases of privatization, accountability is not in fact an appropriate locus of concern at all. Consider four different paths by which a government can make use of privatization:[12]

1. It can abandon or let lapse some state-provided services or goods, so-called "privatization by attrition."
2. It can explicitly sell or lease public assets to private owners.[13]
3. It can "contract out" the production and/or delivery of services to private parties in exchange for government-provided fees. This contracting out can involve transferring funds to a private agency or directly to consumers who can then purchase the service from private and/or public agencies.
4. It can change the regulatory environment, allowing private entities to compete with services that were previously provided only by the government as a monopoly. In this situation, we have mixed provision: private provision complementing or at least coexisting with public provision.

Not all these types of privatization raise the need for increased accountability measures, which are often costly. In cases of the sale of some government assets, for example, it may well be that government has no further interest in monitoring the new owner. Rather, the central issue is getting a fair price and perhaps making sure there is a stock of wealth of the nation going forward, which can be drawn on for social ends. Likewise, in cases where private and social returns coincide, market-based incentives may substitute for accountability, and accountability measures can themselves sometimes impede efficient decision-making. In such cases, the discipline of the market may provide for all the "accountability" that is required. Further, in some cases, the problems with privatization can be attenuated by the existence of a public alternative without changing the nature of accountability with respect to the private contractor.

Interestingly, in some cases, the problem with privatization is not the lack of accountability on the part of private agents; instead, privatization may diminish *government* accountability. For example, the executive branch of the US government has used contracting out to private providers as what Jon Michaels has called a "workaround" with respect to military policy. As the government has faced a scarcity of troops for deployment and redeployment, it has been able to elicit help from a large contingent of private contractors.[14] This has allowed the government to engage in unpopular military operations without reinstituting a draft, it has diluted the number of casualties since contractor fatalities are not officially tallied or reported, and it has allowed the government to avoid the need to seek outside support from coalition partners.[15] Rather than weakening government, such privatization extends its power and alters the policies in place. Improving the accountability of the contractors to the government would not address this concern; here the accountability that is important is that of the government to the public.

The cases I am interested in—such as the increasing privatization of national security, prisons, and education—are typically cases of privatization through "contracting out," although each of the other forms of privatization in these areas can be found. In these three cases, the government typically continues to financially support, but not operate, certain services. The motivations for this contracting out are varied—weakening the power of public sector unions and shifting costs to the private sector is often a key reason—but costs are almost always a key part of the equation.[16] I will consider two concerns we should have about such privatization, beyond that of accountability and efficiency. To be clear, since I reject abstract claims for and against privatization in the overwhelming majority of cases, how worrying these concerns are will depend on the background details, the regulations in place, and the policy alternatives that are possible.

## II. Broadening the Discussion

### *Inequality*

One of the great benefits of using a system of market-based competition is that it allows people to buy the goods they wish to at the level that they desire. Not only does that tend to make for efficient exchanges—people buy and sell to each other only when they each have something to gain—but it also promotes diversity. In the market place, people segment themselves and develop distinctions in their consumption and production. These distinctions give rise to a rich panoply of skills, talents, and goods among social cooperators. In many contexts this diversity and differentiation is a good thing even beyond its efficiency effects. Just as we would not want an entire orchestra composed of bassoonists, so we would not want a society with everyone buying and producing the same goods, having the same interests, developing all of the same skills.

Nonetheless, sometimes diversity undermines the shared nature of a provided good and gives rise to fragmentation, inequality, and sectarianism. Consider, in this light, the provision and distribution of K-12 education. In *Capitalism and Freedom*, Milton Friedman builds on the diversity effect of markets, arguing that while there is a good case for the government paying for schooling—based on the negative third-party effects that come from having an illiterate and innumerate population[17]—there is no good argument for the government being the monopolistic provider of education, or indeed playing much role in provision at all.[18] Instead, Friedman proposes that the government should provide all parents with a voucher and let them purchase education from any provider—public or private—who meets some minimum standards (specifically, those that address the negative third-party externalities). Vouchers, he argues, would make greater school choice effectively available to parents, and school curricula could then be partly shaped by parents' values. Parents could also withdraw from schools that deliver poor educational results, thus creating a race to the top as schools try to find a way to keep children from exiting and retain the funds the voucher provides. Friedman believes the "privatization" scheme he proposes—where the government supplies financing but contracts out provision—would lead to greater diversity and better quality education at lower cost.

Admittedly, Friedman's proposal goes beyond most public school privatization proposals today, since these typically use vouchers only in the context of public (charter) schools. Nonetheless, a few cities—Milwaukee and Cleveland—have experimented with allowing parents to use public vouchers in private schools, including in some cases religious schools. And there have been ballot measures in some states to go further, including in California.

Why not adopt Friedman's proposal? In addition to enabling valuable forms of diversity, there are many things that might be said in favor of arrangements that allow public schools to face competition, from each other and from private schools. Perhaps such competition can overcome the bureaucratic sclerosis that characterizes many school administrations; perhaps choice might empower poor parents who now have few alternatives if their child is stuck in a failing and dysfunctional school. But three egalitarian concerns are explicitly missing from Friedman's treatment of education, and those of many other voucher advocates,[19] which are worth rehearsing here.[20]

The first concern is internal to Friedman's own proposal and concerns the design of the voucher system. Since Friedman's educational privatization scheme allows parents to "top up" the amount provided by the government voucher, already advantaged parents sending their children to private schools will be able to improve the education that those schools can offer. This can further increase the gaps among different children's education, an important concern for those who believe that the educational opportunities children have in life should not depend on their family's financial resources. While it might be said in reply to this worry that, at least in the United States, we already allow parents to send their children to private schools, in the case of this kind of privatization, this inequality in education—to the extent it occurs—is being furthered through state-supplied resources.[21]

Moreover, whether or not the voucher system raises the level of the lowest performing schools and so improves education at the bottom end of the distribution will also depend on other details of the privatization plan. One important question would be whether or not the non-governmental schools are allowed to reject and/or expel hard-to-educate students and if so, what kind of education those children would have access to. This is already a problem with many private and charter schools: while private and many charter schools can reject applicants, public schools cannot. The voucher proposal advocated by John Chubb and Terry Moe in *Politics, Markets and America's Schools* (Brookings, 1990) attempts to address this by requiring a fail-safe principle whereby every child needs to be placed in some school. But a school of last resort may not benefit such harder-to-educate children.

The worries above can be addressed through the design of a voucher system: one can forbid top ups and use lotteries to select students from schools that are oversubscribed. A second and more fundamental concern is that pluralism in K-12 education—differentiation and segmentation—has limits. While Friedman's proposal widens the scope of school choice beyond that of choosing what neighborhood to live in (most often not a choice at all given family resources), by throwing open choice so widely it also raises the concern that children with parents who are bad choosers—either because they lack information, because they are narrow minded, or because their own preferences do not match up with the fundamental interests of their children—will not receive an adequate education. Educational choice differs from other market choices in that children do not themselves make choices but are dependent on their parents' choices.[22] It is surely of concern that some forms of education that parents can choose might leave children vulnerable and servile.

It might be argued in reply that this worry can be addressed through regulation, through constraining the types of schools that can qualify to accept vouchers. Friedman, after all, did not deny the need for ensuring some minimum standards. But the state has interests that go beyond ensuring Friedman's own standards that all its citizens are numerate and literate.[23] The state's interests include turning children into good citizens, capable of living and working in a diverse democratic society and an even more diverse world. This concern goes beyond narrow content standards and includes the makeup of the school's children.

While segmentation and differentiation have a place in many contexts, too much of them in education undermine forms of cooperation and solidarity on which society depends. One of the key concerns about privatizing education is the extent to which it threatens to diminish a needed commonality; this commonality is important for equality. Where students are segregated on the basis of race and class, it is harder for them to view each other as equals. They are strangers to each other's lives and concerns.

A market-like arrangement for distributing students to schools might do a good job in matching children with schools, but a very poor job in matching students with each other. Would a Friedman-style voucher plan decrease or increase segregation along race lines, religious lines, and class lines? Would it allow the children of poor families to attend schools with middle-class students who live in different school districts? Would the diverse types of schools be able to prepare students to live peacefully and profitably with people from other ethnic groups, nationalities, and religions? These are urgent questions, in the United States and indeed increasingly around the globe. Here, the concern is not so much with private school accountability to some specified content standards, but with ensuring that our collective interests in integrated educational institutions are upheld in circumstances where the private and social returns on education may not be aligned.[24]

In circumstances where parents do not agree on the purposes and values of education, it is hard to predict what the consequences of opening up greater diversity in the provision of education would be. If, in trying to address failing public schools, our lack of agreement on common educational standards led to a default to a low minimum standard for an increasing set of education suppliers, and greater school segregation, this would be of concern.

Third and finally, the Friedman-style plan changes the structure of governance. Voucher proposals such as Friedman's empower a new set of special interests, lobbyists, and powerful actors focused on making education profitable.[25] (To be sure, current arrangements are vulnerable to interest group capture as well.) While the voucher plan could be instituted with a ban on for-profit education, the very point of the proposal is for many people to enter the educational marketplace in order to unleash competition. Given the imperfect information about the benefits of education on the part of parents and the weak agency of children in the education decision, there are clear dangers of opening up a system that places so much responsibility in the hands of market actors. While the market might be very good at responding to the preferences of parents as consumers, in education it is not those preferences alone that it is important to satisfy. In particular, leaving the choice of education provision to consumers runs the risk of market providers emphasizing vocational values over citizenship. To the extent that learning citizenship does not result in private benefits and would not be rewarded by the market, the citizenship aspect of education might be further diminished.

It is therefore quite reasonable to worry about the long-term stability of a privatization education scheme with respect to the value of equality. Would education standards unravel over time in the face of private interests diverging from public interests? Would powerful market actors shape the policy space in ways that further segment children on the basis of class and race?

The long-term dynamic effects of education privatization are important in assessing the desirability of introducing vouchers and other market-like mechanisms in education. An additional long-term concern with the Friedman proposal is that it might weaken support for public education for all children. One problem with private schooling and with too much variability in local schools is that allowing exit options for some sometimes undermines the minimum position of others. John Adams describes that when seatbelts were mandated for drivers but not passengers of cars, the result was actually an *increase* in the number of passenger deaths. Because the drivers felt safer, they took more risks, which fell on others for whom the safety situation was different.[26]

Returning to the example of education, work by Susanna Loeb on school finance shows how funding models which allow districts to supplement uniform-per-pupil grants with unlimited additional funds may not be sustainable because high-funding districts lose their incentive to support state funding.[27] Sometimes the best way to protect the interests of the most vulnerable is to put everyone in the same choice situation. Perhaps that is why the captain is supposed to be the last person to abandon the ship.[28]

Making education more like a market leads to externalities where the choices of some affect the choices of others. While externalities are ubiquitous in markets, we especially have reason to be concerned about externalities that affect the vulnerable, in this case children and especially poor children. Moreover, the effect of a voucher program isn't only on the type and level of education that children receive. It affects children's development—who they will become and how they will relate to others in their society.

### Distortion, Fragmentation, and Corruption of Public Purposes

Privatization critics have often targeted the risks of individual corruption—of private contractors lining their coffers at the expense of the public, skimping on the provisions and services they are meant to supply. For example, the literature on private prisons has focused on the ways that the lack of transparency in running such prisons can lead to decreased welfare for prisoners.[29] Unlike public prisons, most private prisons are not subject to the Freedom of Information Act, which provides the public with a mechanism to access prison records. Privatization in these cases allows the government to avoid taking responsibility for the illegitimate use of force and for deteriorating conditions. These are clearly concerns of paramount importance as the privatization of prisons is accelerating.[30] Following on the 2008 economic downturn, some states, including Arizona, debated whether to sell off their entire corrections system to private corporations.

Critics have also documented the waste and inefficiency in US government contracts with private military providers. Indeed, there is some reason to believe that outsourcing increases the cost of military functions, given the lack of a transparent and competitive market among suppliers as well as transparent bidding procedures.

I want to call attention, however, to a different concern: some public purposes may tend to be corrupted over time by a reliance on market-based privatization. In a sense this is a more generalized version of the stability worry I raised above with respect to the value of equality in education. Over time, in some cases, a widespread system of private market-based delivery might subvert or undermine public purposes. As Paul Starr notes in an early paper on privatization, "The potential private owners of public assets and contractors for public services represent specific interests and groups. Privatization is unlikely to be carried out with indifference to those social facts."[31]

Consider a system of private security, where that security is wholly supplied on the market. To simplify matters, assume that in this system, there is no contracting out by the state—no regulatory framework for provision—and all security is purchased on the market. In such a system, not only would people purchase vastly different amounts of security depending on their incomes, but also, security companies could only survive if there is a demand for their services. One way to ensure demand is to try and change consumers' perceptions about threats by engaging in deliberate efforts to increase feelings of anxiety, fear, and insecurity.[32] But this preference manipulation interferes with society's interest, which is in the attainment of an optimal level of security. So the private provision of security through a market *might* undermine the goal of providing optimal levels of protection to people (assuming of course that the state would be able and is willing to supply this). In this case, private agents are empowered in ways that can lead private returns and social returns to diverge.

Larry Lessig has called attention to cases in which some activity that may be harmless in itself—such as making a campaign contribution—tends over time, when it is of sufficient scale and adopted as a widespread practice, to undermine the purposes and goals of the institution.[33] He refers to such cases as "institutional corruption."

How might contracting out prison management to private for-profit entities lead to the undermining and changing of public purposes? While society has a strong interest in reducing the amount of crime, and consequently the number of people in prison, the interests of the private prison industry press in a different direction. One of the largest companies involved in the private prison industry, the Corrections Corporation of America (CCA), regularly engages in lobbying and direct campaign contributions aimed at boosting its market share. To give some telling examples: recently, the private prison industry was secretly involved in drafting Arizona's harsh anti-immigrant law—a law that (by the way) would boost demand for its immigrant detention centers. And the

CCA has offered to relieve the fiscal crises of forty-eight states by buying their prisons—but only provided the states agree to keep the prisons ninety percent full for the next twenty years![34] In its 2014 annual report, CCA worried that changes to American immigration policy would cut the company's profitability.

There is indeed something morally objectionable about viewing human punishment as a moneymaking activity. The attitude we should take to prisoners is one of appropriate resentment towards the wrongs they have done, a hope that they are capable of acting better, and a commitment to foster that capacity. Viewing imprisonment as a revenue stream denigrates the plight of the imprisoned. Private prisons routinely generate profits on such activities as phone calls, financial services, and the like for prisoners and their families. In some cases the fees to prisoners for such services are exorbitant. In a recent article in the *New York Times*, a fifteen-minute phone call by a wife to the prison in Pennsylvania where her husband is incarcerated cost $12.95. The cost for a similar non-prison call within the state would be about 60 cents.[35] While nothing in principle stops the state from such price gouging, in this case prisoners are explicitly seen as a source of profit. Indeed, the CCA is now one of the largest employers in the country and is publicly traded on the New York Stock Exchange. As in the case of children with respect to schooling, prisoners are not free transacting agents in these arrangements.

We might also suspect that private prisons put little emphasis on rehabilitation and decreasing recidivism. Rehabilitation is likely to be costly and the industry has no interest in diminishing recidivism. While regulations could help address this, a system that unleashes private parties with powerful interests might lead to changes in the regulatory regime itself. And if privatization itself leads to changes in law and even in social norms, to what standards should private actors be held accountable?

When we replace a government agency with many competitive actors, we change the decision-making situation. There is an important distinction between monopolistic and competitive situations. In the latter, many single agents take action but with the understanding that their individual actions cannot affect the outcome. (Thus, in an idealized market, no one agent has the power to set prices.) In such a situation, it makes sense for every individual to do what she most prefers from her own standpoint. She cannot set the behavior of the other market players by her actions. By contrast, a monopolistic agent can consider actions from the perspective of a "we."

While monopolistic agents can and do act in their own interests as well, the state is a special kind of monopolistic agent. It not only has the ability to aggregate the preferences of diverse individuals, it can provide the opportunity for reasoned evaluation of these preferences. Thus for example, the state can decide to give more weight to the preferences of vulnerable parties (e.g., the poor), it can decide to give no weight to some preferences (e.g., in racial discrimination), and it can unilaterally establish rules and regulations that shape the environment.

My point here is not that states are inherently pro-social and markets anti-social. In assessing the best policy with respect to privatization, we also need to be careful not to idealize the government's role in prisons (or security) by contrast. Many public prisons are very bad places, with little emphasis on prisoner education or welfare.[36] Politicians sometimes seek to manipulate fear for their own purposes, states rush to build new prisons to secure jobs for their citizens and the state-provided prison system is rife with practices that do not serve important social goals. But the dynamic effects of empowering private market actors is clearly a concern and one that goes beyond accountability *since the concern is precisely that the standards to which prisons are to be held accountable might themselves change.*

### III. Why Accountability Is Necessary but May Not Be Sufficient to Address These Problems

It might be thought that if the problem is the propensity of markets to promote private interests over social interests in cases where these diverge, and to worsen forms of inequality, then regulations that increase transparency and public oversight might be enough to fix, or at least contain, the problem. We can hold private agents accountable for ensuring that our public purposes are met, including our purposes in equality. Privatization is, after all, only a means.

But the cases above suggest that privatization is not only a means for delivering goods and services; privatization also creates a decision path for deliberating about the common good. This path itself can influence the structure of social interactions and thus affect the evolution of norms.[37]

There are two features of schools, security and prisons that are especially relevant:

The first is that in these contexts individual consumer choice is not the best mechanism for decision-making. In particular, those who are most affected—children and prisoners—are not those making the choice. Others are choosing on their behalf and may not choose wisely. Moreover, turning parents more explicitly into private consumers might change the ways that they—and we— think of education.[38] A private delivery system that gives increased scope for segmentation and differentiation might erode the idea of a common interest in education and push harder on the idea of education as a purely private good—aiming at purely private ends—and thus change social norms.

We know that market mechanisms can sometimes change social norms. A wonderful (if overused) example is an experiment that was run with six Israeli day care centers. Because parents typically came very late to pick up their children, the centers each instituted a fine. The result was that the parents came even later! What had been seen as an obligation shared by all the parents came to be seen as an individual good to be purchased at a price. (Interestingly, when the centers abandoned the fines, the late behavior persisted for many months.) This is an example of how a market mechanism can crowd out pro-social motivation.[39]

Second, we might worry about the path that privatization opens up for powerful private actors to manipulate the regulatory environment. This is a real worry, as I pointed out, with prison privatization. While there is nothing illegal about the prison industry lobbying for stricter immigration laws, the public ought to be worried about such initiatives and the effects they might have. By expanding the market's role in service delivery, privatization also changes the path by which we determine social welfare.[40] While one might argue that the ends are set by such deliberation, and privatization is just a means for delivering those ends, that response overlooks the ways that the choice of means can affect our ends.

To be sure, these two concerns are speculative and it is possible that institutional design or regulations could fully address them.

There is no axiom showing that private means cannot advance public ends.

My analysis picks out two values beyond accountability and efficiency as relevant to the privatization decision: inequality and the nature of the public purpose that is at stake. With respect to both of these values, our concerns should be amplified in contexts in which agents are weak decision-makers (children, prisoners, soldiers) and in which the potential for harms to our social fabric is greatest. We have ample evidence now that current forms of prison privatization produce poor consequences for prisoners and raise the concern about the corruption of public purposes; for schools and military contractors, while much depends on the design of the regulatory environment and the alternatives on offer, I have tried to sound alarms about some fragile and important values at stake.

I have left aside in this paper discussion of the main political forces supporting privatization today. No assessment of privatization's consequences can overlook this factor.[41] To the extent that those forces also support cutbacks in social services, taxes, and public goods provision, then privatization may go hand in hand with rising economic inequality. While this is not a necessary consequence of privatization, and indeed privatization can hypothetically be used as a tool to enhance economic equality, any analysis of consequences has to take into account the times in which we live.[42]

## NOTES

1 Some cases of privatization do not involve market actors—as when the government outsources some of its functions to non-profit organizations, including religious organizations such as churches. Such cases raise important concerns but they will not be my focus here, although some of the arguments I canvas do apply to such cases. See Chiara Cordelli, "The Institutional Division of Labor and the Egalitarian Obligations of Non-Profits," *Journal of Political Philosophy* 20, no. 2 (2011).

2 Joseph Stiglitz, *The Price of Inequality: How Today's Divided Society Endangers our Future* (New York: Norton, 2013), 221–23.

3 There is an important question of whether the monitoring capacities of the government and its own regulatory capacities are diminished by some of this outsourcing. See the essay in this volume by Henry Farrell.

4 Since I will be concentrating on the "contracting out" form of privatization (see below), I leave aside here another important consideration

that arises when privatization takes the form of selling off public assets: the potential depletion of national wealth. This is especially a concern when those assets are underpriced. And what happens when resource-constrained governments run out of assets to sell? See Anthony Atkinson, *Inequality: What is to be Done?* (Cambridge, MA: Harvard University Press, 2015) for a discussion of this issue.

5  It might be argued that such concerns fall under the rubric of public accountability, but I will argue below that these are independent concerns. I also leave aside additional concerns relevant to privatization such as feasibility and paternalism.

6  See the concerns raised by the recent *New York Times* editorial (Nov. 7, 2015) "Arbitrating Disputes, Denying Justice" on whether private arbitration paid for by large corporations can dispense justice to claimants.

7  See *Office of Management and Budget* Circular A-76, August 4, 1983 (revised 1999), www.whitehouse.gov, on inherently governmental functions. Examples include the determination of budget policy and combat.

8  See Avihay Dorfman and Alon Harel, "The Case Against Privatization," *Philosophy and Public Affairs* 41, no. 1 (2013) for a different view that emphasizes dispensing punishment and military operations as an intrinsically governmental function. I have elsewhere expressed skepticism about this: the welfare of those affected in such cases has significant weight. See Debra Satz, "Markets, Privatization and Corruption," *Social Research* 80, no. 4 (2013).

9  See Nicolo Machiavelli, *The Prince* and *The Discourses* (New York: Modern Library, 1950).

10 See Albert Hirschman, *Shifting Involvements: Private Interest and Public Action* (Princeton, NJ: Princeton University Press, 1982).

11 Martha Minow, "Public and Private Partnerships: Accounting for the New Religion," *Harvard Law Review* 116: 1129–70, at 1259.

12 Here I follow Paul Starr, "The Meaning of Privatization," *Yale Law and Policy Review* 6, no. 1 (1988): 6–41.

13 The sale of "council" housing in Britain under the Thatcher government would be one such example.

14 T. Christian Miller, "Contractors Outnumber Troops in Iraq: The Figure, Higher than Reported Earlier, Doesn't Include Security Firms. Critics Say the Issue is Accountability," *LA Times,* July 4, 2007.

15 Jon Michaels, "Privatization's Pretensions," *University of Chicago Law Review* 77 (2010): 717–80.

16 I am leaving aside cases of outright corruption, such as selling off assets to friends or political supporters. There are also good reasons to be concerned about the attempt to weaken unions—particularly concerns about inequality—but I do not address these here.

17 Notice that an argument for education in terms of externalities does not show why society should educate *all* children: it is possible to live in a highly productive society where some people form a permanent underclass. Nor can the externalities-based argument explain why society should educate those who may never be capable of contributing to a productive economy.

18 Milton Friedman, *Capitalism and Freedom* (Chicago: University of Chicago Press, 1962), chapter 6. Friedman was of course not the first person to propose a voucher system for education, nor to think that such a system could promote diversity as well as efficiency. John Stuart Mill had earlier advocated moving away from a state run education system. Other noted advocates of vouchers include John Chubb and Terry Moe, *Politics, Markets and America's Schools* (Washington, DC: Brookings, 1990); Christopher Jencks, "Education Vouchers: Giving Parents Money to Pay for Schooling," *New Republic* 163, no. 1 (1970): 19–21.

19 There are, to be sure, egalitarians who advocate voucher programs. But not all of these egalitarians give sufficient weight to the governance issues that I am highlighting here. See Harry Brighouse, *School Choice and Social Justice* (Oxford: Oxford University Press, 2000) for a nuanced discussion of the issues.

20 In this discussion I am addressing only contracting out privatization in the context of K-12 education. An earlier type of voucher scheme that also allowed vouchers to be used at private institutions—the American GI Bill—does not include the same concerns I raise here.

21 This is, of course, already a concern with existing arrangements that allow tax-deductible contributions to private (and public) schools and more importantly with our system of financing education through local property taxes. See Rob Reich, "Philanthropy and its Uneasy Relation to Equality," in *Taking Philanthropy Seriously: Beyond Noble Intentions to Responsible Giving*, eds. William Damon and Susan Verducci (Bloomington, IN: Indiana University Press, 2006): 33–49.

22 See Debra Satz, *Why Some Things Should Not be For Sale* (New York: Oxford University Press, 2010) for a discussion of weak agency in the context of markets.

23 Friedman writes that the role of government is simply to insure "that the schools met certain minimum standards such as the inclusion of a minimum content in their programs, much as it now inspects restaurants to assure that they maintain minimum sanitary standards." (*Capitalism and Freedom*, 89).

24 Some have suggested attaching a different value to educational vouchers depending on the demographic and economic characteristics of each family to address this worry. See Harry Brighouse, *School Choice*

*and Social Justice* (Oxford: Oxford University Press, 2000) for one such proposal.

25 Consider the emergence of for-profit higher education institutions with minimum standards and regulatory oversight.

26 John Adams, *Risk* (London: UCL Press, 1995).

27 Susanna Loeb, "Estimating the Effects of School Finance Reform: A Framework for a Federalist System," *Journal of Public Economics* 80, no. 2 (2001): 225–47. A voucher system without top ups permitted might address this concern.

28 Jonathan Wolf discusses safety in *Ethics and Public Policy: A Philosophical Inquiry* (London: Routledge, 2011).

29 See Rebecca McLennan, *The Crisis of Imprisonment: Protest, Politics and the Making of the American Penal State, 1776–1941* (Cambridge: Cambridge University Press, 2008) for a fascinating history of the intertwining of profit and prisons.

30 According to the Sentencing Project, more than 8% of state and federal prison populations were incarcerated in private facilities as of 2015. Nearly half of all immigrant detainees in America are now held in privately run prisons. See "Private Prisons in the United States," Sentencing Project, August 28, 2017, www.sentencingproject.org.

31 Starr, "The Meaning of Privatization," 34.

32 I take this example from the fine essay by Rutger Claasen, "The Marketization of Security Services," *Public Reason* 3, no. 2 (2011): 124–45.

33 For example, campaign contributions can enhance the goods of political competition and citizen representation. But contributions are rightly viewed as corrupt when they are of a type—a size and/or frequency—that tends to undermine such processes and thereby damage the core purposes and nature of our institution of representative democracy. See Dennis Thompson, "Ethics in Congress: From Individual to Institutional Corruption," (Washington, DC: Brookings, 1995).

34 I draw on this example in Satz, "Markets, Privatization and Corruption."

35 Timothy Williams, "The High Cost of Calling the Imprisoned," *New York Times*, March 30, 2015.

36 Indeed, if privatization improved the welfare of prisoners and decreased recidivism, this would be a powerful argument in its favor. I do not preclude such a possibility, but I believe that an additional concern would be the stability of the system over time.

37 Clearly market mechanisms affect the evolution of norms, sometimes in a positive way.

38 See Maia Cucchiara, *Marketing Schools, Marketing Cities* (Chicago: University of Chicago Press, 2013) for a subtle exploration of one city's educational measures that appealed to parents as consumers.

39 See Uri Gneezy and Aldo Rustichini, "A Fine is a Price," *Journal of Legal Studies* 29, no. 1 (January 2000).

40 All three cases involve individuals who are vulnerable and are weak agents: children, prisoners, and combatants and non-combatants in war. In each of these cases, others are making choices that centrally affect the interests of vulnerable non-choosers.

41 In Starr's words, "in the extreme case, privatization is an instrument of class politics" ("The Meaning of Privatization," 39).

42 I am grateful to Eric MacGilvray and Laura Dickinson for their insightful comments and audiences at Yale, Sonoma State, and the Rocky Mountain Philosophy Conference. Melissa Schwartzberg pushed me to be clearer and more explicit on a few key points that improved the paper (I hope). Thanks also to Jose Armando Perez-Gea and Rob Reich for discussion of the paper and to Andy Sabl for a stimulating set of written comments.

# 2

# IN DEFENSE OF ACCOUNTABILITY AS A LENS TO PERCEIVE PRIVATIZATION'S PROBLEMS

## SOME EXAMPLES FROM MILITARY AND SECURITY PRIVATIZATION

### LAURA A. DICKINSON

Scholars and policymakers writing on privatization have generally focused their attention on the problems of efficiency and account-ability.[1] They have analyzed the efficiency claims of various priva-tization projects on the one hand, and on the other, debated the lapses in accountability that these projects can produce. Debra Satz, in the lead article in this volume, laments the narrow lens that this preoccupation produces: it distorts the privatization debate and impoverishes potential normative proposals that aim narrowly to control "bad" private actors who cheat, commit fraud, or engage in other types of abuses. While Satz does not disparage such efforts, she suggests they obscure broader structural prob-lems inherent in privatization that go far beyond simply weeding out bad actors. In particular, she shows how privatization fuels soci-etal inequality and corrupts public practices.

While I am sympathetic to Satz's aims, I would nonetheless like to steer the conversation back to accountability. Satz surely makes a valuable contribution by attempting to broaden the privatization debate and focus on structural problems and consequences that may exist even in situations when privatization is efficient and even if well-meaning policymakers carry out reforms to rein in contractors. As she points out, we might still be concerned about privatization even in "best-case scenarios." This is an important perspective.

Yet, accountability potentially encompasses more than Satz acknowledges. Just as Satz wants to broaden the gaze from efficiency and accountability, I think it would be useful (and completely consonant with her aims) to broaden her conception of accountability a bit. Upon closer inspection, accountability can consist of more than just the control of abusive private actors by tightening the reins of the principal-agent relationship through careful *ex ante* management and oversight. Accountability also includes *post hoc* mechanisms of redress. Such after-the-fact measures seek not only to deter (and thereby control) bad actors, but also to punish or provide recompense to victims. Accountability can also have expressive functions, such as signifying the government's commitment to oppose and condemn categories of abuse. And accountability can acquire a political dimension by creating an opportunity for public debate about privatization, a crucial issue given that outsourcing reduces the ability of the elected branch to supervise and check the president or the executive branch bureaucracy more broadly. Accountability is a big tent.

Indeed, by examining the ways that privatization can disrupt accountability in its multiple guises, we can observe the profound impact of privatization on precisely the sorts of structural crises that Satz describes, and perhaps even open our eyes to some additional problems besides. Rather than blinders that give us tunnel vision, the framework of accountability, I would argue, potentially provides a wide-angle lens that can expand our focus.

In addition, Satz's important discussion of how privatization can corrupt public purposes might benefit from being viewed in the context of a wider conversation about the way privatization changes the very structure of governance itself. In particular, we may find that the turn to privatization not only empowers government contractors within the political process, as Satz notes, but it may also alter the separation of powers framework of the U.S. government itself. An accountability framework might help us see a loss of political accountability, because privatization diminishes Congress's ability to scrutinize and check the executive branch and therefore reduces voters' ability to scrutinize Congress.

Additionally, privatization fragments decision-making within agencies, potentially shielding such decision-making not only from hierarchical control inside the governmental bureaucracy but also from democratic deliberation in the elected branches. Thus, although Satz seeks to broaden our conception of privatization's structural problems, those problems may be even larger and more varied than even her analysis suggests.

In this essay, I seek to amplify Satz's argument by making two interventions. First, I lay out a more nuanced conception of accountability in its various guises, suggesting that we might find within the accountability discussion some of the sorts of structural concerns Satz seeks to uncover. Second, using examples from my area of expertise, the military and security context, I highlight two ways in which privatization alters the structure of governance beyond the corruption of public practices that Satz describes. I argue that, with respect to the decision to use military force abroad, military and security privatization tilts the historical balance of power between Congress and the executive branch towards the executive because privatization helps the executive branch skirt constitutional and statutory limits on the president's war-making powers. In addition, privatization fragments authority and decision-making *within* the executive branch. Thus, although governmental bureaucracy itself breaks up decision-making among multiple actors, those actors still remain connected within a hierarchical organizational structure. In contrast, by parceling out duties across an array of actors not linked within clearly defined organizational roles, privatization fundamentally alters, and diminishes, responsibility for decision-making and decreases the possibility for democratic deliberation and control. Both effects of privatization might fruitfully be seen as diminishing political accountability. And each amplifies the problems that Satz rightly highlights as crucial factors in the privatization debate.

## I. UNDERSTANDING ACCOUNTABILITY

Satz's efforts to bring the privatization debate beyond accountability and efficiency are important. Yet Satz's analysis might benefit from a more complex understanding of accountability itself because such an understanding would actually help identify additional structural problems inherent in privatization beyond the ones she addresses. Significantly, she does not precisely define what she means by accountability, instead simply seeing it as a by-product of the principal-agent relationship. She notes critics' concern that transfers to the "private" sector bestow increased power to "unaccountable agents" and laments that it is therefore "not surprising . . . that discussions of privatization generally wind up arguing over whether the main concerns can be dealt with through systems of increased accountability that give the principal added power over its agent." This narrow focus, she maintains, "runs the risk of turning the task of taming privatization into one of controlling bad private actors."

Accountability is a much richer concept than Satz acknowledges, however, and consists of more facets than just principal-agent control. My own work on privatization has focused extensively on accountability issues, in particular the impact of growing military and security privatization on the public values embedded in human rights and humanitarian law.[2] I note that some critics have called for an outright ban on military and security outsourcing,[3] but instead I have advocated for new means of regulation, such as the use of contracts and public-private accreditation regimes that attempt to bring the public values embedded in public international law into this newly privatized realm.[4] To some extent, these reforms fit into the principal-agent paradigm Satz wants to move beyond. By calling for reforms of the government contracts regime to rein in private actors, for example, I have argued in favor of expanding principal control over private actors.

Yet Satz, like many others focusing on privatization, conflates two aspects of accountability that can be distinguished from one another: accountability as redress, on the one hand, and accountability as managerial oversight, on the other.[5] In the first form of accountability, an authoritative individual or entity imposes a penalty if a person or organization has failed to comply with a particular rule or standard. This form of accountability is essentially backward-looking, involves a specific sanction, and occurs at a relatively discrete moment in time (though it could have deterrent effects in the future). In the second form of accountability, an authoritative individual or entity evaluates the performance of a person or organization and encourages that person to observe a particular rule or standard. This form of accountability is essentially forward-looking, does not involve a particular sanction or penalty, and is ongoing. When Satz refers to accountability, it is primarily in this latter form of managerial oversight, supervision, and control.

Accountability as redress, which Satz largely ignores, delivers important consequences beyond the limited type of supervision and control that she maintains unduly narrows our view of the impact of privatization. This type of accountability, which can take many forms—from a criminal trial, to civil litigation, to administrative sanctions—has important punitive, compensatory, expressive, and symbolic effects that transcend the mere refinement of the principal-agent relationship. To be sure, such forms of accountability can, of course, help manage that relationship by deterring misconduct. But they also send broader messages. Thus, when a U.S. court convicted Blackwater security guards who fired into a crowd of civilians in Baghdad's Nisour Square,[6] that decision not only played a role in deterring future security contractors from similar conduct, but also punished the individuals involved and gave some measure of redress to the victims. Furthermore, it signaled to the U.S. public, Iraq, and other countries around the world that the United States was accepting responsibility for, and condemning, the kinds of actions that those guards took.

The impact of civil litigation likewise extends beyond oversight and control. Again, tort liability imposes a measure of deterrence: nothing focuses the mind of corporate executives so much as the prospect of big losses in civil suits. The fear of such judgments is likely one of the factors that has mobilized military and security firms to defend themselves vigorously against a mushrooming array of such cases. But beyond deterrence, such suits can provide victims with some measure of compensation, and also signal official condemnation of contractors' misdeeds. Though such disapprobation differs from a prosecutorial decision to initiate criminal charges in the name of the polity, it nonetheless reflects a form of officially recognized sanction through the judicial system. The impact of these cases thus goes far beyond stigmatizing individual bad actors, as such suits can also reveal more systemic problems with privatization itself. For example, a case against the contractors who largely designed the CIA's program to torture terrorism suspects at black sites around the globe aimed not only to deter but to shine a spotlight on the breakdown of the rule of law in a time of national security crisis.[7]

And even accountability as managerial oversight does more than tame agents who might misbehave. Accountability of this type also involves a kind of continuous, collective re-evaluation of the underlying values and goals that govern publicly funded services. Thus, when policymakers reveal the breakdown of this form of accountability, they reach more broadly than advocating the control of individuals who go astray. For example, the final report of the Commission on Wartime Contracting, which described in great depth the waste, fraud, and abuse rampant in the military outsourcing that pervaded the Iraq and Afghanistan conflicts, served just such a role.[8] To be sure, the report highlighted gross supervisory failures of the principal-agent variety—the sharp cuts in contract-monitoring personnel just as the numbers of contractors soared to 260,000, at times exceeding the number of troops; the no-bid contracts drafted hastily with vague terms; the abysmal training of many contract personnel. Yet the report's disturbing overview of these lapses served not to narrow the reform efforts but rather to paint in broad strokes the contours of much larger structural governance problems triggered by privatization. For example, the report questioned the very boundaries between "inherently governmental functions" and tasks amenable to outsourcing. It highlighted the massive transparency failures that this widespread privatization engendered, making it difficult for Congress to exercise its oversight role. It called for "major" reforms— not simply minor regulatory tweaks. And by attaching a more than $30 billion price tag to the problem, the Commission sought to grab the attention of Congress and the public, spark collective outrage, and spur significant action.

Thus, the consequences of not providing adequate accountability mechanisms over private security contractors are even more worrisome than just the failure to punish a few bad actors. Yet, both criminal and civil accountability mechanisms remain sorely lacking. On the criminal side, despite the conviction in the Blackwater case, U.S. law remains riddled with jurisdictional loopholes for criminal conduct by security contractors overseas. For example,

the Military Extraterritorial Jurisdiction Act, which confers jurisdiction on U.S. courts to try such cases, does not clearly apply to
contractors working for agencies other than the U.S. Department
of Defense.[9] Meanwhile, civil cases against private actors also face
significant hurdles, including the political question doctrine[10] and
a variety of theories of contractor immunity and the federal law
preemption of state law claims.[11] In addition, privatization interferes with the substantive claims underlying some of these cases.
In one category of cases, brought under the Alien Tort Statute,
many "torts in violation of the law of nations" potentially encom-
passed within the statute require a connection to governmental
action. For example, the definition of torture in international law
mandates a link to official governmental actors, and it remains at
best disputed whether government contractors qualify. A case in
the Washington, DC, circuit against the U.S. contract interrogators
and translators at Abu Ghraib prison in Iraq foundered in part
on this basis.[12] Steering the privatization conversation away from
accountability risks weakening important initiatives to implement
reforms in these areas.

Privatization also diminishes another form of accountability left
out of Satz's analysis, accountability that we might deem "political." This form of accountability could be said to include the electorate's ability to weigh in on governmental action, as well as the
checks and balances that the multiple branches of government
apply to limit overreaching. Accountability of this type involves
much more than control of individual wrongdoers, but goes to
the kind of structural problems that privatization produces in a
democratic society. One way in which privatization wreaks havoc
here is its tendency to diminish transparency, making it hard for
the electorate to scrutinize the privatized sector and vote its preferences accordingly. Discussed in more detail below, this is just
one of the many pathways by which privatization reduces political
accountability.

By criticizing the privatization debate for focusing on accountability, and then framing accountability narrowly, Satz misses some
of the broader implications of privatization's impact on accountability. Accountability is far more than a process for controlling
bad actors. It can also have larger symbolic effects and can reflect
the public's collective judgment of the values that ought to govern

publicly funded services—even those that are provided by private actors. An examination of the way privatization affects accountability, therefore, actually does reveal broader structural problems posed by privatization—both the sorts of structural problems Satz herself describes and others beyond.

## II. PRIVATIZATION'S EFFECT ON THE STRUCTURE OF GOVERNANCE AND DEMOCRACY

Privatization profoundly unsettles the structure of democratic governance. Satz, in carrying the privatization debate beyond a mere discussion of malfeasance and waste, explores the impact of privatization on inequality and the corruption of public practices. Her analysis of education illuminates particularly clearly the corrosive impact of privatization on societal equality. And she skillfully unpacks the example of prisons to illustrate how privatization can establish powerful interest groups that undermine the collective public decision-making process. Yet, both problems— inequality and the corruption of public practices—might be viewed within a larger class of consequences of privatization: those that alter the structure of governance itself. As discussed above, accountability can actually be a lens to view these disruptions. While there are multiple ways in which privatization can affect democratic governmental structures and practices, in this section I'd like to focus on two, using examples from military and security privatization: first, the expansion of executive power in relationship to Congress, and second, the fragmentation and diffusion of governmental authority and its impact on democratic participation and deliberation.

### *Expansion of Executive Power v. Congress*

The growing use of U.S. military and security contractors to perform a broad range of functions overseas is upending the allocation of power between the president and Congress in deciding whether to use military force abroad. Such contractors, who numbered 260,000 at the high point of the conflicts in Iraq and Afghanistan,[13] have performed a myriad of roles, including constructing military bases and refugee camps, cutting soldiers' hair, serving meals in mess halls, maintaining weapons on the battle-field, interrogating detainees, guarding diplomats, and maintaining military facilities.[14] While the numbers of U.S. contractors in conflict zones has dropped considerably in recent years, many policymakers acknowledge that they are now a permanent fixture of the U.S. military and security establishment.[15] Indeed, military and security privatization has spread to other areas that receive relatively little media attention and public scrutiny, including multiple roles for contractors in the program to operate unmanned aerial vehicles or drones,[16] intelligence-gathering,[17] and the development and operation of new military technologies.

The use of military and security contractors, as well as the growing use of drones and other new military technologies, reduce the political costs of war. Contractor casualties don't count in the same way as those of troops in uniform. The military simply does not include these deaths and injuries in their tallies,[18] and the public does not generally regard contractors as making the type of sacrifice as soldiers.[19] The lower casualty counts, combined with the reduced transparency of privatized military and security operations that masks the full extent of U.S. involvement, has made it easier for the president to deploy force unilaterally.

At the same time, by harnessing private contractors, the executive branch has been able to make legal arguments that the use of force is itself not significant enough to warrant congressional involvement under the existing constitutional and statutory framework. The U.S. Constitution explicitly and purposefully divides responsibility over the use of force overseas between Congress and the president. Under the constitutional scheme, Congress declares war[20] and holds the purse strings,[21] while the president is Commander-in-Chief of the armed forces.[22] Debates about the scope of the president's power in relation to Congress date back centuries[23] and have grown more fraught in the last fifty years now that formal declarations of war are largely a historical relic.[24] Some scholars and government lawyers have asserted broad theories of the president's inherent power to use force unilaterally,[25] while others have taken a more restrained approach, articulating a view of continuing shared responsibility between the president and Congress.[26] After the Vietnam War, Congress tried to protect its position by enacting the War Powers Resolution, which requires the president to halt "hostilities" if Congress has not approved them within sixty days.[27] But since then, while Congress at times has spoken loudly to authorize the use of force—as it did in 2001 to allow a muscular response to Al Qaeda[28] and in 2003 to authorize the war in Iraq[29]—at other times Congress's voice has been muted at best.

The rise of contractors, combined with the growing deployment of unmanned systems and other new technologies, has enabled the president to claim greater legal scope for unilateral action, particularly in the face of congressional silence. Three recent cases illustrate this phenomenon. In Kosovo in 1999, Libya in 2011, and the current campaign against ISIS in Iraq and Syria, the president has staked out broad legal authority to use force in the face of congressional inaction, and the availability of contractors has fueled this legal argument. The consequences of this development are profound and threaten to upend the constitutional separation-of-powers framework.

### A. Kosovo (1999)

Slobodan Milosevic's brutal campaign of ethnic cleansing in Kosovo sparked calls for the United States to intervene militarily on humanitarian grounds. Yet, with the humiliating deaths of U.S. troops in Mogadishu still raw in American minds, President Clinton aimed to act in Kosovo in a way that would minimize the risk of U.S. casualties, primarily through an air campaign carried out jointly with the North Atlantic Treaty Organization (NATO).[30] This strategy had a double goal: stop the killing, but without spilling U.S. blood.

Contractors formed a crucial element in the military strategy. During the air campaign, contractors provided intelligence support, served as linguists, transported fuel from barges on the Adriatic Sea to locations inland, and built three refugee camps for displaced Kosovars.[31] After the primary air campaign ended, military contractors poured into the region, augmenting the U.S. contingent of peacekeepers. And the contractors performed an unprecedented variety of roles—from logistics, to construction, to training to policing.[32] Significantly, their presence allowed the U.S. military to contribute a much smaller number of troops (7,000) than might otherwise have been needed.[33] Overall in the Balkans, the number of contractors far exceeded the number of troops, at a ratio of approximately 1.5 to 1.[34] Drones were also a part of the story that helped the U.S. military to reduce its footprint and cut back on the risk of casualties. Although at this point they had not developed the broad-ranging capabilities they now possess, their capacity to convey live video feeds for "real-time targeting" was important.[35]

This strategy of waging war from a safe distance, made possible in part by contractors, combined with new technologies, gave the president more political leeway to act without clear approval from Congress. Congress debated the Kosovo conflict extensively, but neither explicitly supported nor opposed it because those in favor of military action never mustered enough votes to pass a resolution permitting the use of force.

The military strategy also emboldened Clinton administration lawyers to justify the unilateral use of force as a legal matter. At the time, the Department of Justice Office of Legal Counsel (OLC) did not explicitly explain the constitutional basis of the president's authority to conduct the Kosovo campaign in the absence of Congress's authorization. Instead, an OLC memo articulated in general terms the purpose of the military action:

> To demonstrate the seriousness of NATO's purpose so that the Serbian leaders understand the imperative of reversing course; to deter an even bloodier offensive against innocent civilians in Kosovo; and, if necessary, to seriously damage the Serbian military's capacity to harm the people of Kosovo.[36]

Moreover, the memo contended that the president had not run afoul of the sixty-day clock imposed by Section 5b of the War Powers Resolution. Although that provision limits the president from using force in "hostilities" without congressional approval, OLC argued that Congress had in fact authorized the use of force by funding the campaign, even though Section 8(a) of the War Powers Resolution purports to disallow such an approach.

Significantly, despite the ambiguity at the time, a decade and a half later, when OLC lawyers sought to explain the legal basis of President Obama's use of force in Libya in 2011, they drew a comparison to Kosovo, arguing that the Kosovo campaign avoided the difficulties of withdrawal and risks of escalation that may attend commitment of ground forces—two factors that this Office has identified as "arguably" indicating "a greater need for approval [from Congress] at the outset."[37]

The memo also emphasized that, "as in prior operations conducted without a declaration of war or other specific authorizing legislation, the anticipated operations here served a 'limited mission.'" Thus, OLC suggested that Clinton never needed to get Congress's blessing in part because the risk of casualties was so minimal. And of course, the casualty count was so low largely because harm to drones and contractors are not tallied in the official casualty figures.

B. Libya (2011)

A decade after the Kosovo intervention, President Obama joined a coalition of other nations to initiate an air campaign to prevent atrocities in Libya. But the president pledged that he would not deploy U.S. ground forces, except possibly for search and rescue missions, and he asserted that the risk of substantial casualties for U.S. forces would be low.[38]

As in Kosovo, contractors played a key role after the international air campaign ended. Because the new Libyan government expressed concerns about an extensive contractor presence, the contractor footprint was lighter.[39] Yet the U.S. Embassy in Libya did employ contractors, and the CIA also used contractors extensively.[40] Due to significant innovations, drones assumed an even larger role in Libya than they had during the Kosovo campaign.[41] Thus, while the contractor involvement in Libya may have been more muted, as in Kosovo the deployment of contractors, combined with the use of drones, enabled the military to shrink its visible image. This seemingly smaller footprint both emboldened the president politically to take action without congressional approval, and lent credence to legal arguments that he was neither constitutionally nor statutorily required to do so.

Indeed, as the president proceeded with the operation, his lawyers made the case that as a legal matter,

under these circumstances, the President had constitutional authority, as Commander-in-Chief and Chief Executive and pursuant to his foreign affairs powers, to direct such limited military operations abroad, even without prior specific congressional approval.[42]

More specifically, the OLC memo justified the use of force by arguing that the reduced risk of casualties—enabled by the deployment of drones and contractors—exempted the operation from Congress's exclusive authority to declare war. The memo reasoned that a particular use of force is a war "for constitutional purposes" only if there are "prolonged and substantial military engagements, typically involving exposure of U.S. military personnel to significant risk over a substantial period." In contrast, the military action in Libya, the memo argued, was "limited in scope and duration."[43] Again, the so-called limited scope was made possible by the expanded role of drones and contractors substituting for military personnel.

In addition to the constitutional arguments in the OLC memo, administration lawyers Harold Koh and Robert Bauer (over OLC's objections) also contended that the Libya campaign did not fall within the War Powers Resolution's sixty-day limit on "hostilities" without congressional authorization. Crucial to their reasoning was the fact that manned planes had moved quickly into a mere supporting role, even though "unmanned forces" continued to carry out strikes up to the very day Muammar Qaddafi was killed. In other words, so the argument went, because U.S. blood would not be at risk, it didn't count as warfare.

## C. ISIS (2014–15)

These military engagements in the Balkans and Libya have set the stage for the current campaign against ISIS in Iraq and Syria, where the combined impact of contractors and drones, as well as the use of contractors to operate drones, have further expanded the scope of executive power. Drones have played an even more significant part of the current campaign against ISIS than they did in Libya. U.S. Central Command has reported that drone strikes constitute about 15% of the overall number of strikes,[44] and drone surveillance capabilities have greatly expanded conventional air capabilities by enabling eyes on the ground, particularly in denser urban areas. Moreover, demand for drones is so high and the drone pilots are so overworked that the U.S. Air Force has announced a crisis of drone "pilot fatigue."[45] As a consequence, the military has temporarily reduced the number of combat flights to sixty per day.[46]

Contractor involvement is also significant. U.S. Central Command reported as of July that the Department of Defense employs 41,900 military contractors in the area within Central Command's responsibility.[47] Moreover, this figure does not include the State Department contractors who are providing security to U.S. diplomats and other services, as the State Department does not release data on contractor numbers.[48] And the United States has recently sought to hire more military and security contractors in Iraq to buttress the now small number of U.S. troops there and to help stop the advance of ISIS.[49]

Additionally, contractors are providing extensive support to the drone operations themselves. Contractors are performing maintenance on the unmanned vehicles, loading bombs into them, analyzing the intelligence feeds they provide, piloting the unarmed drones, and in some cases steering the takeoff and landing of armed drones.[50] And although contractors do not select targets, some of their activities, such as intelligence analysis, may at times effectively determine target selection. Certainly contractors are performing virtually the entire panoply of tasks associated with the operation of the unmanned vehicles.

As in the Kosovo and Libya conflicts, the use of contractors combined with the widespread use of unmanned systems enabled the Obama administration to maintain the appearance of a small military footprint with minimal risk of harm to U.S. troops. Indeed, although he increased the number of special operations forces on the ground, President Obama repeatedly stressed that he would not deploy significant ground combat units to fight ISIS, maintaining that U.S. troops cannot fix the underlying political problems that ultimately have caused the crisis.[51]

The administration's legal justification for the military intervention rested on the pre-existing Authorization to Use Force against Al Qaeda, from 2001[52] (as well as to a lesser degree the Authorization to Use Force in Iraq).[53] This legal theory balances on a tenuous link between ISIS and Al Qaeda, two terrorist organizations that are literally fighting each other on the ground in Syria.[54] The Obama administration put forward an alternative authorization to use force, but action on that authorization has stalled.

I would suggest that, even if the existing AUMF cannot be stretched to cover all aspects of the current operation, the precedent now exists for administration lawyers to contend that the current operations would not necessarily even require congressional authorization. While many administration lawyers might not go that far, the legal groundwork exists for the claim that a low risk of troop casualties, made possible by contractor and drone involvement, could justify U.S. engagement without congressional approval. Relying on previous actions in Kosovo and Libya, the executive branch could in theory argue that the military's current footprint, in part due to the combined impact of drones and contractors, is not big enough to trigger the need for congressional authorization.

The implications of such an argument are profoundly unsettling for the historical constitutional tradition of "mutual participation" between the president and Congress in waging war.[55] To be sure, Congress's abdication of its role and the corresponding swelling scope of presidential authority is a continuing storyline from the Korean War to the present.[56] Yet, the combined force of new, increasingly automated military technologies, alongside growing military privatization, has arguably catapulted the phenomenon to another level. Not only have these new technologies and methods of warfare strengthened the executive's political hand to use force unilaterally, but the twin trends of automation and privatization have made possible legal claims that the use of force is so limited that congressional assent is neither constitutionally nor statutorily necessary. In so doing, the new technology has disturbed the very architecture of U.S. governance.

### Fragmenting Authority and the Problem of Democratic Deliberation

The military and security example also highlights how privatization has fragmented governmental authority, changing the nature of responsibility and democratic deliberation. By dividing decision-making up among multiple actors, many of whom fall outside existing or clear governmental hierarchies, privatization diffuses responsibility. At the same time, decisions often become more opaque than in ordinary bureaucracies. Democratic deliberation and input into decision-making becomes more challenging.

The potential democratic deficit of bureaucratic governance is a fundamental concern of administrative law, because the delegation of authority from Congress to the executive branch potentially removes decision-making from a democratically accountable body and renders the decision-making less transparent.[57] Many administrative law procedures and mechanisms, such as those established within the Administrative Procedure Act, are designed to address these problems. Significantly, the administrative law view of public participation is not simply about making sure a voting polity ratifies all governmental decisions. Rather, it is concerned with ensuring that there is some sort of dialogue, even if informal, between the government and the governed to act as a check on power and guard against the possibility of capture by interest groups.[58]

When the executive branch then outsources a broad range of functions to private actors, and in particular discretionary functions that include the provision of services, it is essentially a double delegation. First, the legislature delegates functions to an agency, and second, an agency delegates those functions to a private body. This second-step delegation removes the privatized functions from many of the processes aimed at injecting democratic deliberation into the first-step delegation. For example, many legal frameworks designed to foster transparency and dialogue, such as the Freedom of Information Act (FOIA), whistleblower protection statutes, civil service conflict-of-interest rules, notice-and-comment rule-making, and judicial review of agency decision-making under the APA apply unevenly, if at all, to contractors.[59]

Furthermore, portions of the decision-making process often pass from governmental employees within defined bureaucratic hierarchies to a myriad of individuals employed by private firms or non-profit organizations with a variety of organizational structures and cultures. The multiplicity of actors with ill-defined roles can cause problems. And because the decisions themselves are parceled out into multiple pieces, responsibility becomes muddied. It is true the first-step delegation can also result in fragmented decision-making. But arguably the second-step of delegation to private actors results in fragmentation that is different in kind, because decisions are now made outside bureaucratic structures.

The atrocities at Abu Ghraib prison in Iraq provide a stark example of this problem. In addition to the uniformed troops who

beat and humiliated detainees, contract interrogators and translators participated in, and in some cases reportedly supervised,
abuses. After-action military reports concluded that the multiplicity of actors created confusion on the ground as to the chain of
authority, and this confusion itself contributed to the abuse.[60]

Private military and security outsourcing also diminishes transparency, which is a prerequisite for deliberation. It is, of course,
true that bureaucracies often suffer from a lack of transparency,
particularly in the national security arena. Yet, privatization
increases the transparency problem exponentially. For example,
private contractors can shield themselves from Freedom of Information Act requests by invoking not only the act's exemptions for
national security–related information, but also by arguing that the
information is protected as confidential business information. This
is an exception that is unavailable to governmental actors. And the
multiplicity of actors providing privatized services outside bureaucratic hierarchies also makes it far more difficult for governmental
or not-for-profit entities to keep track of the range of privatized
activity. Indeed, the U.S. government's continuing inability to even
count the number of military and security contractors working in
Iraq and Afghanistan is almost comical.

Thus, we can see that privatization creates structural problems
of democratic accountability, fragmentation, and loss of control.
And these structural problems exist even beyond the ones Satz so
aptly describes.

### III. CONCLUSION

Satz quite rightly wants us to question the structural impact of
privatization separate from the question of efficiency and separate
from the question of whether we can plausibly weed out the most
venal actors from the privatization scenario. Thus, she argues,
even in the best-case scenario, with private actors performing efficiently and honorably, we might nevertheless be concerned that
the very privatization itself creates serious structural problems that
cannot readily be solved.

This response paper adds additional structural concerns to the
ones Satz rightly identifies. By considering the multiple roles that
systems of accountability can play, we can recognize what is lost

when such systems are thwarted. And by understanding the way in which privatization complicates both our constitutional separation-of-powers framework and our mechanisms for transparency and democratic deliberation, we can see that the problems posed by privatization are profound indeed. Fortunately, scholars like Satz are pushing to identify such problems and point us towards a fuller understanding of this era of privatization in which we live.

## NOTES

1 See, e.g., Jody Freeman and Martha Minow, eds., *Government by Contract: Outsourcing American Democracy* (Cambridge, MA: Harvard University Press, 2009).

2 Laura A. Dickinson, *Outsourcing War and Peace: Preserving Public Values in an Era of Privatized Foreign Affairs* (New Haven, CT: Yale University Press, 2011). Such privatization has engendered a rich debate. See generally: Lindsay Cameron and Vincent Chetail, *Privatizing War: Private Military and Security Companies under International Law* (Cambridge: Cambridge University Press, 2013); Sean McFate, *The Modern Mercenary* (Oxford: Oxford University Press, 2015); Freeman and Minow, *Government by Contract*; Simon Chesterman and Chia Lenhardt, *From Mercenaries to Market: The Rise and Regulation of Private Military and Security Companies* (Oxford: Oxford University Press, 2009); Peter Singer, *Corporate Warriors: The Rise of the Privatized Military Industry* (Ithaca, NY: Cornell University Press, 2007); Paul Verkuil, *Outsourcing Sovereignty: Why Privatization of Government Functions Threatens Democracy and What We Can Do About It* (New York: Cambridge University Press, 2007); Deborah Avant, *The Market for Force: The Consequences of Privatizing Security* (New York: Cambridge University Press, 2005); International Committee of the Red Cross, *The Montreux Document on Pertinent Legal Obligations and Good Practices for States Related to Operations of Military and Security Companies During Armed Conflict* (2009).

3 See, e.g., Sarah Percy, *Mercenaries: A History of a Norm in International Relations* (New York: Oxford University Press, 2007).

4 Dickinson, *Outsourcing War and Peace*; Laura A. Dickinson, "Regulating the Private Security Industry: The Promise of Public/Private Governance," *Emory Law Journal* 63, no. 2 (2013): 417–54.

5 For a more extensive discussion of this issue, please see Laura A. Dickinson, "Privatization and Accountability," *Annual Review of Law and Social Science* 7 (Dec. 2011): 101–20.

6 Matt Apuzzo, "Ex-Blackwater Guards Given Long Terms for Killing Iraqis," *New York Times*, April 13, 2015, www.nytimes.com.

7 *Salim v. Mitchell*, CV-15–0286-JLQ, Memorandum Opinion and Order Denying Defendants' Motion to Dismiss, April 28, 2016.

8 Comm'n on Wartime Contracting, Final Report, "Transforming Wartime Contracting: Controlling Costs, Reducing Risk" (2011) (hereinafter CWC Final Report).

9 The statute confers jurisdiction over crimes committed by contractors whose employment relates to supporting a DOD mission overseas. 18 U.S.C. 3261, 3267.

10 See, e.g., *Lane v. Haliburton*, 529 F.3d 548 (5th Cir. 2008).

11 See, e.g., *Saleh v. Titan*, 580 F.3d 1 (D.C. Cir. 2009). For a good overview of these issues, see generally Rebecca DeWinter-Schmitt, ed., *Montreux Five Years On: An Analysis of State Efforts to Implement Montreux Document Legal Obligations and Good Practices* (2013, available online) (section on civil liability in the United States).

12 *Ibrahim v. Titan Corp.*, 391 F. Supp. 2d 10 (D.D.C. 2005).

13 CWC Final Report.

14 Ibid.

15 See James Risen and Matthew Rosenberg, "Blackwater's Legacy Goes Beyond Public View," *New York Times*, April 14, 2015, www.nytimes.com.

16 See, e.g., Abigail Fielding-Smith and Crofton Black, "Drone Warfare: Reaping the Rewards: How Private Sector is Cashing in on Pentagon's 'Insatiable Demand' for Drone War Intelligence," Bureau of Investigative Journalism, July 30, 2015, thebureauinvestigates.com; Laura A. Dickinson, "Drones and Contractor Mission Creep," Just Security, August 5, 2015, www.justsecurity.org; Laura A. Dickinson, "Drone Contractors: An Oversight and Accountability Gap," Just Security, July 21, 2015, www.justsecurity.org.

17 Jon Michaels, "All the President's Spies: Private-Public Intelligence Gathering in the War on Terror," *California Law Review* 96, no. 4 (2008): 901–66.

18 Steve Schooner and Colin Swan, "Dead Contractors: The Unexamined Effect of Surrogates on the Public's Casualty Sensitivity," *Journal of National Security Law & Politics* 6 (2012): 11–58.

19 Mateo Taussig-Rubbo, "Outsourcing Sacrifice: the Labor of Private Military Contractors," *Yale Journal of Law & The Humanities* 21, no. 1 (2009): 105–64.

20 U.S. Constitution Article I, sec. 8, cl.11.

21 Ibid., sec. 8, cl. 12–13.

22 Ibid., sec. 2.

23 *Compare The Prize Cases*, 67 U.S. (2 Black) 635 (1863) (upholding constitutionality of President Lincoln's unilateral decision to impose a na-

val blockade during the Civil War, when Congress was not in session); with *Little v. Barreme*, 6 U.S. (2 Cranch) 170 (1804) (concluding that a U.S. naval captain's seizure of a ship sailing from a French port during the naval war with France was unjustified because Congress had only authorized seizures of ships sailing to French ports).

24 The United States has not formally declared war since World War II. See "Joint Resolution Declaring That a State of War Exists Between the Government of Rumania and the Government and the People of the United States and Making Provisions to Prosecute the Same," ch. 325, 56 Stat. 307 (June 5, 1942) (the last declaration of war by the United States).

25 See, e.g., Leonard C. Meeker, "The Legality of United States Participation in the Defense of Viet-Nam," Dep't St. Bull. 54 (1966): 474–89, reprinted in *Yale Law Journal* 75, no. 7 (1966): 1085–108; John C. Yoo, "The Continuation of Politics by Other Means: The Original Understanding of War Powers," *California Law Review* 84, no. 2 (1996): 167–305.

26 See, e.g., Harold Hongju Koh, *The National Security Constitution* (New Haven, CT: Yale University Press, 1990); David J. Barron and Martin S. Lederman, "The Commander in Chief at the Lowest Ebb—Framing the Problem, Doctrine, and Original Understanding," *Harvard Law Review* 121, no. 3 (2008): 689–804.

27 "War Powers Resolution," 50 U.S.C. sec. 1541–48 (1973); see Pat M. Holt, *The War Powers Resolution* (1978).

28 "Joint Resolution to Use the United States Armed Forces against Those Responsible for the Recent Attacks Launched against the United States," Pub. L. No. 107–40, sec. 2(a), 115 Stat. 224 (2001).

29 "Authorization for Use of Military Force against Iraq Resolution of 2002," Pub L. No. 107–243, 116 Stat. 1498 (October 16, 2002).

30 See President William Jefferson Clinton, Statement on Kosovo, March 24, 1999; President William Jefferson Clinton, "Letter to Congressional Leaders Reporting on Airstrikes against Serbian Targets in the Federal Republic of Yugoslavia (Serbia and Montenegro)," 35 Weekly Comp. Pres. Doc. 527, 527 (March 26, 1999); see also North Atlantic Treaty Organization, "The Kosovo Air Campaign: Operation Allied Force," November 11, 2014, www.nato.int.

31 Department of Defense, "Report to Congress Kosovo/Operation Allied Force After Action Report," January 31, 2000, at 116, www.dod.mil (hereafter known as "Report to Congress").

32 Moshe Schwartz and Jennifer Church, "Department of Defense's Use of Contractors to Support Military Operations: Background, Analysis and Issues for Congress" (Congressional Research Service, May 17, 2013).

33 Department of Defense, "Report to Congress."

34 See Richard Fontaine and John Nagl, "Contractors in American Conflicts, Adapting to a New Reality" (Center for a New American Security, December 2009), www.cnas.org; see also Office of Defense Procurement and Acquisition Policy, "Contingency Contracting Throughout U.S. History," www.acq.osd.mil.

35 During Operation Allied Force in Kosovo, the unmanned vehicles operated as "remote-controlled intelligence and surveillance platforms" (Department of Defense, "Report to Congress"). The Defense Department after-action report to Congress highlighted the significance of the new technology, emphasizing that they were used at "unprecedented levels" and "played an important role in our overall success" (Ibid.). Specifically, the report noted, drones "enabled commanders to see the situation on the ground without putting aircrews at risk and provided continuous coverage of important areas. See Fontaine and Nagl, "Contractors in American Conflicts"; see also Office of Defense Procurement and Acquisition Policy, "Contingency Contracting Throughout U.S. History."

36 "Authorization for Continuing Hostilities in Kosovo," 24 Op. O.L.C. 327 (2000), justice.gov; see also "Proposed Bosnia Deployment," 19 Op. O.L.C., 333 (November 30, 1995).

37 Memorandum Opinion for the Attorney General, "Authority to Use Military Force in Libya," April 1, 2011 (hereafter known as Memo, "Authority to Use Military Force in Libya,").

38 Ibid.

39 James Risen, "Benghazi Attack, Private Security Hovers as an Issue," *New York Times*, October 12, 2012, www.nytimes.com; see also Ahol Mehra, "Time to Put Security Contractors Under the Gun," *Huffington Post*, February 28, 2013, www.huffingtonpost.com.

40 Associated Press, "New Benghazi Investigation Finds No Fault in Response," *New York Times*, November 21, 2014, www.nytimes.com.

41 Drones enhanced the Air Force's capabilities to better gather information for targeting because of their greater ability to fly low for extended periods, hover in densely populated areas, and transmit high-quality information in real time. See Cheryl Pellerin, "Gates: Obama OKs Predator Strikes in Libya," Department of Defense News, April 21, 2011, www.archive.defense.gov; see generally James Igoe Walsh, *The Effectiveness of Drone Strikes in Counterinsurgency and Counterterrorism Campaigns* (Carlisle, PA: Strategic Studies Institute and U.S. Army War College Press, 2013). This capacity increased the precision of conventional air power and helped reduce civilian casualties. Even more significantly, in addition to providing intelligence, drones could themselves drop bombs.

42 Memo, "Authority to Use Military Force in Libya."

43 Ibid.

44 Eric Schmitt, "Obstacles Limit Targets and Pace of Strikes against ISIS," *New York Times*, November 9, 2014.

45 Christopher Drew and Dave Philipps, "As Stress Drives Off Drone Operators, Air Force Must Cut Flights," *New York Times*, June 16, 2015, www.nytimes.com.

46 See Missy Ryan, "Air Force Struggles to Keep Pace with Explosion in Use of Combat Drones," *Washington Post*, June 17, 2015, www.washington-post.com.

47 Department of Defense, "Contractor Support of U.S. Operations in the USCENTCOM Area of Responsibility," July 2015, www.acq.osd.mil.

48 See Risen and Rosenberg, "Blackwater's Legacy Goes Beyond Public View."

49 Ibid.

50 See discussion at notes 16 and 17.

51 Christopher M. Blanchard and Carla E. Humud, *The "Islamic State" Crisis and U.S. Policy* (CRS Report No. R43612) (Washington, DC: Congressional Research Service, 2015), https://perma.cc/CV2E-PV9A.

52 "Joint Resolution."

53 "Authorization for Use of Military Force."

54 See, e.g., Dan Byman, "Testimony before the Subcommittee on Counterterrorism and Intelligence of the House Committee on Homeland Security," April 29, 2015.

55 See *DaCosta v. Laird*, 448 F.2d 1368 (2d Cir. 1971); see also Koh, *The National Security Constitution*.

56 See John Hart Ely, *War and Responsibility: Constitutional Lessons of Vietnam and Its Aftermath* (Princeton, NJ: Princeton University Press, 1993). Indeed, during the Korean War, Truman administration officials referred to the conflict as a "police action," despite the deployment of more than five million U.S. troops to the region.

57 See, e.g., Benedict Kingsbury, Nico Krisch, and Richard B. Stewart, "The Emergence of Global Administrative Law," *Law & Contemporary Problems* 68, no. 3 (2005) 15–61; Alfred C. Aman Jr., *The Democracy Deficit: Taming Globalization Through Law Reform* (New York: NYU Press, 2004): 154–55.

58 See, e.g., Cary Coglianese, "Administrative Law," in *International Encyclopedia of Social & Behavioral Sciences* (Amsterdam: Elsevier Science, 2001): 85–88.

59 See, e.g., Dickinson, *Outsourcing War and Peace*, 105.

60 See, e.g., Maj. Gen. George R. Fay, "AR-15–6 Investigation of the Abu Ghraib Detention Facility and 205th Military Intelligence Brigade" (2004).

# 3

# WHY PRIVATIZATION MATTERS

# THE DEMOCRATIC CASE AGAINST PRIVATIZATION

## ALON HAREL

A private person cannot lead another to virtue efficaciously: for he can only advise and if his advice be not taken, it has no coercive power, such as the law should have, in order to prove an efficacious inducement to virtue . . . But this coercive power is vested in the whole people in some public personage, to whom it belongs to inflict penalties.

—Thomas Aquinas, *Summa Theologica*[1]

## I. INTRODUCTION

Privatization is a contentious issue among political theorists and citizens. Like other contentious issues, both advocates and opponents of privatization conceptualize the debate in instrumental terms. Under the traditional view, the privatization debate is primarily concerned with the competence of the relevant agent and her capacity to achieve desirable ends that are independent of the identity of the agent. The decision whether or not to privatize therefore requires us to compare the performance of a public functionary with that of her private counterpart.[2] Both advocates and opponents of privatization assume that there exists a "desirable end" (i.e., a just or correct decision) that is in principle independent of the identity of the agent which brings it about. The appropriateness of privatization hinges on the answer to the question as to who is most likely to make the just or correct decision and bring about the most desirable ends.[3]

This article challenges the traditional approach to the issue of privatization, noting its failure to address other important concerns triggered by the shift of responsibilities from government to private entities. More specifically, privatization severs the link between decision-making processes and citizens, eroding the prospect of meaningful political engagement and civic shared responsibility. The privatization debate is not only about the quality of the decisions which private entities make on behalf of the state. At times, the identity of the decision-maker (public or private) is significant independently of the justness or correctness of her decision. Therefore, concerns about privatization are not only empirical or pragmatic. There is more at stake than a positive or negative appraisal of the performance of a particular decision-maker. In fact, privatization is, at least sometimes, *necessarily* undesirable, not merely contingently undesirable (such as where private decision-makers are shown to perform poorly).[4]

My contention is based on a simple observation: at times we care not only about whether a decision is right, just, efficient, or desirable; we also care about *who* the decision-maker is. A public institution differs from a private one not only with respect to the probable quality of the resulting decision. It also differs in that the decisions of a public institution are attributable to the polity and to citizens. Hence, massive privatization, which significantly shifts decision-making away from public institutions to unaccountable, private entities, can detrimentally affect public responsibility and, in turn, adversely impact political engagement. It is worth noting that, in this article, "public responsibility" and "political engagement" are purely normative terms, rather than descriptions of psychological phenomena. In other words, they refer to whether individuals *ought* to see themselves as responsible, rather than whether individuals do in fact possess particular subjective states of mind.

In analyzing privatization through this lens, one needs to consider whether decisions of the polity can be said to be made in the name of citizens and whether citizens can be held responsible for these decisions. What makes a decision a "public decision"? What enables us to say that a particular public decision is made by or in the name of members of the polity? Could private entities also operate in the name of the members of the polity? What institutional features facilitate attributing responsibility to citizens? This chapter will address these questions.

Section II examines the traditional view of privatization, according to which privatization is evaluated on the basis of instrumental considerations. Under this view, the quality of the decision is paramount, not the status of the decision-maker. The agent who makes the decision is only a *means* for implementing publicly oriented decisions, but nothing more. Section II also establishes that this view conflicts with foundational legal principles and with common sense intuitions. Section III examines the concept of publicness and, in particular, defends the view that decisions made by public entities can be attributed to the public as a whole. Section IV draws normative conclusions from this observation and identifies the hidden costs of privatization. I then conclude by arguing that massive privatization necessarily undermines public responsibility and political engagement. The costs of privatization should be measured not only in terms of the quality of the privatized goods or services, but also in wholesale terms—by gauging its impact on the relationship between citizens and the polity, and between citizens themselves. Aside from its contingent impact, massive privatization is detrimental to the polity *as such*.

Importantly, my analysis does not in any way imply that the privatization of a particular good or service is undesirable. It only suggests that policymakers often fail to account for the non-monetizable costs of privatization.[5] My focus is not on the discrete effects of privatization on the provision of a particular good or service. Instead, my focus is on massive privatization—a profoundly transformative process that has the potential to reshape society, the political system, and public culture, with robust shared responsibility and political engagement eclipsed by fragmentation and sectarianism.

## II. THE VICES OF INSTRUMENTALISM

Why does privatization matter? The prevailing view is that privatization matters because the decisions made by private entities are likely to be different from the decisions made by public entities. In particular, it is frequently argued that the incentives operating on public officials differ from those operating in the market, and that these different incentives result in different decisions. The decision-maker is selected on the basis of competence, namely the capacity and likelihood to make appropriate decisions, act rationally, and promote the public interest. To the extent that a public entity is likely to make better decisions than a private entity, it should be assigned the task of decision-making, and vice versa.

This view is shared by both advocates and opponents of privatization. Advocates of privatization often emphasize efficiency-based reasons in favor of privatization. They argue that private entities are superior to public entities because they can provide high-quality goods and services at a lower cost, thanks to market forces and market discipline.[6] These economic hypotheses are confirmed by empirical studies that establish that private actors outperform public actors in the provision of certain goods and services.[7] But economists are careful to point out the problems of private entities. Market failures, such as monopolies, externalities, and informational failures, can and do affect the provision of goods and services by private entities. Economists predict that in this scenario public entities will outperform private actors. In either case, however, the desirability of privatization turns solely on considerations of efficiency.

Efficiency is typically considered to be blind to the goals of privatization. Economists argue that whatever goals we wish to achieve, we can achieve them by privatizing the provision of certain goods.[8] Yet opponents of privatization challenge this view on a variety of grounds. One standard challenge is that economic considerations do not capture certain objectives (e.g., accountability and impartiality); these objectives are typically better captured by public entities.[9] One prominent advocate of this view is Martha Minow, who argues that competitive forces are sometimes detrimental to "public commitments." The term "public commitments" includes taking steps to "ensure fair and equal treatment and to prevent discrimination on the basis of race, gender, religion, or sexual orientation."[10] Public commitments are also concerned with the fact that privatization can impair the set of public norms required from state action, such as freedom and equality.[11] Lastly, Minow describes public accountability as a major concern that should guide decision-makers and that, in her view, can typically be better promoted by public entities.[12]

The controversy surrounding the positive and negative effects of privatization relies on empirical conjectures. On the one hand, advocates of privatization harness standard economic theory to maintain that private entities are, generally speaking, more likely to operate efficiently. On the other hand, opponents of privatization maintain that private entities fail to pursue public commitments; public entities are more likely to reason in a way that is conducive to the fulfillment of public commitments.

These empirical observations are often treated as gospel among theorists, but at times they can be challenged. For instance, opponents of privatization point out that public entities are not necessarily (or even typically) less efficient than private entities.[13] Further, advocates of privatization argue that private entities can promote public commitments. In a response to Minow, Trebilcock and Iacobucci argue that private entities are characterized by market-based accountability. Under this view, "market forces often compel private firms to act as though governed by public accountability rule."[14] More generally, Trebilcock and Iacobucci argue that "the phrase 'public accountability' can easily induce a slide to unreflective thinking that the more accountability and the more public it is, the better. In the real world of policymaking we should resist this temptation to indulge the 'nirvana fallacy'" (the fallacy of dismissing a realistic solution as a result of comparing it with an unrealistic idealized alternative).[15]

In an even more ambitious effort to reconcile privatization with public commitments, some theorists have developed the concept of publicization. Publicization refers to a process whereby private entities endorse public interest reasoning and modify their decisions accordingly. Jody Freeman outlines the normative implications of publicization:

> Instead of seeing privatization as a means of shrinking government, I imagine it as a mechanism for expanding government's reach into realms traditionally thought private. In other words, privatization can be a means of "publicization," through which private actors increasingly commit themselves to traditionally public goals . . . So rather than compromising democratic norms of

accountability, due process, equality and rationality—as some critics of privatization fear it will—privatization might extend these norms to private actors through vehicles such as budgeting, regulation and contract.[16]

Freeman's observation is not utopian. In describing what might prompt private entities to pursue public commitments, Martin Sellers explains that "private companies become like the public agencies because competition for contracts is keen and they must be perceived by the contacting agent, government, as being agreeable with the government's demands in order to be contracted with again."[17]

This analysis poses a grave challenge to the opponents of privatization. The term "public commitment," as understood by Minow and other opponents of privatization, is only contingently related to public institutions, public officials, or public agents. Minow's public commitments and public values include values such as fair and equal treatment, public participation, public control and review, equality, due process, and democracy. And it is possible that, in some circumstances, private entities could actually protect these lofty values more effectively than public entities.[18] Now, if we assume that private entities can pursue public commitments (accountability, impartiality, etc.), what makes these ideals in any way "public"? Why, for example, is the value of efficiency less "public" than the value of equality or due process?[19]

One way of addressing these questions is to concede that the term "public" does not refer to the identity of the decision-maker, but to a decision that is grounded in appropriate reasoning. Dorfman and I termed this view the "reason-based characterization of publicness."[20] According to the reason-based characterization of publicness, a decision is public if it meets certain conditions of equality, impartiality, and accountability—irrespective of whether the decision-maker is an organ of the government or a private entity. The underlying rationale for the reason-based characterization of publicness is clear: the status of the agent is a technical matter. What really counts is the reason(s) why a decision was made and what its effects are likely to be. The agent who makes the decision is merely a vehicle for implementing publicly oriented decisions or carrying out public acts. If she successfully implements public policy, her decision is public irrespective of her institutional affiliation. If she fails to do so, her decision is private.[21]

This is a seductive idea, and while seductiveness is at times the boundary of horror,[22] one ought to at least sometimes be willingly seduced. Yet, this seductive suggestion should be resisted for two reasons. Firstly, as the rest of this section will demonstrate, the reason-based characterization of publicness is inconsistent with legal realities and common sense intuitions. Secondly, section III proposes an alternate understanding of publicness based not on the reasons underlying the decision but on the institutional identity of the decision-maker. This understanding of publicness implies that a public decision must be made by a public institution. Consequently, the publicness of a decision is not gauged solely by the quality of a decision and/or its adoption of "public commitments," but also by the identity and the status of the decision-maker.

The view (which I defend in section IV) that the identity of the decision-maker is important independently of the quality of its decision has been recognized by both political and legal theorists and by the courts. It is often argued that in order to justify delegating decision-making or other powers to a private agent, it is not enough that the agent be likely to make the right choice or act properly. The agent must also be a public entity. A few examples will help demonstrate the importance of the identity of the decision-maker.[23]

In his classic discussion of punishment, John Locke argues:

> To justify bringing such evil [i.e. punishment] on any man two things are requisite. First that *he who does it has power and commission.* Secondly that it be directly useful for the procuring of some other good . . . Usefulness when present (being but one of these conditions), cannot give the other, which is a commission to punish.[24]

For Locke, to justify the infliction of punishment, it is not enough that the agent "is useful for the procuring of some other good." In addition, the agent who "brings such evil" as punishment needs to have "a commission," i.e., an authorization or a mandate to impose sanctions. This view is also shared by contemporary political theorists such as Malcolm Thorburn:

> Those who are acting in the name of the polity as a whole are enti-
> tled to do things . . . that private citizens may not, and they have the
> power to decide questions . . . that private citizens do not; but in all
> this, they are answerable to others for their conduct and their deci-
> sions in a way that private citizens are not . . . All of these rules are
> concerned not merely with the quality of an individual's acts but,
> first and foremost, with her legal standing to undertake it in the
> first place.[25]

Thorburn, like Locke, believes that publicness hinges both on
the quality of the reasoning and values behind a decision and on
the "public" status of the agent. Not only are public agents more
likely to be guided by public reasons, but they are suitable decision-
makers *because* of their public status. This view is advocated by theorists, legislators, and judges alike. The Federal Activities Inventory
Reform (FAIR) Act of 1998 refers to the concept of "intrinsically
governmental functions." An intrinsically governmental function
is "a function that is so intimately related to the public interest as
to require performance by Federal Government employees." Similarly, courts have insisted that certain goods and services should be
provided by the government, invalidating (even in the absence of
express legislation) government attempts to privatize these. In a
decision of the Supreme Court of Israel, the majority proscribed
the privatization of a prison on the grounds that such privatization
violates the dignity of the prisoners. The Court emphasized that its
decision was based on principled reasoning: it is not that private
prisons are less humane or less effective in rehabilitating prisoners. Rather, the Court argued,

> The special constitutional status of the right to personal liberty and
> the fact that it constitutes a condition for exercising many other
> human rights mean that the legitimacy of denying that liberty
> depends to a large extent *on the identity of the party that is competent to
> deny that liberty* and on the manner in which that liberty is denied.[26]

Publicness is not merely a vehicle for safeguarding impartiality, accountability, equality, or other values. Publicness is an essential feature of state institutions; the public character of the institutions matters *as such*, whether or not it improves the quality of

decision-making or increases the prospects of promoting public values. To borrow Locke's phrase, this paper addresses the following questions: which institutions have a "commission" to pursue public goals, and why is this commission so important? The answer to these questions is that *public* officials have commission, and that commission is important because decisions made by public officials are decisions that are *made in our name*—in the name of the political community. These decisions, in turn, give rise to collective responsibility. To better understand this, I will now turn to examine the nature of public officials and the factors that explain why public officials can act in the name of citizens.

### III. PUBLICNESS AS DEFERENCE

What makes a decision a public decision? In an abstract sense, a public decision is a decision that can be attributed to the public—a decision that is made in the name of citizens or perhaps more broadly members of the political community or the People.[27] Naturally, this does not imply that each and every member of the polity supports the decision or is even aware of its existence. The question is whether a given decision can be considered to be have been made "in the name of members of the polity." It is also worth inquiring whether it is ever possible for a decision of the polity to be made in the name of its members. This section argues that the overarching characteristic of public officials is their deference to the public interest as dictated by the sovereign, which itself decides and acts in the name of citizens. It is this characteristic which enables us to attribute the decisions and acts of public officials to citizens.

The starting point for this discussion is the widespread conviction that decisions made by the state are, at least typically, made "in the citizens' name," and that citizens bear some degree of political responsibility for these decisions. Of course, the degree of responsibility and its practical implications differ from case to case. Ordinarily, political responsibility is not sufficiently powerful or well-defined to justify the imposition of *legal* responsibility. However, political responsibility is (or should be) enough to induce citizens to protest, or at least express their disapproval of and disassociate themselves from, unjust and unsavory decisions.

Citizens always have good reason to struggle against injustice irrespective of who is responsible for it. However, many people believe that there is special reason to do so when an injustice is the work of public officials. This is because it is commonly believed that acts of public officials, including any injustice, are carried out in the name of citizens. A citizen's protest against an injustice committed by a public agency differs from a protest against an injustice committed by an individual, a private entity, or another state. An injustice committed by a public decision-maker can be attributed to ordinary citizens, who can themselves be held responsible for its occurrence.

One telling example of this idea is the name chosen by a group of dissidents that protested against the security measures taken by the US government in the wake of 9/11. The protesters called their organization "Not in Our Name." This label implies that governments typically operate in the name of their constituents. When members of the polity wish to distance themselves from the decisions of their government, they have to vocally disassociate themselves from these decisions. The label "Not in Our Name" would not, however, appropriately describe an organization that protests against the decisions of a private corporation or a foreign state. The decisions of these entities are not made in the name of citizens and cannot be attributed to them. Karl Jaspers was one of the first scholars to articulate the term "political guilt." Jaspers believed that citizens have "to bear the consequences of the deeds of the state whose power governs [them] and under whose order [they] live."[28]

Political guilt is an upshot of the widespread conviction that citizens can be held responsible for the actions of the state to which they belong. As already explained, a decision is considered a public decision where it can be attributed to citizens of a state. But in which cases is such an attribution justified? In order to answer this, let us investigate how this lofty notion of attribution can be translated into institutional terms. What is it that enables certain institutions, and not others, to speak in the community's name?

One intuitive answer is that the power to speak "in our name" stems from the indirect control that citizens exercise over government decisions in a representative democracy. Arguably, as people elect their representatives, people have an opportunity to influence the decisions made by their representatives. By virtue of this public monitoring role, we can attribute the decisions of public representatives or executive bodies to citizens. In speaking about privatization, Paul Starr articulated a more sophisticated version of this position:

> Privatization does not transform constraint into choice; it transfers decisions from one realm of choice—and constraint—to another. These two realms differ in their basic rules for disclosure of information: the public realm requires greater access; private firms have fewer obligations to conduct open proceedings or to make known the reasons for their decisions. The two realms differ in their recognition of individual desires; the public realm mandates equal voting rights while the market responds to purchasing power. They differ in the processes of preference formation: democratic politics is a process for articulating, criticizing and adapting preferences in a context where individuals need to make a case for interests larger than their own.[29]

Starr's observation does not itself establish that the state operates in the name of its citizens. Decisions made by public officials in the public interest are typically made in the absence of direct orders from the political representatives or citizens. In fact, this exercise of discretion is necessary in order to successfully promote the public interest. Therefore, we should ask: if public officials exercise discretion and thereby release themselves from the control of political representatives or citizens, why should their decisions be considered to have been made by (or in the name of) citizens? What makes citizens responsible for the decisions of public officials?

In the past, Dorfman and I addressed this question and argued that the key to understanding what justifies the attribution of decisions and acts of the state to its members is a proper understanding of the concept of a "public official" and the ways in which a public official employs different reasoning (from private actors) in her decision-making. We argued that, despite the difficulties outlined above, only the acts of public officials can be attributed to the state and thereby justify the attribution of responsibility to its citizens. This is because for an act to be attributed to the state, it must be carried out by an actor who shows deference to the polity, and only public officials show such deference. Being a public official is therefore not merely contingently conducive to the performance of a task that, in principle, could be performed by anybody; public officialdom is a *sine qua non* for acts to be carried out in the name of the state.[30]

Our present challenge is to show that, despite the fact (overlooked by Starr) that citizens may often disagree with the decisions of public officials or remain unaware of the decisions of public officials, public officials still act in the name of the polity.

Before confronting this challenge, we should note an important qualification. The way Dorfman and I characterized public officials is invariably an idealized depiction and does not necessarily account for each and every feature of public officials. Our characterization of public officials is designed to capture the normative significance of the distinction between private and public officials. Moreover, I do not claim that this characterization captures the "real" essence or nature of public officials. It is possible that in other contexts different characterizations may be preferable.[31]

Dorfman and I identified two conditions that must be satisfied in order for a person to be considered a public official whose acts and decisions are attributable to citizens:

1. There must be a practice which dictates what decisions are made; and
2. The institutional form of the practice. The practice must show deference.[32]

To speak or act in the name of the state, one must be guided by a practice that prioritizes the public interest as viewed from the perspective of the sovereign (as opposed to that of the decision-maker herself). A public official does not engage in independent reasoning with respect to the public interest; instead, a public official adopts the public point of view, which is that of the sovereign.

I will now elaborate on the first condition required for a person to qualify as a public official—the existence of a normative practice that dictates how individuals ought to decide and act. In order to make decisions and perform acts *from the perspective of the state*, there must be a fixed framework or ongoing coordinative effort

that facilitates participants (public officials) systematically working together to create a common policy perspective. The process
is coordinative in that participants respond to the preferences and
activities of each other as decisions are made. In fact, this process
has the potential to place free-standing constraints on the deliberations of participants. For instance, what an official decides in a
particular matter will depend on how her colleagues approached
similar matters. This responsiveness to the deliberation of others
is founded in the joint commitment to implement laws in light
of the decisions and acts of other public officials. It is hoped that
this analysis reveals that the decision-making of public officials is
not truly discretionary, nor is it captive to the caprice or personal
desires of any particular official. Even if public decision-making is
not governed by rigid norms, the practice described above con-
strains the activity of public officials.

Of course, this kind of constraint on the discretion of decision-
makers does not only affect public entities; it also affects private
entities. Therefore, assuming the operation of such a constraint is
a prerequisite for a decision being a public decision, our central
question—what makes a decision a *public* decision—remains unan-
swered. We still face the challenge of establishing precisely how
decisions and acts that conform to existing normative practice can
be performed in the name of the polity.

In the abstract, a decision that conforms to existing normative
practice is a public decision if, in making the decision, the agent
suppresses her own judgment and endorses the judgment of the
sovereign with respect to the public interest. Under this view,
only a judgment that is reached *from the perspective of the sovereign* is
public. Truly public decisions of the official are characterized by
unqualified deference to the judgment of the sovereign. On this
conception of deference, recruiting assistance from public officials amounts to increasing the available *means* by which the sovereign governs.

Before examining whether this perspective is feasible, we
should note the difference between this perspective and the
instrumentalist perspective discussed above. The instrumentalist perspective assumes that public decisions are characterized by
consequentialist standards such as enhanced impartiality, transparency, or accountability. Under the instrumentalist view, public

officials are at least sometimes simply those who are more likely to make better decisions or bring about better outcomes. In contrast, under the view developed in this chapter, public officials are defined by their deference and fidelity to the sovereign. It is their loyalty that explains why they are seen to act in the name of the state.

Yet, for this view to be feasible, we must be able to demonstrate that the abstract analysis developed in this chapter can be implemented on an institutional level. We must scrutinize the specific institutional tools used to gauge the judgment of the sovereign and enable decision-makers to defer to them. This is no simple task. Unlike deference in the context of less developed polities, deference to a modern state is not deference to the actual will of a particular, identifiable, natural person. Arguably, the sovereign is too vague a concept; identifying its true will and urging public officials to be guided by it is not feasible, for both epistemic and conceptual reasons.[33]

To properly defend the view that public officials act in the name of the people by deferring to the sovereign, one cannot rely on a spurious factual conjecture, such as the belief that citizens effectively control and monitor the decisions of public officials. Instead, one should consider more likely assumptions about public institutions and take into account the fact that most citizens have little knowledge or understanding of the operation of public institutions. To do so, one should identify the features that distinguish public entities from private entities. Only then can one explore whether these features properly support the claim that public entities defer to the sovereign and, in so doing, speak in the name of the citizens.

I will now discuss two different ways by which deference can be effected. Firstly, "integrative practices" give politicians the opportunity to intervene in public decision-making; thereby the practice gains its publicness from the interventionist potential of the decisions. Secondly, "insular practices" require public officials to make decisions in conformity with the long-term public interest, protecting their decisions from political intervention. Insular practice gains its publicness by subjecting the activity of public officials to detached, professional norms. I will proceed to argue that neither of these institutional frameworks apply to private entities.

*Integrative Practices:* Dorfman and I argued that what makes a practice a public practice is the potential for direct involvement and intervention on the part of politicians.[34] We defined integrative practices as practices that involve both bureaucrats and politicians. Further, we argued that the integration of political officers into the community of practice does not limit the role of politicians to that of establishing the basic rules of conduct and operational framework for bureaucrats. Nor does it limit politicians' role to that of monitoring and supervising (either directly or indirectly through other state officials) the participants of the practice. Ultimately, integrative practices are public by virtue of the *potential for intervention* by representatives of the sovereign. The inclusion of politicians in sovereign decision-making forges an important bond between decision-making rules and the general interest (considered from the public point of view). The deference of public officials in such cases is a simple byproduct of the Hohfeldian power to change the rules governing the practice. Privatization of an integrative practice would cut off political officials from the community of practice and bar employees of private firms from accessing and implementing the state's conception of the public interest.

Critically, this characterization of integrative practices does not depend on how much (or to what extent) politicians actually take advantage of their ability to influence practice. In many cases, and particularly in certain spheres of state action, politicians seldom utilize their interventionist powers. That said, it is the combination of the potential to intervene and the actual readiness of politicians to do so that counts. Accordingly, the actual intervention of politicians does not itself indicate whether or not political officers are sufficiently integrated into the community of practice. Only an assessment of the *potential* for intervention can do this.

*Insular practices:* As Dorfman and I noted, integrative practices are not the only form of publicness.[35] Some public officials should not be influenced, let alone be subject to politicians; instead, they should be insulated from politicians. I will argue that, as a matter of fact, the Hohfeldian immunity of public officials from political intervention is at times necessary for the practice to gain its publicness.

Consider, for example, the case of courts, a central bank or an independent election committee. Granting greater autonomy to bureaucrats in such cases may well be necessary to promote the public interest (as perceived by the sovereign). The Hohfeldian immunity granted to public officials is often the best, if not the only, way for a bureaucrat or an expert to show deference to the public interest. Under this view, participants in an insular practice are just as deferential as participants in an integrative practice. Public officials engaged in insular practice are expected to defer to the long-term public interest as defined by professional norms of the community to which they belong. Participants in insular practice are expected to make decisions on the basis of professional expertise. The public interest as understood by the sovereign requires that the responsibility for certain spheres of action be allocated to experts. The deference of these actors requires them to operate exclusively on the basis of such norms. Hence, such actors show deference precisely by resisting political intervention.

To sum up, this section has identified two types of public officials, both of which are characterized by deference to the sovereign: (1) integrative practices whose publicness hinges on the potential for intervention by politicians; and (2) insular practices whose publicness relies on deference to professional, expert norms. It is also evident why this understanding of public officials can be regarded as democratic understanding: the deference of public officials to the sovereign is the mark of complete control of the people over the decisions made by the state. But the analysis would not be complete without examining the differences between public entities and private entities. Cannot private integrative practices or private insular practices also fit the bill?

Let us answer this question by contemplating a typical privatization agreement.[36] A government begins by stipulating (in general and underspecified terms) the desired ends and then proceeds to impose basic constraints on the means that the private executor can employ to pursue those ends. It then, perhaps predictably, makes some room—an arena of permissibility—for the private entity to meet the designated ends by employing whatever means necessary, provided that they are consistent with the basic constraints set out by the original contract.

Clearly, the acts and decisions of a community of private practice acting within the arena of permissibility do not meet the requisite standard of deference (to the general interest as judged from the sovereign's point of view). The so-called arena of permissibility simply authorizes private contractors to promote their own views as to what the public interest requires. It enables them to pursue the general interest but only as filtered through their own lens. Significantly, the arena of permissibility is no accident; it did not come about and characterize privatization by accident. The arena of permissibility is in fact a prerequisite for achieving the goals of privatization, and in particular, efficiency.[37] A private actor which is completely constrained, i.e., has no "arena of permissibility," is more akin to a public actor, and should be so classified for the purposes of this article. The arena of permissibility therefore remains a defining—and not merely contingent—feature of private entities.[38]

This analysis demonstrates that private actors cannot form integrative communities and, for similar reasons, nor can they form insular communities. If they do so, they thereby become public entities. The power of private entities (in this context) depends solely on the contract between the government and the private entity. The arena of permissibility not only protects certain decisions from intervention by politicians; it also protects the private firms from being fully committed to professional or expert norms. Unless deference is enshrined in contract, a formally defined arena of permissibility ultimately authorizes private contractors to contravene professional norms.

On the whole, private entities differ from public entities in that they cannot be described as deferring to the sovereign. Private entities belong in neither integrative communities of practice nor insular communities of practice. Assuming they take place within the arena of permissibility, decisions made by a private entity should be tolerated even when these decisions run afoul of the public interest. The arena of permissibility empowers private actors to negate the public interest.

Before examining the normative implications of this analysis, I will address one final objection to our understanding of the term "public." Under this objection, perhaps surprisingly, private entities can be just as committed to the public interest (as seen by the sovereign) as public officials. To deny this objection by defining public officials as agents that must defer to the sovereign is to win the debate by fiat.

Needless to say, the term "public official" can indeed be defined in different ways. My definition of "public official" draws on institutional realities and the ordinary meaning of the term. Further, as I show in section IV, different definitions help to ground different normative convictions or sensibilities with respect to privatization. In principle, private employees of a private firm can defer to the sovereign. In such a hypothetical case, I would not hesitate to characterize them as public officials. This use of the term "public official" captures important normative aspects embodied in our legal and political practices and should therefore, where appropriate, shape our understanding of the term.

To sum up, this section defined public officials in terms of deference. Public officials are characterized by their deference to the public interest (as viewed by the sovereign). Such deference takes different forms. At times, the deference is effected by the interventionist potential on the part of politicians. At other times, the deference is effected by adherence to professional norms and to insular practices grounded in these norms. Unlike public officials, private actors retain some degree of discretion to act against the public interest, so long as they operate within the arena of permissibility. It is this deference that explains why we can attribute responsibility to citizens for the deeds of public officials.

## IV. The Hidden Costs of Privatization: Public Officials, Public Responsibility, and Political Engagement

It is now time to explore the implications of my view with respect to the desirability of privatization. I will argue that massive privatization erodes shared responsibility and, in so doing, threatens political engagement. Privatization undermines shared responsibility by creating protected spheres of decisions—decisions that are not guided by deference to the sovereign. Massive privatization transforms our political system and public culture, replacing robust shared responsibility and political engagement with fragmentation and sectarianism. Notably, this argument does not relate to political solidarity; it does not rely on the psychology of joint activity or its advantages. Instead, it is a purely normative argument concerning the nature of the polity and the collective responsibility resulting therefrom.

Section III established that because public officials defer to the sovereign, decisions made by public officials are decisions made "in our name" as members of a political community. Such decisions promote the public interest as viewed by the sovereign. The control exercised by the sovereign over the polity has immediate normative implications, in particular the attribution of decisions by a legitimate sovereign to the citizens. It is therefore easy to see why democracy is so compelling. In a democracy citizens govern the polity. Their responsibility for the acts of the polity is a byproduct of their power (and duty) to govern. In the absence of such power and obligation, there is no shared responsibility and decisions made by private entities would not be attributable to citizens. In contrast to public officials, private contractors are afforded discretion by the "arena of responsibility." When private contractors act within the arena of permissibility, they need not defer to the sovereign with respect to issues that are not specified in the contract. Privatization, therefore, divorces the polity from at least some state decisions. By privatizing the provision of a good or service, the polity distances itself from the privatized activity, or at least from the decisions of a private entity acting within its arena of permissibility. Thus, for example, to the extent that the activities of a private company tasked with running prison facilities fall within its arena of permissibility, the activities would be private matters and citizens would be absolved of any associated responsibility.

One might, however, protest that it is the polity that *voluntarily* decides to delegate its powers to a private entity; the polity should therefore remain responsible for any decisions made within the arena of permissibility. The initial delegation means that the private entity continues to operate in the name of the polity. The authority of the private entity, after all, derives from that of the polity. According to this view, the polity bears responsibility for the decisions of a private entity to whom authority is delegated, just as it bears responsibility for its own decisions.

I disagree. Let me begin by stating that the polity and its constituents do indeed bear responsibility for their initial decision to privatize a given activity, select the appropriate contractor, and perhaps monitor its conduct. Nonetheless, the view articulated above fails to account for the polity's loss of control over the manner in which a private entity acts. Even if we assume that the polity had a specific vision and objective(s) when it privatized a particular activity, it is thereafter barred from reconsidering its purpose or otherwise changing course. Consequently, where citizens protest against decisions made by private bodies, the relevant decisions cannot be said to have been made in the name of those citizens and those citizens are not responsible for the relevant decisions. It is this feature that fundamentally distinguishes between public officials and private entities: the former defer to the sovereign and so act *in the name* of citizens, while the latter, at best, act *for the benefit* of the citizens. This might explain why organizations that protest against injustices perpetrated by corporations have not adopted the label "not in our name." After all, there would be no need to do so; the decisions and acts of private entities are not attributable to citizens, and there is therefore no need for citizens to distance themselves from these decisions.

Yet, shared responsibility is not in and of itself desirable or undesirable. To complete my argument against privatization, it is necessary to show that civic detachment and the shunning of responsibility for major decisions is at least sometimes undesirable. To do so, I will stress the significance of collective responsibility. By acting as a polity—that is, by using public officials to perform certain tasks—citizens become responsible for the decisions made by these officials. Citizens regard the acts of the polity as their own, creating connections with other members of the polity who share similar responsibilities. The deference of public officials to the sovereign is a social adhesive that binds together members of the polity.

On this view, privatization undermines an important dimension of our moral practices—taking responsibility. In particular, privatization downplays the political dimension of responsibility by absolving citizens of their collective responsibility. As already mentioned, this argument does not turn on the psychology of joint activity and its advantages. Rather, the argument turns on political engagement facilitating citizens taking collective responsibility for sovereign action. The spheres of activity that are privatized are excluded from this collective undertaking and are hidden away behind a corporate veil; they thereby become the exclusive business of the private entity which is assigned with the task of making decisions with respect to them.

The fact that privatization downplays the political dimension of responsibility-taking is not necessarily problematic. This is because the provision of some goods might not, in the first place, give rise to political engagement. Goods the provision of which does not give rise to major normative questions or trade-offs (such as between equality and efficiency, domestic and cosmopolitan justice, and so on) do not contribute to civic engagement. In the absence of such trade-offs, the value of public provision can only be justified instrumentally—that is, it can only be justified if the goods in question are better provided by public officials. But what remains problematic is the massive privatization of goods whose provision *does* raise major political and ethical concerns. Massive privatization leads to fewer decisions being made in the name of the community and, in turn, undermines the value (if not the existence) of the political community as it becomes devoid of a sphere of decisions that are made in the name of the community.

However, importantly, our emphasis on the public provision of goods and services does not imply that privatization should be categorically ruled out. The argument developed in this article does not deny that sometimes, and perhaps often, privatization is desirable for any number of reasons, including the traditional instrumental reasons. My argument only asserts that considerations of political engagement and responsibility-taking should be balanced against conflicting considerations. Privatization on a large scale distances citizens from direct and immediate control over the provision of privatized goods and services. The gradual transition to a privatized society has grave costs in terms of political engagement and shared responsibility. And, although these costs are not monetizable, they should not be ignored.

My argument differs radically from previous discussions concerning privatization. Typically, advocates and opponents of privatization do not evaluate the desirability (or undesirability) of privatization *as such*; instead they evaluate the provision of a particular privatized good or service.[39] They compare the good or service when it is provided by a public entity to when it is provided by a private entity. But, even from a purely economic perspective, this method is lacking. Privatizing the provision of one good or service may well affect the provision of other goods and services. For instance, privatizing the provision of some goods and services may decrease the appeal of working in the public service and the willingness of individuals to enter the public sector. It may also harm the reputation of the public service or adversely affect the provision of other, un-privatized public goods and services. One likely victim, whose harm is not easily translated into economic terms, is a robust public service responsible for providing the goods and services needed to sustain political engagement.

As I have intimated, any assessment of privatization is not just about questioning whether a public prison is better or worse than a private prison, or whether a private forestry is better or worse than a public forestry.[40] Assessing privatization requires us to ask broader questions about whether stripping the state of its powers erodes civic responsibility. I would even venture to say that the erosion of public responsibility has additional consequences, which I will not fully explain in this article. Privatization does not only concern the transformation of detention centers, trains, tax inquiry offices, forestry operations, and so on, on a case-by-case basis. It concerns the transformation of our political system and public culture from an axis of robust shared responsibility and political engagement to a civilization marked by fragmentation and sectarianism.

However, one may wonder whether there might exist an altogether different institutional structure—in place of the distinctively political dimension of responsibility-taking apropos public officials—by which individuals could take responsibility for the actions of private entities. After all, human institutions are not natural creations; they are constructed by our traditions, which, no matter how entrenched, can be re-constructed. In fact, there is reason to suspect that such re-construction is already underway.

One suggestion is that the weakening public sphere is slowly being replaced by private individuals and NGOs, fueled by activists who aim to influence the decisions of private actors, often under the umbrella of corporate social responsibility. This phenomenon of market activism looks likely to expand. There are ample opportunities for market activism in every polity, particularly in connection with privatization. One may even speculate that the more privatization undermines shared responsibility and political engagement, the more market actors will assert control over private and privatized bodies. The proliferation of consumer boycotts and the now entrenched principle of corporate social responsibility suggest that market activism could perhaps compensate for the loss of shared responsibility—the very same responsibility that market activists might have borne in their capacity as members of the polity. In other words, political engagement is being gradually replaced or supplemented by market activism. The evolving transnational community of market participants has begun to eat away at the ever-weakening ties between members of political communities. However, it remains to be seen whether such transformation will prove effective. More importantly, the moral implications on the potential for persons to relate as free and equal beings in the market are as yet unknown.

## V. SUMMARY

Traditionally, privatization has been analyzed in instrumental terms; it is desirable if it is likely to bring about better decisions and outcomes. In challenging this analysis, I adopt the view (which I developed elsewhere) that foundational legal institutions and legal procedures that are typically described as contingent means to facilitate the realization of valuable ends do, in fact, matter *as such*.[41]

I argued that, even if a private entity is better at providing a particular good or service, there are other important consequences when it comes to shifting responsibility away from the state and to private entities—consequences that are not reflected in the quality of the privatized good or service. Privatization detrimentally impacts public responsibility and, in turn, undermines civic and political engagement.

This argument understands publicness as a function of deference. To the extent that publicness is grounded in deference to the sovereign, privatization reduces the control of the sovereign over the polity. While this might sometimes be desirable, massive privatization can altogether erode public responsibility and threaten the very existence of a robust polity capable of acting in the name of its citizens. Most importantly, it undermines the power that the people have in making fundamental decisions concerning their collective life. Privatization should therefore be regarded as detrimental to democracy.

One important upshot of this attempt to explain the opposition to privatization in non-instrumental terms is that it better tracks what lurks beneath the surface, namely our underlying intuitions, particularly the intuitions of those who oppose privatization. As section II demonstrated, there are numerous indications that the instrumental approach to privatization does not accord with common sense intuitions or legal doctrine. I believe that my perspective more precisely identifies the concerns that lie at the heart of political and legal debate about privatization. Throughout this enterprise, I have sought to better understand the fundamental perspectives of both advocates and opponents of privatization. The instrumental account fails to properly capture these perspectives; it simply tries to quantify and rationalize them. My ambition has been to grasp the underlying sentiments of politicians, activists, and citizens and to theorize their concerns as authentically as possible by using academic discourse.

## NOTES

1 Thomas Aquinas, *Summa Theologica*, vol. 2, part 2 (New York: Cosimo Classics, 2007): question 90.

2 See Martha Minow, "Public and Private Partnerships: Accounting for the New Religion" *Harvard Law Review* 116, no. 5 (2003): 1242–55.

3 This conviction is part of a more general approach of contemporary political theory that I have criticized in the past. More specifically, I argued against the view that "to justify an institution or a procedure one needs therefore to identify what the right or correct decision is and then to identify the institution or procedure which is most likely to get it right." Instead, I argued, "At times, institutions are not mere contingent means to the realization of valuable ends, instead such institutions are necessary prerequisites for the realization of certain values." See Alon Harel, *Why Law Matters* (Oxford: Oxford University Press, 2014): 2.

4 For an earlier defense of this view, see Avihay Dorfman and Alon Harel, "Against Privatization as Such," *Oxford Journal of Legal Studies* 36, no. 2 (2016): 400.

5 Non-monetizable costs have been recognized as relevant. See Cass Sunstein, "The Office of Information and Regulatory Affairs," *Harvard Law Review* 126, no. 7 (2013): 1838, 1866; Daniel A. Farber, "Breaking Bad? The Uneasy Case for Regulatory Breakeven Analysis," *California Law Review* 102, no. 6 (2014): 1469.

6  Michael J. Trebilcock and Edward M. Iacobucci, "Privatization and Accountability," *Harvard Law Review* 116, no. 5 (2003): 1422; Ronald A. Cass, "Privatization, Politics and Legal Theory," *Marquette Law Review* 71, no. 3 (1988): 449, 450.

7  William L. Megginson and Jeffrey M. Netter, "From State to Market: A Survey of Empirical Studies on Privatization," *Journal of Economic Literature* 39, no. 2 (2001): 321, 323–26.

8  Cass, "Privatization, Politics and Legal Theory," 452.

9  See Robert S. Gilmour and Laura S. Jensen, "Reinventing Government Accountability: Public Functions, Privatization, and the Meaning of 'State Action,'" *Public Administration Review* 57, no. 3 (1998): 247.

10 Minow, "Public and Private Partnerships," 1230.

11 Ibid., 1248.

12 Ibid., 1236.

13 Johan Willner, "Privatization: A Sceptical Analysis," in *International Handbook on Privatization*, eds. David Parker and David Saal (Cheltenham: Edward Elgar, 2005): 60.

14 Trebilcock and Iacobucci, "Privatization and Accountability," 1448.

15 Ibid., 1450.

16 Jody Freeman, "Extending Public Law Norms Through Privatization" *Harvard Law Review* 116, no. 5 (2003): 1285.

17 See Martin P. Sellers, "Privatization Morphs into 'Publicization': Businesses Look a Lot Like Government," *Public Administration* 81, no. 3 (2003): 607.

18 To facilitate the process of publicization some legal theorists argue for changing legal doctrine in ways that would be congenial to accountability. See Richard Frankel, "Regulating Privatized Government Through § 1983," *University of Chicago Law Review* 76, no. 4 (2009): 1449.

19 Minow says, "The public identity of particular actions can carry traditional, symbolic, or political significance." Minow, "Public and Private Partnerships," 1234. Yet, it seems that besides symbolism or tradition there is nothing which dictates that the values identified by Minow as "public" are more public than the value of efficiency and efficacy.

20 Dorfman and Harel, "Against Privatization as Such," 405. For a defense of such a view, see, e.g., Malcolm Thorburn, "Reinventing the Night Watchman State," *University of Toronto Law Journal* 60, no. 2 (2010): 425, 442.

21 This is the view that is labeled "pragmatist" by Freeman: "To the pragmatic privatizer, it matters little whether the service in consideration is waste collection, power generation, education or incarceration. Similarly irrelevant are the vulnerability of the population being served, its exit options or its political power. Any of these services may be ripe for

privatization if they present opportunities to cut costs and improve service quality through innovation" (Freeman, "Extending Public Law Norms," 1298). As Dolovich points out, the view that privatization is merely a technical change has often been used to legitimize privatization. See Sharon Dolovich, "How Privatization Thinks: The Case of Prisons," in *Government By Contract: Outsourcing And American Democracy*, eds. Jody Freeman and Martga Minow (Cambridge, MA: Harvard University Press, 2009): 128, 145.

22 George Bataille, *Story of the Eye* (London: Penguin Books, 2001): 34.

23 These examples are taken from Dorfman and Harel, "Against Privatization as Such," 409.

24 John Locke, "A Second Letter Concerning Toleration," in *Locke on Toleration*, ed. Richard Vernon (New York: Cambridge University Press, 2010): 100.

25 Thorburn, "Reinventing the Night-Watchman State," 442.

26 See HCJ 2605/05 *Academic Center of Law and Business v. Minister of Finance* 63, no. 2 (2009): PD 545, 612–17 (Isr), www.elyon1.court.gov.il. For a discussion of this case, see Barak Medina, "Constitutional Limits to Privatization: The Israeli Supreme Court Decision to Invalidate Prison Privatization" *International Journal of Constitutional Law* 8, no. 4 (2010): 690. This is not the only case in which courts resist privatization of functions that they regard as essential to the government. The Indian Court emphasized that policing is an essential state function and "cannot be divested or discharged . . ." (*Nandini Sundar v Chattisgarh* [2011] 7 SCC 547 [India]).

27 I shall use the terms "citizens," "members of the political community," and "members of the polity" interchangeably.

28 See Karl Jaspers, *The Question of German Guilt*, translated by E.B. Ashton (New York: Fordham University Press, 2000): 25.

29 Paul Starr, "The Limits of Privatization" *Proceedings of the Academy of Political Science* 36, no. 3 (1987): 124, 132.

30 See Dorfman and Harel, "Against Privatization as Such," 412. See also Avihay Dorfman and Alon Harel, "The Case against Privatization" *Philosophy and Public Affairs* 41, no. 1 (2013): 67, 79–90; Harel, *Why Law Matters*, 86–95.

31 Public officials are often identified on the basis of various benefits they are entitled to, including, for instance, a fixed salary–based structure of official compensation, procedural due process, and the legal protection against termination of civil service employment except for cause. Those characteristics are important for various purposes, but to establish the argument I develop a different characterization—one that rests on deference.

32 See Dorfman and Harel, "The Case against Privatization," 79–89; Harel, *Why Law Matters*, 86–95.

33 The difficulties of identifying the will of the sovereign were pointed out by Hart in his article: H.L.A. Hart, "Positivism and the Separation of Law and Morals," *Harvard Law Review* 71, no. 4 (1958): 593, 603–5. Justice Holmes was also skeptical about the relevance of the will of the sovereign to law and argued that "in a civilized state it is not the will of the sovereign that makes lawyer's law, even when that is its source" (Holmes, Note, *American Law Review* 6 [1871–72]: 723).

34 Dorfman and Harel, "The Case against Privatization," 83–88.

35 Dorfman and Harel, "Against Privatization as Such," 418–20.

36 This section is based on Harel, *Why Law Matters*, 91–92.

37 As one commentator has noted:

The emphasis on outcomes gives private service providers latitude to develop their own strategies for achieving the desired results. If all tasks were specified in the governing contracts, there would be little room for the beneficial effects of competition to operate (Matthew Diller, "Form and Substance in the Privatization of Poverty Programs," *UCLA Law Review* 49, no. 6 (2002): 1739, 1745).

The arena of permissibility is typically broader than is conceived by the government at the time of contracting. See Jody Freeman, "Private Parties, Public Functions and the New Administrative Law" Administrative Law Review 52, no.3 (2000): 813, 823–24.

38 Arguably this is merely a semantic maneuver: winning by fiat. Below I show that this definition is not an arbitrary one; it is one that accords to a large extent with contemporary legal practices.

39 See for instance Dorfman and Harel, "The Case against Privatization," 92–96, where we argued that punishment must be provided only by public officials.

40 For a similar view, see John Gardner, "The Evils of Privatization" (unpublished manuscript), http://papers.ssrn.com.

41 See Harel, *Why Law Matters*, 2.

# 4

# PRIVATIZATION AND THE OUGHT / STATE GAP

## PETER JAWORSKI

Institutions, public and private, have merely derivative value. They are instruments and, as instruments, should be evaluated by the good (or bad) they help us accomplish, or the bad (or good) they help us bring about or realize. Not everyone shares this view, but everyone should.

There are many things that we might want our institutions to deliver. Determining what should be included on the list, what would make it not just comprehensive, but complete, is a normative exercise. We can do this in our armchair. Once we have a complete list of good things, we can then evaluate the institutions on the basis of how well they realize or deliver those goods.

We can argue about whether or not our current list is complete, about whether we have overlooked or failed to consider something important. We can argue about how to weigh the various things on our list. We can argue about what it would take to actually deliver what is on the list. And so on.

Debra Satz wants to expand what we typically focus on.[1] She tells us that, thus far, the debate about privatization has focused too much on accountability and efficiency. In general, people seem to share the view that public enterprises deliver on accountability, while private enterprises are more efficient. We are asked to decide between "public bureaucracy," which is accountable, and "private entrepreneurship," which is efficient. Satz wants to highlight how important it is that we also consider the effects of private and public enterprises on equality, as well as the possible effects of privatization on corrupting public purposes. She wants us to expand what we think matters in the debate about privatization.

Satz is right. Equality and corruption of public purpose matter in addition to common worries about accountability and efficiency. There are many other "good" things that would be beneficial for our institutions to deliver, including liberty and security.

No matter what ends up constituting the complete list—what features or functions we settle on as good or desirable—whether we ought to pick public or private enterprises to deliver them will not be settled in principle. This is because there is no necessary or essential connection between this list, and their realization through one or another particular institution, including the government. There is a gap between the functions and features on our complete list, and their realization through the state.

I call this the ought / state gap, but it could just as easily be called the ought / institution or ought / enterprise gap. The right question to ask is whether or not some or another institution, including government institutions, more reliably delivers on the list; whether or not this or that institution makes it more likely that we discharge our obligations, or realize our duties. Questions about reliability invite social scientific inquiry. Bridging the gap requires an appeal to empirical facts; we cannot get there by reflection in our armchairs alone. Our armchairs can get us as far as determining (at least some of) what should be included on our list—the obligations and duties—but no further.

In this contribution, I also want to highlight the many ways in which our armchair is not up to the task of deciding whether or not to privatize some enterprise. Just as there is probably always a gap between what we ought to do and our using a state instrument to get it done, so there is probably always, but at least often, a gap between the desirable features and functions of institutions, and the state in particular. There is probably no conceptual, nor any other necessary, bridge between any plausibly desirable function or feature on our list and the state.

In saying that there are no conceptual or other necessary bridge principles, we leave open the possibility that many if not all enterprises could be privatized. Whether or not we should privatize in practice, however, is a different question. That some private institution could, in principle, fulfill some function in a better way does not mean that it will. That a public institution is currently fulfilling a morally important function without that fulfillment coming at the expense of something of moral importance is a very good reason to keep doing it that way. At the very least, we should recognize that changing institutions has costs.

With those preliminaries out of the way, I want to do the following:

First, I want to show that very many of the desirable features or functions that we typically associate with state-owned enterprises (SOEs) are contingent. For every desirable feature or function that is thought to be connected to an SOE, there is at least in principle, and probably always in practice, a privately owned enterprise (POE) with that feature. In addition, the fact that we are convinced that a non-state enterprise will fail at delivering some morally important feature does not rule out privatization. We can always mandate or require the specific feature as a regulatory requirement.

Second, I want to remind us that the division between public and private is a division based on ownership. To say that something is a public or state enterprise is to say that it is owned by the government, and to say that it is a private enterprise is to say that it is not so owned. When we talk about privatizing some function performed by a state enterprise, we are just talking about a non-state enterprise taking over that function. Discussions about accountability, equality, governance, partiality, the public interest, and so on are conceptually distinct issues.

Third, and finally, I want to show why one attempt at bridging the gap without relying on any empirical evidence fails. This is a strategy by Alon Harel (sometimes with Avihay Dorfman) that attempts to show that the state is the only institution that can punish, that judges must be agents of the state, and that prisons must be state run. I think this argument fails, but it fails in a way that is instructive for anyone else who wishes to make a case for states doing certain things without appealing to any empirical claims.

## I. INSTITUTIONAL ARCHITECTURE

*"Marketization" Is Not Privatization*

Consider the following complaints about public education in the U.S.:

Some people complain that, in fact, rich people get better education, because they are able to move to expensive neighborhoods and send their kids to better schools. Some people complain that public schools are not able to fire bad teachers, and this makes those schools worse. Sometimes, the complaint is that bad schools don't go out of business, which at least sometimes would be an improvement. Some complain that public schools have very little incentive to improve, because they don't face competition.

None of the above are arguments against public education as such. Instead, they are at best arguments against those specific features. The reason why there are better schools in wealthy neighborhoods is, in part, because a portion of the funding for schools comes from local property taxes (obviously there are many other reasons as well, but this is one). Schools in wealthy neighborhoods have more resources as a consequence of the funding mechanism. In addition, in some cases a child can only attend a particular public school if she is within the catchment area of that school. If you are wealthy, you can afford to move, and you can afford to move to whatever public school district has better performance. It is these features, and not the fact that the education is provided by the government, that partly explain why wealthy children get better public schools.

Neither of these features are necessary features of public schools. For example, some states in the U.S. have public schools without catchment areas (like magnet schools), while some public schools have school finance systems that do not solely rely on property taxes, like the use of vouchers. Public universities accept students from all over the world, not just from their area, and their funding is not tied to property taxes at all. So in fact there are public schools without these features and so, in principle, we could change them. Getting rid of a catchment area is not tantamount to privatization, and neither is changing the funding mechanism.

The same is true of the other complaints. It is relatively difficult to fire bad teachers, not because the government operates the school, but because of the terms found within the labor contract teachers' unions have secured. But in practice, teacher tenure policies differ in different states, and many include a probationary period during which it is relatively easy to fire a teacher. In Florida, for example, the probationary period during which a teacher can be fired even without just cause is ninety-seven days; in most other states, the probationary period is two to three years. Some public universities make use of adjuncts or other non-tenured teachers whose dismissal is not difficult. And even if all public schools were uniform in making it difficult to fire teachers, it would be true that, in principle, we could eliminate this feature. The relative security of an employment contract is not what makes something "public" as opposed to "private."

So too with closing poorly performing schools and competition between schools. There are in fact cases where closing public schools is not difficult, and besides this is a reform that could be incorporated within a recognizably public school system. There are other cases where public schools compete with other public schools, and we could have public schools compete for students without changing the nature of the school from a public to a private one. This is so in higher education, for example. The University of California competes with other public universities for students and teachers, and competes with private universities as well. Competition may be a typical feature of markets, but it is not what distinguishes public enterprises from private ones.

Competition between enterprises, competition for customers or employees, relative ease of firing poor performers, and relative difficulty of securing funding for continued operation are each constituents of market discipline. They are typical features of the traditional private sector model. They may be among the features that explain efficient (or inefficient) outcomes, but instituting some, even all, elements of what is part of the traditional private sector model into a state-owned enterprise does not amount to privatization. At best it amounts to marketization, but marketization is not the same as privatization.

### "Publicization" Is Not Nationalization

Something very similar can be said to privatization opponents. There are very many privately owned enterprises that have features in common with state-owned enterprises. In addition, where we do not see a desirable feature or do see an undesirable one, we can often either recommend that it be included, or require it through regulation.

To illustrate, consider the following complaints about private schools:

Some people complain that only the wealthy can afford to send their children to private schools. Some worry that they will hire charlatans, rubes, or otherwise ignorant teachers. Some worry that these schools will discriminate on the basis of gender or race in their acceptance and hiring decisions. There are many others, but these will be sufficient to make the point.

Just as in the case of complaints against public schools above, so too with these complaints: They are not complaints about privatization as such, but about contingent features that not all private schools share, and features that, in principle, we could design away.

It is true that very many private schools are expensive, but not all of them are. Very many are inexpensive. Many private schools provide need-based scholarships for students. Expensiveness may be a common feature of private schools, but it is not essential. It is also not exclusive to private schools. If you would like to send your child to Thomas Jefferson High School for Science and Technology in Fairfax, Virginia, you will first have to buy a house in one of the six eligible, but high-priced, counties. Thomas Jefferson is an expensive public school. We can also recommend a different model or eliminate this particular worry by having the government pay for tuition, as they sometimes do, in the form of vouchers or other systems, or by subsidizing those students who could not otherwise afford it. Subsidizing students does not amount to nationalizing the school.

The worry that private schools will hire charlatans is not true of, for example, Princeton University or Harvard University. It is also not true of very many actual private high schools, or an exclusive problem for private schools. In Texas, Louisiana, and Tennessee, teachers are permitted to teach "alternatives" to evolution, like creationism, and at least some do. Charlatanism is a problem for both the public and the private school system.[2] We can recommend different licensing or certification systems, or require them through regulations, and in a way, we do. For example, you have to have a Ph.D. from an accredited university in order to fill most of the permanent faculty positions at most private universities. The fact that we do have these regulations in place even for private schools does not mean that those schools are therefore public schools.

When it comes to discrimination, we can always point to private schools that are not subject to this criticism. It need not be a feature of all private schools that they so discriminate. Discrimination is also not a problem exclusive to private schools. Segregation was legally imposed on all schools in the U.S. in the not-too-distant past, and when the Supreme Court ruled that schools must desegregate, George Wallace, the then-governor of Alabama, stood in front of the University of Alabama to try and stop the enrollment of black students. We can recommend that schools follow a different course, and try to persuade private agents to behave differently. And in principle, if we don't trust that private agents will so act, we can require non-discrimination in hiring decisions, and in decisions about which students to accept.

At this point, the strategy should be clear: First, none of the complaints mentioned are necessary features of a private school; they are all contingent. Second, some actual private schools do not have those features, while some actual public schools do. Third, we can always recommend that the feature be changed. Finally, for any of these features, we may be able to regulate them away without thereby nationalizing the school.[3]

Requirements on who may be hired, how difficult it is to fire them, prohibiting certain forms of discrimination, subsidizing consumers through tax revenues, and so on are each features common to the public sector. Some of them are typical features of the traditional public sector model.[4] They may be part of the features that help explain the performance of private schools. But instituting some of these elements, or one or another of the constituents of the traditional public sector model, into a private enterprise does not amount to nationalization. At best it amounts to "publicization," but publicization is not the same as nationalization.

Let me offer some more concrete examples.

## Other Contingent Features

In Canada, every election includes a discussion about the status of the Canadian Broadcasting Corporation (CBC). The CBC provides local and national news, television shows, and sports coverage, as well as music and talk shows, on radio and television. The mission of the public broadcaster is to promote the public interest. It does so through three principles, captured in their vision statement: "It should focus on citizens and creators, reflect Canadian identity and promote democracy, and support social and economic innovation."[5]

None of the features we might point to are unique to the public broadcaster model. There are many private enterprises that subsidize certain business units that operate at a loss in order to promote the public interest.

The Cable Public Affairs Channel (CPAC), for example, covers Question Period in the House of Commons, various briefings and panels, debates between political opponents, and more in order to inform Canadians on what their government is doing, which is taken to be in the public interest, on television. It is financed by several cable companies, each of which are for-profits, but operates at a loss.

Apple is a technology company that makes attractive computers and tablets, mobile phones, and devices that let you listen to music and podcasts. It has a business unit dedicated to making gadgets for people who are visually and hearing-impaired, which it operates at a loss, in order to promote the well-being of visually and hearing-impaired people, which is part of the public interest. Apple is a for-profit company.

These are business units with a significant public interest component operating within for-profit enterprises, but a profit orientation is not a distinction between SOEs and POEs. There are many charities, not-for-profits, and, in the U.S., public benefits corporations. National Public Radio (NPR), for example, provides local and national news, various storytelling shows, a car show, a game show, and so on, on the radio. Their mission is to promote the public interest. It is funded by grants from large private granting bodies and through contributions from listeners like me. They receive some funding from the government but, nevertheless, they are a not-for-profit private company. Underwriters Laboratories (UL) "certifies, validates, tests, verifies, inspects, audits, advises and educates." They do this for various products in order to "facilitate global trade and deliver peace of mind," which is in the public interest. They are a non-profit company that charges the products they certify a fee. Meanwhile, there are SOEs that are for-profit enterprises. Fannie Mae and Freddie Mac are SOEs that are supposed to help realize the goal of expanded home ownership, which is taken to be in the public interest, through the provision of home mortgages. Both are for-profit enterprises.

Promoting Canadian identity through Canadian content does not require a public broadcaster. We can imagine a regulation that requires private enterprises to include a certain percentage of Canadian content on their private radio and television shows and networks. In this case, we don't have to be very imaginative since this is what the Canadian government does through Canadian content (CanCon) laws overseen by the Canadian Radio-television and Telecommunications Commission (CRTC). Similar regulations exist in Australia, Mexico, Israel, South Africa, and New Zealand. France, meanwhile, has a quota system that requires not French content, but European Union content more broadly. These regulations restrict what private enterprises may do, but this particular restriction does not make these enterprises state-owned or public, not even de facto.

## II. Privatization Is About Ownership

It is worth reminding ourselves that what demarcates public from private is ownership. Something counts as public if and only if it is owned by the state, and counts as private if and only if it is owned by a non-government enterprise. As far as enterprises go, what we mean by privatization is that something that is currently owned by the government comes to be owned by a non-governmental entity.

Privatization is about ownership, but ownership is a complex concept. Above, I've said that, in principle, we could always regulate some feature of a private enterprise without thereby nationalizing it. But a sufficient number of regulations on what it is legally permissible for a private enterprise to choose to do will amount to nationalization.

This complication is consistent with the best analysis we have of the concept of ownership, which is A.M. Honoré's account of ownership as consisting in a bundle of rights (sometimes called "sticks").[6] These include the right to use, to transfer, to earn income from the good, to destroy, to exclude others, and so on. If someone has one of these rights, we say that they have a "property in" whatever it is that right is associated with. Only when we have a sufficient number of the individual rights can we say that we own that thing. So the government, through regulations, can have a property in a private enterprise's decision about whom to hire, or can remove the legal permission for a company to charge whatever price it wants, or can determine the price itself, etc., but if it removes enough of what an enterprise can legally do, that enterprise becomes a public enterprise.

There are interesting questions, then, about de facto public and private. An enterprise might be "private" in name, but public in practice.[7] We should understand that in the following way: The government, through regulations or requirements of a contract or other means, has taken a sufficient number of incidents away such that it is justified for us to say that the government "owns" the enterprise. There is a significant legal literature on the issue of regulatory "takings" in the U.S.[8]

Honoré left unexplored whether any incidents are essential or necessary to ownership. Subsequent scholars have insisted on some of these incidents being necessary, the most popular of which is the right to exclude.[9] I'm not sure whether something similar should be said in this context. Perhaps there is an incident such that, without it, we cannot say you are the owner. But I, too, will leave this issue unexplored.

### Contingent Features: Judges

Here is a concrete recent example:

Debra Satz maintains that we do not want judges to be motivated by financial considerations, something she calls an instance of "intrinsic corruption."[10] This intrinsic corruption is a problem, she maintains, with the idea of privatizing the criminal justice system, which is essentially, and not contingently, a public good. She writes, "For example, it is essential to the proper workings of the criminal justice system that officers of the court not be motivated by financial considerations when they consider punishments. Privatization[11] of the system wouldn't work—not because competitive markets in judicial opinions couldn't be developed but because the buying and selling of judicial services is (automatically, as it were) a corruption of the process of dispensing justice."[12] This is a reason to prefer a state-owned enterprise to a privately owned enterprise, and it is an intrinsic feature that would presumably pervade all private criminal justice systems.

But, in the first place, that is too narrow. What we don't want is for judges to render decisions based on whether or not they are attracted to the defendant or prosecutor, or whether or not they are hungry and tired just now, or because they're afraid that the defendant will harm them or their family, or to decide based on a prediction about how instrumentally useful this decision might be for climbing the judicial ladder or getting a spot on the Supreme Court.

That it is too narrow is important. It is important because it allows us to more easily see that there are undue pressures that judges will confront regardless of whether we have private or public judges. If there is a difference, it will be found in either the degree or the kind of undue pressure, rather than in its being due or undue, and it will be a result of the specific features of the enterprises responsible for criminal justice, rather than their being state- or privately owned.

Different states select judges differently. In several states, although not at all in Canada, judges are elected rather than appointed. Elections are a form of pressure that might cause judges to rule based on what they think is popular, rather than just.[13] Appointing judges replaces the pressure of satisfying the electorate, or some financial interest, with the pressure of satisfying the politicians or political parties who appoint judges.[14] Moreover, some judges are not satisfied with their judgeship, and aspire to join the Circuit Court, or the Supreme Court. This common desire to climb that ladder means judges will feel pressure to render verdicts in ways that at least do not undermine the climb.

In the second place, it is not a necessary feature of a private system. Satz and I are judges of a sort—we judge students. We both work in private institutions, Stanford and Georgetown Universities. For whatever reason, possibly precisely because of worries about corruption, these private institutions do not pay for our services by having students hand us a bag of money after each class. We don't get paid based on something like a commission. Instead, students pay tuition, and we get a salary from that. Since we consider it important to evaluate students without certain kinds of undue pressures, we insist on certain ways of paying for the service.

It may or may not be a good idea to privatize the criminal justice system. But, in principle, the worry that judges will decide based on financial pressures is a contingent feature. Only if judges feel pressure to deliver a particular result that conflicts with how they ought to make decisions will this be a worry, and that depends on how they are chosen and paid, how they advance in their careers, and how they get removed. If we think we know what features avoid bad pressures, we can insist on them through regulations. We can say, we will privatize the system, but you cannot pay judges in this way.

Similarly, it may or may not be a good idea to privatize the CBC, but it should be clear that we can preserve all of the desirable features of public broadcasting within private enterprises, either by selecting private enterprises that already have whatever features we think desirable, or by requiring it through regulations. In theory, we could privatize the CBC.

It might be objected that private enterprises are unreliable promoters of the public interest. But this is an empirical question. Again, we can check. But notice that we should also check when it comes to the state. Just how reliable are actual public agents at promoting the public interest?[15] Just as maybe most private enterprises are not good at this, neither are most governments. Probably a small minority of all governments in history have even sincerely *attempted* to promote the public interest, rather than some narrow sectarian or private interests. Maybe public sector employees and the enterprises they work in now, in countries like Canada, Australia, New Zealand, France, Denmark, the U.S., and so on, are sincerely devoted to the public interest. But maybe employees of the Red Cross, Harvard University, National Public Radio, St. Jude's Hospital, and Starbucks are also sincerely devoted to the public interest. To find out, we have to check.

## III. NON-CONTINGENT BRIDGE

Alon Harel (sometimes with Avihay Dorfman) has suggested that there are at least a few cases where we do not have to check, where privatization is ruled out necessarily and not contingently. In a series of papers, as well as in a book, he has argued against privatization of, among other things but especially, the criminal justice system.[16] His argument depends, in part, on a "pretheoretical intuition" that there is a difference between vigilante justice and punishment.[17] That distinction is grounded in the difference between imposing a harm or suffering on someone for having done something wrong, and doing that while also communicating or expressing the body politic's condemnation or disapproval.

Suppose we have an official list of crimes and a list of punishments that correspond to the crimes. Now suppose Frank Castle (the protagonist in Marvel Comics's *The Punisher*) witnesses someone doing one of the things on the first list. Frank springs into action, capturing the offender. He then carefully checks the second list, and delivers precisely that penalty. You and I may approve of what Frank has done, but we will have to agree that his actions do not constitute punishment. He could choose to call himself The Vigilante, and maybe we approve of what he has done, but he could not call himself The Punisher. Or, he could, but he wouldn't actually be doling out punishment.

How could The Vigilante become The Punisher? First, we would need a list of crimes. That list cannot be arbitrary, and must be composed by appealing to the interests of the relevant corporate entity—the body politic. Our list of crimes, then, must be consonant with, or at least not contrary to, the General Will, or the Common Good, or the Public Interest.

Once we had our list of crimes, we would need to capture the expression of condemnation (the "resentment and indignation"[18]) of the body politic at the commission of a crime on our list. This expressive or symbolic act of communication requires a communicator, someone or some group who may speak on behalf of the body politic, on behalf of the state. The only person or group who speaks on behalf of the body politic is a legislator or legislature (in this scenario, Rex).

Since Rex cannot punish everyone personally, we will need agents who can act on behalf of Rex. The action taken by an agent must be an action properly attributed to Rex, rather than to the agent (or to someone or something else). This requires a particular kind of reasoning. An agent's actions are "of" Rex, rather than

"for" Rex (or for themselves, or for some other entity) when the
agent demonstrates fidelity of deference. The agent must defer
not only to Rex's judgment about the content of the Public Interest, but also defer to Rex's judgment about the best way to bring
it about. The question must be, "What would Rex do?," not "What
should Rex do?" or "What is the best thing to do?" It turns out
that only state agents can use fidelity of deference in this way, since
non-state agents have an "arena of permissibility" that permits
them to reason according to their own judgment (otherwise, they
would just be state agents).

Finally, it has to be the case that the person punished does
not feel alienated from the punishment. This lack of alienation
is guaranteed when she is a member of the corporate entity on
whose behalf an agent acts. In principle, her interests are captured
in the Public Interest, and so the punishment is undertaken also
on her behalf.

The Vigilante, it turns out, would have to be a state agent to be
The Punisher. Not only would he have to be a state agent, so would
The Judge, as well as The Warden. The Judge, in having to make
normative decisions about what constitutes impartial and fair punishment, and The Warden, in having to make normative decisions
about the correct treatment of a prisoner, would each have to use
fidelity of deference. So, when it comes to the criminal justice system, we simply cannot privatize these particular functions, because
if we did we would not succeed at punishing anyone. We would
simply be imposing suffering and harm on them.

## Arena of Permissibility

Harel and Dorfman want to highlight an "arena of permissibility" that distinguishes the private from the public realm. We can
reflect on what it means for something to be private to see that it is
precisely in virtue of a broader arena of permissibility that we call
something private. It is public, on the other hand, when that arena
of permissibility is, in principle, restricted.

There are, however, two different kinds of permissibility. If it is
an arena of legal permissibility, then we can all agree that private
companies are private in virtue of having greater legal permissions
in making choices about what to do within that arena. To count as

private, they have to have a sufficient number of incidents from the bundle of rights so that it is accurate to say that they are "owners" of those decisions. If the state were to restrict or regulate away a sufficient number of the possible choices they are free to make according to their own best judgment, then, at some point, they would be de facto state (or public) agents, rather than private ones.[19]

It might be said that public agents are given significant arenas of legal permissibility as well. For example, Supreme Court members have wide immunity from being removed by Rex, as do Attorney Generals, and as do members of Parliament or Congress. The difference, say Harel and Dorfman, is that *in principle* any one of these agents of the state *should* be removed from office as soon as they fail to defer to the sovereign's judgment and act on their own judgment. That is, they should be removed whenever their actions become actions for the state (or for a non-state entity or person), rather than actions of the state. So while they might have an arena of legal permissibility, this arena is sharply circumscribed by their role morality. Whenever they violate their role morality as agents of the state, they are subject to being removed and should be removed.

An action is to be individuated as public or private on the basis of whether the action is properly understood as an action of the state or not. If the former, it is public, and if the latter, it is private. But not only must the ends sought be determined by the state, but also the means. Dorfman and Harel write:

> On this conception of fidelity, recruiting assistance amounts to increasing the available means by which Rex can govern his subjects on the basis of his, and only his, conception of the general interest and the best ways to bring it about (including, of course, setting appropriate punitive responses to crimes). Unlike fidelity of reason (on which more below), deferential fidelity is assessed not by reference to the general interest as impartially identified from the assistant's own point of view, but rather by reference to the assistant's success in retreating from his point of view and in adopting Rex's point of view.[20]

This combined view—the conception of the general interest plus the best way to bring it about—invites the following objection.

Rex says murder is wrong and contrary to the public interest. He says that in order to decrease murder, the state will give all murderers seven houses and seven horses. Rex is a fool who thinks this will dissuade murder. Foolishly, but unintentionally, Rex has offered an incentive to murder, rather than a disincentive. What should judges do? Should they defer to the object of the law, or the means (because they cannot do both)? They can try to reduce murders, in which case they cannot defer to Rex's judgment about the way to bring it about, or they can defer to what Rex says they are to do when confronted with a murder, in which case they will incentivize more murders.

Dorfman and Harel might concede as follows: The question about means in this hypothetical is a non-normative question about a matter of fact. When it comes to matters of fact, we don't need to reference the body politic. Unlike matters about what the public interest consists in, matters of fact can be delegated to private agents. Indeed, during criminal trials, the state often relies on private agents for just these sorts of determinations—like a private DNA lab to tell us whether or not this DNA matches the accused, or asking for expert testimony from a private psychologist, and so on. So if there is a non-normative fact of the matter about what would disincentivize murder (or what would best bring about the end that Rex wants brought about), then it is within the arena of permissibility for the judge to defer to the ends without having to defer to the means.

For Dorfman and Harel, there appear to be three conceptually distinct elements of a trial. First, there is the non-normative question of guilt—did this person in fact do what we are accusing her of doing? Second, there is the question of how much punishment should be doled out. Sometimes, that requires judgment by the judge, but other times Rex might give a specific punishment ahead of time requiring no independent judgment ("all murderers get the death penalty, no exceptions whatsoever"). When it's the latter, it is a non-normative question of finding the crime on the list, and reading the punishment that corresponds to it.

The final element is condemnation. Once you are found guilty, you are condemned not by any of the persons who participated in your court trial, but by the body politic. It is this last bit that appears to metaphysically require Rex's "Joints" or "Nerves."[21] The body politic is represented by Rex, so when a representative of Rex says or does something in such a way that it is the doing of the state, she represents the body politic as a whole. Perhaps a verdict of "guilty" would not require a state agent if it were merely a matter of fact, but it comes bundled, insist Dorfman and Harel, with the community's judgment of condemnation.

## Symbolism

This is a good place to pause for a moment and consider other cases. Dorfman and Harel's analysis of the criminal justice system has formal features that might help us explain similar sorts of judgments by others. So, for example, some would like education to be public, to be operated and funded by the state. Others would like the health care system to be public. While instrumental considerations might count in favor (or not) of public education or health care, so too might there be a non-instrumental reason for preferring public versions of these enterprises. Public education and health care permit us to communicate or express that we, as a body politic, care about the education of fellow citizens, and care about the health of our community. We do this when agents of the state teach our children and run our hospitals. They are the unique and exclusive kinds of agents who may speak on our behalf as a body politic. So one value that is always lost to us when we have private education and health care is the symbolic value of expressing our judgment, as a body politic, that education and health care matter. It is true that, if we were all shareholders in one company, club, or church, we might be able to express collective judgments. But then we would do so qua shareholders, club members, or church body, not qua citizens, or as the body politic.

Now, of course, we should consider the price of this symbolic value. Supposing that private education or health care were significantly superior to the public version, we might then prefer the former. But it would be a shame, goes this argument, because it would come at the expense of this symbolic value—we would lose, and always lose, something that belongs on the comprehensive list of good things.[22]

This argument, however, fails in at least two ways. The first way is this: If the private education system was better in any way, then we would in fact fail to express our collective judgment that we value education if we were to pick the public education system. We would instead communicate that we value appearing to look like we value education. Suppose I was feeding my child medicine. The medicine is called "I care about my child's health" medicine. A convention arises, over time, that identifies caring for your child's health with giving them "I care about my child's health" medicine. Now suppose that it turns out that this medicine is harmful to the child. Even if the harm is minor, if we actually cared for our child, we would stop giving them "I care about my child's health" medicine.[23] If we didn't, then we would show that we do not care about our child's health, but would demonstrate that we care about the totem that symbolizes it. It is a way of fetishizing the symbol over the meaning of the symbol. We should care about our children's health, not care about appearing to care about it, nor about expressing our collective commitment to caring. Actual caring always beats expressing caring.

The second way in which it fails is in failing to see that expressing the collective judgments in some symbolic way is multiply realizable. One way may very well be through public education. But a different way is to, for example, have a state representative pick up an extraordinarily dazzling scepter (the Symbolic Scepter of the State), and, while waving it in a circle precisely eight times, say the words "We care about the education of our children" eight times, each utterance corresponding with each full circle of the scepter.[24] There is no conceptual connection between a) the claim that we, as a body politic, ought to express a commitment to the education of our children or the health of our fellow citizens, and b) the state having to provide the good through state-owned enterprises with state agents.

Will this response work for criminal justice? We might think that the polity's attitude of condemnation captured in a punishment reduces criminal behavior. But then this would just be a contingent reason to keep the symbolic communication, not a necessary one. A non-contingent reason would be grounded in our conviction that punishment is made only when it communicates condemnation from the body politic. And perhaps we need to do this in every instance. While we might be able to symbolize and express our collective commitment to education or health care with a scepter and a ritual or a statue, we do not appear to be able to do this with punishment.

Even if so, however, and returning to the three-part conceptual distinction of a trial, there does not appear to be any metaphysical requirement for each of these elements to be embodied in one natural person. Indeed, during jury trials, the finding of guilt or not is determined by the jury, and the judge decides on a sentence. There also appears to be no reason for why these particular matters of fact (guilt and type of punishment when it's on a list) require state agents. In which case that leaves open the possibility of introducing a third natural person, a state agent, whose job it is to communicate condemnation. Perhaps, after a finding of guilty by a private judge, this person is given fifteen minutes to pick up the Symbolic Scepter of the State, which he uses to methodically and significantly thump the ground while intoning, "Shame!"—thump—"Shame!"—thump—"Shame!"—thump.

### Exclusive and Unique?

The reason why this scepter matters so much is because, as I'll try to show presently, something like the Symbolic Scepter of the State is, in fact, the only unique and exclusive feature of a state that Dorfman and Harel can point to.[25] For all other features that they identify, private enterprises either do in fact share in them, or could in principle.

First, consider the formal features. It is not that only state entities can have agents whose actions can be described as "of" the entity. All collective entities have "arms" of the entity, arms whose movements can rightfully be described as actions of the entity. Provided that an employee of Coca-Cola, say, demonstrates fidelity of deference within the relevant Coca-Cola community of practice, her actions are of Coca-Cola and not just for Coca-Cola.

Non-state collective entities also cannot have a take-it-or-leave-it attitude towards their role morality. All agents working within some collective entity, whether state or non-state, have obligations that befall them in virtue of the nature of the relevant enterprise. Tenured professors who have managed to work out a contract where they no longer have to teach students, and who also decide to no longer publish, spending their days flying kites instead, are immune from legal prosecution and may be immune from being fired by their university, but they are not immune from the judgment that this is not, in fact, within the arena of their moral permissibility and from the further judgment that therefore *in principle* they *should* be removed. They may have the legal right to do wrong, but they do not have the moral right to do wrong. No one does. And the judgment that the truth about one's role morality should set the standard by which we can judge whether or not some agent in principle should be removed is a judgment that applies across state and non-state entities.

Next, consider the content of the role morality. Public agents in Dorfman and Harel's sense are required, in part, to treat all members of the public in an equal, impartial, and fair way. These constitutive features of what makes someone a public agent are not exclusive to state enterprises. So, for example, teachers are obligated to treat their students equally, impartially, and fairly. And we know this not from an inquiry into the nature of "public" or "private," or state or non-state, but from an appeal to the nature and good of the enterprise itself.

When we ask what makes someone a good teacher, we do not first ask whether or not they work in a public or private school. Similarly with schools: To find out what makes a school good, we do not first ask whether it is public or private. The standard is set by what we want from schools and teachers, what the point of the enterprise of education is. If the nature of the enterprise sets the standard then, in principle, we can always ask, when comparing public and private schools, whether the former or the latter has features—governance, decision-mechanisms, incentives, and so on—that more reliably deliver the good of education. We can then see whether or not reforming public or private schools is better than privatizing or nationalizing schools by appealing to the complete list of good things.[26] But when we reflect on the nature of education and our complete list of good things, we will see that none of them make any essential or necessary contact with the state. Potentially, an all-private education system could deliver on everything on our complete list. When we get all the items on that list, we leave nothing of value on the table.

*Cosmopolitan*

Perhaps it is in virtue of what makes you a member of the public. In the case of a firm, one becomes a member of that firm's public (whose interests are to be taken into account), obligating the taking of a public point of view (where the public is at least the shareholders), when one purchases shares in the firm.[27] But the firm is in no position to say that they represent anyone other than that subset of a broader group of people who have chosen to buy shares. But in the case of the body politic, the state gets to claim you as a member in its public if you were born there or follow whatever procedure they put in place for becoming a member if you weren't born there.[28] Presumably there would be no problem if, say, a shareholder in a private justice company were criminally harmed by a different shareholder in the same company, and the company presumed to adjudicate and execute a punishment on behalf of the first shareholder. It would not be a problem because both of these shareholders are members of the company's public, and the company is bound by their role morality to consider each of their interests from the company-public point of view. Each of the shareholders are appropriately represented by the company. All decisions about each member, in principle, are done with shareholders' interests in mind (and if a company decision-maker fails to do so, she should be removed). No shareholder is a mere spectator, but is a full participant in that her interests are accounted for in the company-public point of view, and she has a say in what that company-public point of view consists in.

But no company could have a monopoly on the legitimate use of force in a given jurisdiction, or else it would just be a de facto state, rather than a private company. So there is always the question of what happens when a member not in the company-public is subjected to the company's adjudication or punishment—it looks like in that case this person is alienated from the relevant public, and is subject to mere violence. She is not a member of the company-public, and her interests are not included in the company-public point of view. Call this the "not my company" problem. The resolution of this problem is found in the body politic. The body politic is a broader public that represents shareholders and non-shareholders alike, and its jurisdiction trumps any sub-jurisdictions. Companies may punish their members, but that punishment cannot conflict with the state's punishments, and the state always reserves the right to trump the company's punishment proceedings. So we take all of the companies, clubs, groups—all corporate entities—in our jurisdiction, and we incorporate them into a bigger corporate entity that rules them all. That's Rex. Rex solves the "not my company" problem.

This actually raises, rather than settles, many questions. For Dorfman and Harel, the arena of permissibility—not just legal but moral permissibility—includes the right of a company to exclude persons from the company-public point of view. They have permission, in fact and in principle, to treat persons partially, unequally, and, possibly, unfairly, on the basis of whether or not they are members of their company-public. This moral permission to be so partial seems on its face to be correct. We typically don't think that parents do something wrong when they favor their own children; in fact we think that this is part of what makes someone a good parent. If you flip a coin every time you choose between giving your child a sandwich, or your neighbor's child a sandwich, you are a bad father. It doesn't have to be 100/0, but it shouldn't be 50/50 every time.

This applies to states as well. While all of us are owed equal, impartial, and fair consideration and representation by Rex, it is also true that only us are owed this by Rex. All and only us. So one interesting question is what is to be done when one of Lex's citizens comes and visits us, and commits a crime on our list of crimes, but not on the list of crimes of her state, while she is in our jurisdiction? It seems right to say that this person is then punished by our polity, rather than merely exposed to violence at our hands. But she is not a member of our polity. She's just visiting. She is alienated from us—she would literally be called an "alien" in the U.S. Dorfman and Harel have a "not my sovereign" problem that is the same as the "not my company" problem above.

To solve the "not my sovereign" problem, Dorfman and Harel can either go cosmopolitan, or they can invoke explicit or implicit agreement between states. Neither are going to work.

Let's take the options in reverse order. Maybe Rex is permitted to punish one of Lex's subjects only with Lex's implicit or tacit permission. After all, Lex can pick up the phone and call Rex whenever Lex feels as though what Rex is doing is contrary to Lex's polity's public point of view. In fact, we might be tempted to say that only when what Lex's subject does is also a crime on Lex's list, should Lex permit the proceedings to go on. Otherwise, Lex should insist that Rex not so proceed, on pain of some sanction or, at the extreme, war. So, in principle, Rex can punish her just in case it does not violate Lex's public point of view. Maybe we say the same thing about constitutional governments as well. Constitutional law is different from criminal law, but the criminal law is subject to the Constitution. Exactly who are we deferring to? What happens when there is a disagreement between Rex and the judiciary about the meaning of some constitutional provision as it applies to this criminal statute? We might want to respond to this challenge by invoking the possibility of a Constitutional amendment. The legislature retains its superiority because any part of the Constitution could be changed by the current legislature. The deference given to the Constitution is actually implicit, captured by the fact that, if the legislature changes its mind about what the Constitution should say, they can change it.

But if that's all it takes for the punishment to be a bona fide punishment, then we could privatize the whole criminal justice system. Notice that, in theory, Rex can nationalize anything. Every private enterprise's arena of permissibility is necessarily constrained by Rex's current judgment that what they are doing is at least not in conflict with the public interest. If at any point Rex thinks an enterprise is acting contrary to the public interest, as Rex sees it, he could, and in principle should, nationalize it.[29] This strategy would not work because it would remove fidelity of deference as a necessary requirement. We wouldn't need Rex's arms and joints and nerves, we would only need Rex's implicit or tacit permission to carry on.

Instead, maybe Rex and Lex can sit at a special table and hammer out an explicit agreement. Both must retreat to their respective public points of view and, in deference to those points of view, come to terms. If they do not come to terms, then it looks like they must ban travel between the states.[30] But if they do come to an agreement, then it is this agreement that binds. But then why couldn't the "not my shareholder" problem be solved in the same way? If explicit agreement is a solution, then it's a solution that allows us to have private criminal justice systems. All we would need is explicit agreements between private justice companies.[31] Does this agreement then constitute a new super-state? Does the agreement thereby create a super-polity of which Rex's and Lex's polities are a smaller part? It cannot be, and the reason why is because Rex and Lex have actual criminal justice systems with actual punishments that appeal not to the super-polity's point of view, but to their own separate polities' points of view, which are not identical, except incidentally, with what would be the super-polity's point of view.

Finally, then, maybe what we need is precisely to construct this super-state with a super-Rex. A Rex to rule us all. A public point of view that is not the country-public point of view, but the global-public point of view. A view that captures every person in the world, a view from which no one is alien. After all, these are precisely the footsteps we laid down in charting a path that solved the "not my shareholder" problem, and this move simply follows in those footsteps, footsteps that take us to a cosmopolitan view. And if we make contact with actual aliens who are moral agents, then these very same footsteps would necessitate the incorporation of the global-public into the universe-public, leading us to a cosmopolitan view. But this does not vindicate our ordinary use of the concept of "punishment" (which is explicitly one of the goals of the argument) but, rather, comes at its expense.

### Lex Iniusta Non Est Lex

Maybe what we want to say is this: It is punishment only when our body politic punishes a member of our body politic, but something else when violence is done against one of us by one of them, and vice versa. It is indexed to the relevant body politic. When, for example, Michael Peter Fay, a U.S. citizen, was sentenced to four months in jail, a fine of 3,500 Singaporean dollars, and six strokes of the cane in Singapore for theft and vandalism, many Americans complained. The U.S. government intervened and, while conceding Singapore's right to punish, thought caning was excessive. Singapore reduced the sentence to four strokes in place of six, but Americans remained upset by it. From the American (including, possibly, Fay's) point of view then, the caning did not constitute a punishment, but the imposition of violence, while from the Singaporean public point of view, it was punishment.

But if so, we have the following worry: The Singaporeans know that Fay is alien to their public. And yet it is plausible to think that, from their point of view, Fay is actually punished. And the same is true for Americans. Americans will think that, when Singaporeans are arrested and jailed in the U.S. for American crimes that are not crimes in Singapore, using methods that are foreign to Singapore, Americans will think that the Singaporeans were actually punished. When Rex punishes subjects of Lex, members of Rex's public think it's punishment. When Lex punishes subjects of Rex, using crimes or methods not on Rex's lists, Rex's public will think Lex is just imposing violence.

The same may be true historically. Subjects of Rex now might look back on their own history and think that, in the past, there were cases where they failed to punish, despite it being true that, in the past, they thought they were punishing, and not just imposing violence. This is not about the punished being alienated from their punishment. It is possible, after all, for a person who was "punished" to think herself punished in Dorfman and Harel's sense. This is possible because of a different, possibly pretheoretical and possibly also deeply held intuition that many people appear to have. Namely, that an unjust law is no law at all. It is a "schlaw." The list of crimes derived from a schlaw are schrimes, and the punishment they receive is just schpunishment.

We can wonder whether or not this pretheoretical intuition is weightier or more significant than the pretheoretical intuition about what constitutes a "punishment." As the above example shows, they can conflict. We may, alternatively, attempt to argue against the former intuition, and insist that the latter one stands up to scrutiny. Finally, we can try to account for both by appealing to an alternative explanation for the intuitions. In what follows, I will try to construct an alternative explanation that accounts for both intuitions, and does so by appealing to a Rex- and body politic–independent list of crimes.

On the one hand, we can wonder whether Rex makes a criminal act wrongful, or if there is a Rex-independent list of wrongs that ought to be criminal. If the latter, then Rex might be wrong about what ought and what ought not be a crime.

Suppose Rex chooses laws and crimes out of the "hats of justice." He asks his agents to write down all the things that people might do, and then puts all of these things into ten hats. Once a week, he goes to each hat in order, picking one sheet of paper from each hat, and makes that action criminal. Rex sincerely believes that this is a good way of figuring out what ought to be crimes. He believes Lady Justice herself guides his royal hand. Rex is a deluded fool, but a fool with a scepter. In a case like this, however, the scepter seems powerless. I find that I would not condemn anyone found guilty and punished of any of these crimes. If that's right, then Rex has to bend at least somewhat to some reliable procedure for determining what is to be a crime.

Now suppose Rex arms his agents with five "coins of truth" and tells his agents to go door-to-door to figure out who is and who is not guilty of the ten crimes he has pulled out of his hats this week. He tells us to flip the "coin of truth" to determine who is guilty and who is innocent. Police go door-to-door, and flip the coin of truth. They end up finding that roughly half the people are guilty, and they all go to jail. Coins are impartial, says Rex. And Rex sincerely believes that they render a true verdict. Rex is a fool, but a fool with a scepter. In a case like this, does his scepter do the trick? Knowing that my neighbor went to jail because of the flip of a coin hardly moves me to think her condemnable. So even if Rex thumps his scepter or spins it in a circle eight times, he is simply powerless in generating condemnation. If that's right, then Rex has to bend at least somewhat to a reliable procedure for determining who is guilty.

We cannot insist on the view that Rex makes things wrongful because Rex is powerless at making crimes wrongful, and only those crimes which we think are wrongful will be condemned. The very same is true for the method chosen to pick out the guilty from the innocent. We need to believe that crimes are wrongful, that procedures track guilt, before we are moved to condemn. Condemnation is essentially, not contingently, connected with acting wrongly. If we think that someone has done nothing wrong, but has committed a crime, we will fail to condemn. But Rex is only contingently, and not essentially, connected with the truth about what is wrong. What is non-contingent is Rex's role as a communicative device on our behalf as a body politic.

Dorfman and Harel don't insist on it anyways. Harel, in a different paper, argues that there is a duty to criminalize certain kinds of actions.[32] He clearly believes that there is a Rex-independent fact of the matter about what ought to be a crime. What ought to be a crime is also a body politic–independent fact.[33] There are things that are in the public interest, or facts about what is and is not wrongful, and whether the body politic sees that or not is a separate fact of the matter. Caning is or is not a just punishment independently of what the Singaporean body politic thinks.

If there is an independent fact of the matter about what ought to be a crime, then there is an independent fact of the matter about what ought to be condemned. In which case, we have, in principle, an independent fact of the matter about what ought to count as "punishment."

We might think that we still need the scepter because punishments must express our "resentment and indignation"[34] as a body politic. We might think that "sanctioning a wrongdoer is an expressive/communicative act of condemnation. It is a public manifestation of condemnation and disapprobation of the criminal deeds."[35] And only an appropriate agent can deliver this. But if we know what ought to be a crime, and what ought to count as punishment, then we know what we ought to be resentful and indignant about. We don't need an intermediary to tell us what we already know, or an embodied convention for its expression.

The following are open to criticism: We can challenge what criteria we use for expressing our condemnation, and what convention we accept for communicating our condemnation, as well as what we take to be the right corporate body on whose behalf we express it. None of these are immune from criticism. None of these are fixed points that serve as immutable premises in our argument.

So, for example, is the body politic the right corporate body to do the work Dorfman and Harel want it to? States do not carve nature at her joints and, more importantly, they do not carve people into corporate entities on the basis of shared values. Nations, on the other hand, are conceptually distinct from states, often cross state lines, and are individuated on the basis of certain shared values and practices.[36] These shared values obviously play a role in what members take to be justified and unjustified violence done against one of their members, and so play a role in what they find condemnable. Sometimes, when a state agent insists something is a crime, a nation within the state might balk at the idea of condemning. So, at least sometimes, members of nations within countries are alienated from these decisions, and states will be powerless at communicating condemnation.

Nations would be better than states for Dorfman and Harel's purposes. Indeed, we might say that what they ought to have had in mind were nations all along. States don't, of necessity, deliver on the shared values that ground our current practices of calling something "punishment" or just mere violence. Nations might.

But nations get what ought to be crimes right contingently. All they deliver on are the descriptive facts about when members of the nation are liable to call something a "punishment" rather than mere violence, based on their shared conviction about what ought to be condemned. But if there is a nation-independent list of what ought to be crimes, then there is a nation-independent list of things that are to be condemned. If a nation fails to condemn what ought to be condemned, the nation is criticizable.

What matters is that we condemn what is condemnable. The truth about that is a Rex-independent fact. It is a corporate body–independent fact. If so, then what we are looking for is an agent who can speak on behalf of Justice. If Lady Justice herself showed up and told us what ought to be a crime, we had better conform our list to hers. And if our community is not already busy condemning what is on her list, we had better start doing so. If we're worried that someone will feel alienated, we need only remind that person that all of us, in virtue of being moral agents, are members in the Justice League anyways.

If this is so, then we need to ask what is the most reliable mechanism for getting as close as possible to *this* list. We also need reliable procedures for determining what ought to be on the list, reliable procedures for determining who has and who hasn't done something in violation of the list, and a reliable system for delivering on the punishment.

This suggests an alternative account for both pretheoretical intuitions that something is a punishment only when it, among other things, communicates condemnation on behalf of some relevant corporate entity, as well as the intuition that an unjust law is not a law. We would have to change the corporate entity from the body politic to the Justice League. We would have to accept the view that in principle each of us, when we reason according to fidelity of deference (to Justice), can be Agents of the League. We would then need to know a) what system (or what methods or procedures) most reliably conform to Lady Justice's list of crimes, b) what methods or procedures reliably distinguish the guilty from the innocent, and c) what system (or what methods or procedures) most reliably treat the guilty how they ought to be treated. Often, we think that the state does this. However, a private criminal justice system could deliver on each of these as well. And so the question of whether or not we ought to privatize any (or all) of the criminal justice system is not settled by any conceptual or necessary bridge between an ought and the state.

## IV. Conclusion

The state is just an instrument. There are many reasons to wield this instrument. Our armchairs can deliver the comprehensive, maybe complete, list of good things. The armchair is for oughts. But our armchairs cannot tell us whether this or that institution will best deliver on the oughts. Those require answering some armchair-independent empirical questions. To answer those, we cannot reflect on the nature of a practice, nor on any symbolic question; we need to go out there and check. Since this is so, everything can, in principle, be privatized.

## Notes

1 Debra Satz, "Markets, Privatization, and Corruption," *Social Research: An International Quarterly* 80, no. 4 (2013): 993–1008.

2 The difference might be captured in the number of people in a jurisdiction who are attracted to charlatanism. If the number is small, then perhaps this will mean that some students are taught nonsense if we have private schools. Having a government mandate a curriculum or only having public schools would mean that these students would not be taught nonsense. But if the number is large, or a sufficiently large and motivated political interest group gets involved, then that means very many students will be exposed to nonsense if we have a standardized public school mod-

el. In this latter case, permitting private schools and not mandating non-sense into the curriculum means that at least some students avoid being taught nonsense.

3 A "sufficient" amount of regulation will result in de facto national-ization. However, it is not plausible to suggest that requiring, for example, non-discrimination in hiring means that the state has effectively national-ized all private enterprises. A regulated private enterprise is not a contra-diction in terms. See more on this below.

4 The "traditional public sector model" typically includes three ele-ments: The good or service is delivered by state agents, it is subsidized or paid for through taxes, and consumption of the good or service is priced at $0.00.

5 CBC Radio-Canada, accessed Nov. 4, 2016, www.cbc.radio-canada.ca.

6 A. M. Honoré, "Ownership," *Oxford Essays in Jurisprudence* 107 (1961): 107–47.

7 The very same might be said vice versa. There are enterprises that are "public" in name only, but private in practice. An enterprise that has privatized a sufficient number of incidents from the bundle of rights has effectively become private and the government no longer owns the enter-prise.

8 See, for example, Richard A. Epstein, *Takings: Private Property and the Power of Eminent Domain* (Boston: Harvard University Press, 1985).

9 See, for example, Carol Rose, "The Comedy of the Commons: Cus-tom, Commerce, and Inherently Public Property," *University of Chicago Law Review* 53, no. 3 (1986): 711–81. See also David Schmidtz, "Property," in George Klosko, *The Oxford Handbook of the History of Political Philosophy* (New York: Oxford University Press, 2011): "At the heart of any property right is the right to say no: a right to exclude non-owners. In other words, a right to exclude is not just one stick in a bundle. Rather, property is a tree. Other sticks are branches; the right to exclude is the trunk" (at p. 600).

10 Satz, "Markets, Privatization, and Corruption," 996.

11 One possibility is that what Satz means by "privatization" here is "marketization." It may very well be an instance of intrinsic corruption if we marketized this particular element within the broader enterprise.

12 Satz, "Markets, Privatization, and Corruption," 996.

13 Except contingently: Voters who bother to cast a ballot for judges care about that, know enough about the track record of a judge (or can accurately project based on campaign materials and other past actions what a candidate for the office of judge will do once elected), and cast a ballot on that basis. And there are very many reasons to believe that they

don't, casting ballots instead for judges who are perceived to be very strict, especially on minor drug dealers who happen to be minorities.

14 Moreover, some judges aspire to be appointed to higher courts. This aspiration may lead a judge to rule in accordance with the preferences of the political party that either now or will in future be in a position to appoint a Supreme Court Justice, say.

15 As Satz warns, "We have to be careful not simply to assume that public employees display more pro-social altruistic behavior than private sector employees. In both private corporations and in large bureaucracies, employees are motivated by a mixture of altruism and self-interest" (Satz, "Markets, Privatization, and Corruption," 1000).

16 See Alon Harel, "Why Only the State May Inflict Criminal Sanctions: The Arguments from Moral Burdens," *Cardozo Law Review* 28, no. 6 (2006): 2629; Alon Harel, "Why Only the State May Inflict Criminal Sanctions: The Case against Privately Inflicted Sanctions," *Legal Theory* 14, no. 2 (2008): 113–33 (hereafter referred to as "The Case against Privately Inflicted Sanctions"); Alon Harel, "Outsourcing Violence?," *Law & Ethics of Human Rights* 5, no. 2, (2011): 396–413; Avihay Dorfman and Alon Harel, "The Case against Privatization," *Philosophy & Public Affairs* 41, no. 1, (2013): 67–102; Avihay Dorfman and Alon Harel, "Against Privatisation As Such," *Oxford Journal of Legal Studies* 36, no. 2, (2016): 400–27; Alon Harel, *Why Law Matters* (New York: Oxford University Press, 2014).

17 See Harel, "The Case against Privately Inflicted Sanctions," 122–3. See also Dorfman and Harel, "Against Privatisation As Such," 408 ("There is a prevalent intuition that there is a difference between these two cases [private and public prisons] and that this difference is important independently of the empirical considerations described earlier.") In Dorfman and Harel, "The Case against Privatization," 89, they explain that their discussion of fidelity of deference (at that point in the argument) "is merely designed to capture the difference between a group of vigilantes and the police . . ."

18 See Joel Feinberg, "The Expressive Function of Punishment," *The Monist* 49, no. 3 (1965): 400.

19 Dorfman and Harel leave open this possibility. They write, in a footnote, "Whether or not cases of formally private agents that count as functionally public agents exist is a question we do not address here" (Dorfman and Harel, "Against Privatisation As Such," 417n49).

20 Dorfman and Harel, "The Case against Privatization," 74.

21 Citing Hobbes, Dorfman and Harel write, "Subsuming sovereignty into the natural body of Rex renders his '*Joints*' the '*Magistrates*,' and other '*Officers* of Judicature and Execution' and his '*Nerves*' the offices of

'*Reward* and *Punishment*.'" Dorfman and Harel, "The Case against Privatization," 71.

22 Just how valuable symbolic value is is a matter for a separate discussion. All we need to vindicate this view is the conviction that symbolic value breaks ties. If the private and public school or health care systems were just as good, we should then prefer the public version.

23 Suppose the medicine did nothing at all. Would the communicative value break ties? Would we have reason, any reason whatsoever, to keep feeding our child this medicine?

24 Perhaps we could just erect a statue (the Symbolic Statue of the State), as a sort of literal totem to education, sort of like how the Statue of Liberty symbolizes America's love of liberty as a collective. If the statue is a possible way of expressing a collective judgment, then we'll only need the state to do that once, and we won't need them thereafter. Just have them erect statues to all the important things we want expressed, and then we can be instrumentalists again.

25 Jason Brennan pursues this strategy in Brennan, "Consequences Matter More: In Defense of Instrumentalism on Private Versus Public Prisons," *Criminal Law and Philosophy* 11, no. 4 (2015): 1–15. He also goes on a hunt in Harel's work for what he calls the "Special Feature F" that is unique and exclusive to the state, that justifies Harel's insistence on state and not private punishment. His hunt, like mine, comes up empty.

26 We will also have to consider the costs of changing institutions as well.

27 I'm not embracing the shareholder model of business ethics. I'm only using this model to illustrate how this works. If you think customers, suppliers, employees, and other stakeholders, or some of them, count, then just substitute that for "shareholders" and mutatis mutandis throughout the example.

28 But the Roman Catholic Church appears to represent the body Roman Catholic, and presumes to speak authoritatively on behalf of that whole community. They also insist on deference to the Pope whenever he speaks as Pontiff, and it is expected that priests and other agents of the Church use fidelity of deference rather than their own judgments about what God wants. We are not alienated from these decisions, since we are all God's people. While the Church may speak on behalf of Catholics, and may adjudicate disputes, we typically do not think it legitimate for the Church to enforce the Will of God even on members of the Church with the use of coercive violence. The reason why not is going to be important for my purposes. To forewarn: We probably do not allow it because, in the first place, we think the content of God's Will is controversial, we think it controversial that the Roman Catholic Church actually represents

God's Will (rather than just saying so), and we may not trust that agents of the Church will use fidelity of deference to God's Will rather than fidelity of reason. Indeed, our choice between democratic and nondemocratic governments appears to be based on our no longer trusting that non-democratic regimes give a hoot about the General Will—never mind God's Will—but can be made to so care through elections that encourage politicians to defer to that Will on pain of losing their job.

29 Notice that this is true of private enterprises in general, and not just in the criminal case. As long as we have a sovereign of some sort, it is always an option for them to nationalize something when it fails to be consistent with the public interest as they regard it. We could privatize health care and education and just about everything, but keep a legislative body which stands ready and is empowered to nationalize. All of these private enterprises would then operate privately just in case they are regarded as operating at least not in conflict with the public interest as the legislative body sees it. Dorfman and Harel write:

> It is the combination of the potential for intervention in and guidance of the practice, on the one hand, and the readiness of politicians to intervene whenever they are unsatisfied with the ways in which the practice operates, on the other, that counts. Accordingly, the realisation of this potential, namely the de facto intervention on the part of politicians, is not in and of itself crucial to determine whether the political offices are sufficiently integrated into the community of practice. Instead, what is crucial is the participants' Hohfeldian liability to the power of political officials to place them under a duty to act in certain ways and the willingness to exercise this power whenever they are unsatisfied with the ways in which the practice operates (Dorfman and Harel, "Against Privatisation As Such," 417).

Later, they write, "Sometimes politicians should defer to the decisions made by the private entity insofar as they fall within the arena of permissibility *even when* these decisions run afoul of the public interest. This is because, and insofar as, the private entity has acquired a right to so act" (Dorfman and Harel, "Against Privatisation As Such," 420). This is a practical matter. We offer this arena of permissibility since we agree that the state may, in practice, be wrong about the content of the public interest. In principle, however, we can say that all private enterprises operate conditionally on the judgment of Rex that they are operating not in conflict with the public interest. That there is a Constitution in the U.S., for example, that enshrines an arena of permissibility prohibiting America's Rex from infringing is a separate matter. The Constitution itself is to be approved of only on the condition that it promotes the public interest. If it failed to do so, or if we decided that it undermines it rather than promotes it, then we could, in principle, get rid of it.

30 I don't know what happens if someone ignores the ban and travels anyway. Would they be punished, or would it just be violence?

31 Notice that saying that this is unlikely in practice is not an objection here. If we say that private companies are unlikely to come to these agreements, while states are more likely to do so, all we are saying is that we should prefer states for contingent, rather than necessary, reasons.

32 See Alon Harel, "The Duty to Criminalize," *Law and Philosophy* 34, no. 1 (2015): 1–22.

33 A Euthyphro dilemma could be regenerated here: Is it wrong because the body politic thinks so, or do they think so because it is wrong? Without going into detail, I recommend grabbing hold of the second horn here as well.

34 Harel, citing Feiberg (1965), writes, "Punishment is a conventional device for the expression of attitudes of resentment and indignation, and of judgments of disapproval and reprobation, on the part either of the punishing authority himself or of those 'in whose name' the punishment is inflicted." This function can only be performed by the state, since "punishment expresses the judgment . . . of the community that what the criminal did was wrong" (Harel, "The Case against Privately Inflicted Sanctions," 121).

35 Dorfman and Harel, "The Case against Privatization," 92–93.

36 See, for example, Colin Woodard, *American Nations: A History of the Eleven Rival Regional Cultures of North America* (New York: Penguin, 2011).

# 5

# PRIVATIZATION WITHOUT PROFIT?

## CHIARA CORDELLI

When is privatization morally objectionable? This question has recently received renewed attention by political philosophers. Many are concerned that, given private actors' self-interest and profit-maximizing motives, the privatization of important public functions, from education to defense, is likely to lead to morally objectionable social outcomes, whether defined in terms of inequalities of access to certain goods, or to undesirable changes in the quality of such goods. In this key, some argue that privatization corrupts, through commodification, the nature of some particular goods,[1] or, through profit-maximizing incentives, crucial public purposes.[2] Still others understand privatization as necessarily embodying an objectionable form of "neoliberal rationality"—a totalizing attention to quantification, metrics, and efficiency.[3] And others again locate the wrong of privatization in the very fact that private actors tend to be motivated by morally objectionable considerations, namely profit-making, when discharging sensitive public responsibilities.[4]

All these arguments have something in common. They connect the wrong of privatization to some property or another of markets or market actors, most prominently their self-interested tendency to maximize profits or other personal gains, and their impulse to treat everything as a quantifiable and interchangeable commodity.[5]

The thrust of these arguments is understandable, since advocates of privatization often trumpet the many possible ways in which entrepreneurship and efficiency—qualities often associated with private markets—can benefit society.[6] Yet, their critical power

113

is necessarily limited in scope. This is because privatization need not involve the delegation of functions to profit-maximizing, self-interested market actors, and often, in practice, does not. Many instances of privatization involve civil society actors such as charitable associations, religious organizations, and NGOs (hereafter nonprofits), the primary purpose of which is not, or should not be, to win a market competition or maximize profits.

To illustrate: today, American nonprofit associations are the principal private providers of publicly funded social services.[7] Government social-welfare spending is directed—whether through grants or contracts—to a large number of nonprofit associations that produce and deliver essential goods and services on behalf of government. In 2010, some 33,000 civil society associations were under a total of some 200,000 government contracts for social services delivery, including education, healthcare, childcare, and unemployment benefits.[8] In some states, nonprofit associations can control up to ninety percent of overall social service delivery and up to seventy-five percent of state benefits delivery.[9] Nonprofit organizations provide seventy-one percent of all hospitals nationwide.[10] Beyond service provision, these associations also perform important functions of accreditation, certification, and standards-setting.

True, nonprofit associations do not seem to play a prominent role in those forms of privatization that appear as most objectionable, such as, for example, the privatization of prisons. In the US, all private prisons are owned and operated by for-profit corporations such as Corrections Corporation of America (CCA), which can host more than 80,000 offender beds in sixty-five correctional facilities, and the GEO Group, which has a capacity of 49,000 beds distributed across around sixty facilities.[11] Yet, the role of nonprofits here is also not insignificant. Nonprofits have traditionally run behavioral health agencies, including prison medical care facilities, forensic mental hospitals, civil commitment centers, and home arrest programs. Further, recently there have been calls to convert private for-profit prisons into (still private) nonprofit prisons. For example, Citizens United for the Rehabilitation of Errants—a prison reform group of former inmates in Washington, DC—has started a campaign to convert a private prison in DC into what would become the first nonprofit prison in the US.[12]

Nonprofit actors are (ideally) conceived not as market actors but rather as civil society associations. They are often publicly funded or reimbursed and can thus deliver services or perform public functions without directly charging fees. Additionally, many assume that people who work within these organizations are less self-interested, or even work from altruistic motives. Market-based arguments cannot therefore help illuminate what is objectionable, if anything, with the above cases of privatization.

Therefore it is worth asking whether the only reasons to object to privatization are market-centered, or whether there are important *market-independent* reasons as well. By "market-independent" I mean unrelated to (1) the self-interested (profit-maximizing) motivation and calculating form of rationality often attributed to market actors, and (2) the commodifying tendencies associated with market exchanges. Is there anything wrong with privatization, when those empowered by it are socially minded, perhaps even altruistic, actors, as opposed to profit-maximizing ones?

I aim to develop three market-independent arguments against (some forms of) privatization and to suggest that they provide strong, although perhaps not conclusive, reasons to limit the systematic delegation of important public functions to nonprofit (as well as for-profit) actors. Interestingly, a few of these arguments should lead us to regard some forms of privatization to nonprofits as being even more problematic, morally speaking, than privatization to market actors. Importantly, this is so even if we assume that nonprofits can be both no less efficient than for-profit organizations at performing their assigned tasks *and* that their employees are motivated by other-regarding considerations and not self-interest.

The arguments I will develop appeal, respectively, to three distinctive values and commitments that a liberal political society should pursue or honor: (1) equal freedom, (2) value pluralism, and (3) symbolic reciprocity. More precisely, they relate to three distinctive functions that political institutions must play so as to realize or honor the above values. These functions of political institutions include (i) the establishment of an omnilateral system of public rules, which is necessary to guarantee equal freedom (*the omnilaterality function*); (ii) the externalization of certain social and moral burdens, which is needed to make possible the simultaneous realization of plural and conflicting values (*the externalization function*), and (iii) the maintenance of arrangements through which a valuable relationship of civic reciprocity is not only secured through substantive means but also expressed and rendered visible to all citizens (*the expressive function*). As I will argue, contemporary forms of privatization risk depriving political institutions of the ability to *simultaneously* fulfill these functions, and do so regardless of the specific nature of the agents through which they operate, whether these be profit-seeking market actors or benevolent Samaritans. Before proceeding, a clarification of terms is in order.

Privatization is not a self-evident term. In broad strokes, privatization can be defined as the devolution of public responsibility to private parties. This, however, entails the need for a baseline against which the idea of public responsibility can be specified. Here I should understand "privatization" as the delegation to private actors of public functions (rather than ownership of public assets or utilities), defined according to a *normative,* as opposed to historical or economic, baseline.[13] For the purpose of this paper, I will assume that in a just society government ought to bear, on grounds of justice, the primary responsibility to secure not only a fair distribution of general and neutral resources, including income and wealth, through tax and transfers, but also an adequate (if not equal) provision of certain in-kind goods, ranging from police protection to education and healthcare.[14] This does not per se entail, at least not without further argument, that government should provide these goods directly. Government may fund the provision of in-kind goods, while contracting out their administration and provision to private actors. I shall then use the term *privatization* to identify the process through which justice-based, public responsibilities are systematically contracted out by government to private actors.

A further term that needs clarification is the one of *nonprofit.* The term *nonprofit,* also known as *non-business entity,* refers to a particular organizational form. Like for-profit or business firms, nonprofits can in principle sell goods (they can, e.g., charge fees for services) and their employees are paid a salary. Yet, nonprofits exhibit the distinctive feature of being subject to a *non-distribution constraint.* This means that the organization cannot distribute its surplus revenue to its shareholders as profit. It must use its surplus income to pursue its mission, whatever this may be.[15] Although in many contemporary societies, nonprofits are increasingly subject to market pressure and competition, for the sake of this paper I will assume an idealized conception of nonprofits as voluntary, civil society associations aimed at pursuing particular missions or expressing particular ideals, the employees of which are motivated not so much by greed or self-interest but rather by other-regarding motives. This assumption, even if lacking empirical accuracy, helps isolate those objections to privatization that are independent from market-based factors.

## I. Three Roles of Political Institutions

An account of what is objectionable with (certain forms of) privatization, I believe, must ultimately proceed from an account of what political institutions are for—that is, why we have reasons to attribute certain public responsibilities, however exactly defined, to these institutions in the first place. There are certainly many possible accounts of the function(s) of political institutions. Here I will focus on three main functions that have been particularly prominent in liberal-egalitarian political thought, and assess the desirability, or lack thereof, of privatization with respect to them. Although, due to limits of space, I won't be able to provide a full, independent justification in support of these functions, I will briefly reconstruct and interpret the central arguments that have been adduced in their support by some of the main exponents of the liberal tradition. By adopting this "functionalist approach," my aim is to detach the critique of privatization from accounts of the moral limits of markets, and thus to broaden this critique so as to encompass both for-profit and nonprofit varieties of the phenomenon.

### A. The Omnilaterality Function of Political Institutions

It is a long-standing lesson of social contract theory that political institutions are necessary to both secure and (according to some) even constitute a relationship of equal freedom among those subject to them. They do so by providing, among other things, a unified and omnilateral definition of their rights and duties. Immanuel Kant, one of the founders of contemporary liberalism, develops and powerfully defends this view in *The Metaphysics of Morals*. According to Kant, freedom consists in an interpersonal relationship of reciprocal independence that can only be constituted, let alone realized, through properly functioning political institutions. To be free, for Kant, is not to be subordinated to another person's choice or will.[16] A free person has the ability to establish purposes for herself and to pursue them. Freedom requires certain rights. It requires, for example, that a person be able to acquire and employ usable means as she wishes, according to her own purposes, within the limits imposed on her by the entitlements of others to do the same.[17]

Now, for Kant, in the state of nature, there can only be provisional rights to external resources, not conclusive ones.[18] This is, first, because of what we might call *the problem of unilateralism*. This problem consists in the fact that no one person, through her own private, unilateral judgment, can change the normative situations of others by placing them under new obligations—e.g., not to interfere with their rights—they did not previously hold.[19] Indeed, this would be incompatible with the "original right" to freedom, since it would effectively subject them to the particular will of others.

Second, rights, by conceptual definition, impose reciprocal constraints on freedom and must apply to all equally. But rights are indeterminate and their definition necessitates judgment. A general rule, including a principle of equal freedom, is too general to determine the contours of specific rights. This gives rise to the following problem: if you and I have different understandings of what our respective rights entail, and cannot find agreement, neither of us can have a right, consistent with the freedom of others.[20] If my right to property, or the obligations I acquired by voluntarily entering into a contract with you, were subjectively determined according to my own understanding of my rights and obligations, then your obligations not to interfere with my property and your contractual expectations would entirely depend on my unilateral will. Even if I act in good faith, your ability to pursue your own purposes would still be dependent on my own unilateral choice.[21] Since my judgment and your judgment are equally weighty (for we are moral equals), in case of disagreement, neither of us is required to follow the other person's judgment.[22] If I could unilaterally change your normative situation—your obligations—this would mean, effectively, that I would have title to coerce you into respecting my own rights, as subjectively determined through my own unilateral judgment. But this would violate your freedom. In the absence of a shared public system of rules, therefore, my right to acquire usable means so as to pursue my ends and act as a free agent necessarily remains merely provisional, for I cannot unilaterally impose on you any obligation to respect my own rights. This system fails to secure freedom as independence.

To overcome this situation, the boundaries of rights need to be determined omnilaterally, through a unified body, an arbiter, that is publicly authorized to determine these boundaries "with mathematical exactitude," and in the name of everyone.[23] This is true domestically; it is also true internationally where every state can only derive their security and rights from a "united power and the law-governed decisions of a united will."[24]

Political institutions, in this view, are therefore nothing else than an omnilateral system of laws, which are necessary to define and constitute a relationship of equal freedom among subjects. The state overcomes the limits of unilateralism by establishing, in objective terms and with unified voice, the very boundaries of our rights and by imposing correlative obligations on all of us.

## B. The Externalization Function of Political Institutions

Beyond defining and protecting rights, political institutions can be regarded as playing a further important function. They discharge burdens that would in their absence fall (at least in part) on individuals themselves or on their private associations, thereby leaving the latter with less time and resources to form and pursue their own ends and conceptions of the good. So regarded, one of the fundamental roles of liberal political institutions is to preserve a condition of value pluralism by *externalizing* responsibilities that would otherwise prevent individuals and their associations from forming and pursuing their diverse sets of values and purposes.[25]

This externalizing function is what can be regarded as grounding John Rawls's well-known division of labor between, on the one hand, the "basic structure of society"—the major socio-economic and political institutions of a well-ordered society—and, on the other hand, individuals and private associations, including civil society associations and business firms.[26]

This division of labor is both institutional and normative. It is institutional insofar as the basic structure and private associations are meant to have different *social roles* and to fulfill different functions. As Rawls explains, "If this [institutional] division of labor can be established, individuals and associations are then left free to advance their ends more effectively within the framework of the basic structure, secure in the knowledge that elsewhere in the social system the necessary corrections to preserve background justice are being made."[27] Political institutions have the distinctive role to secure and maintain background justice, while private associations have the role to pursue ends that individuals can, against that background, freely and collectively unite to pursue. This division of labor between state and civil society is often considered a pillar of contemporary liberalism. Will Kymlicka clearly explains the terms of this separation, as it figures in the thought of most contemporary liberals, as follows: "the distinction between state and civil society maps onto the two parts of the liberal-egalitarian ideal: social justice is secured by the state . . . individual freedom is secured in civil society."[28]

From an institutional division of labor, a moral division of labor follows. "[I]t is the distinct purposes and roles of the parts of the social structure, and how they fit together, that explains," Rawls argues, "their being different principles for different kinds of subjects. Indeed, it seems natural to suppose that the distinctive character and autonomy of the various elements of society requires that, within some sphere, they act from their own principles designed to fit their particular nature."[29]

In sum, a normative commitment to freedom and value pluralism—the idea that individuals and private associations (unlike political institutions) have a first order interest to form and pursue their own particular ends and conceptions of the good—together with an empirical assumption about the limited epistemic capacities that private agents have to secure and maintain background justice, provide support for an institutional division of labor between state and civil society. This division of labor, in turn, explains why different principles and moral requirements (duties and obligations) should apply to political institutions and private actors respectively. Once the role of pursuing justice is attributed to the basic structure, individuals and their associations can be left free to act from "their own" principles, as opposed to principles of political morality.[30]

By undertaking the task of securing background conditions of justice, political institutions externalize necessary social burdens, thereby leaving individuals and associations free to pursue their ends and conceptions of the good within the limits set by the basic structure, secure in the knowledge that justice is being collectively achieved. By performing this externalization function, political institutions make possible the simultaneous cultivation of plural and otherwise conflicting values and perspectives, including individual freedom and social justice, partiality and impartiality, particular ends and collective interests.

## C. The Expressive Function of Political Institutions

Liberal political institutions do not simply define rights and externalize collective burdens. A further important role they play is expressive. Institutions instantiate particular kinds of relationships among citizens, and express the corresponding values and ideals that support these relationships. Depending on how they are arranged, institutions can instantiate relationships of hierarchy or domination, or rather relationships of equality. The institutions of a liberal-democratic society should instantiate egalitarian ideals among its subjects and be arranged so as to express these ideals. As Joshua Cohen, under Rousseau's influence, points out, a democratic society is not simply a society where citizens are *treated* as equals by the state but also a society where citizens *see* one another as equals through their common institutions.[31] This is why, for example, an arrangement such as symbolic religious establishment (e.g., allowing crucifixes on the wall of public spaces) can be objectionable from a liberal-egalitarian perspective, even if it neither restricts people's rights (because it is merely symbolic) nor distributes their burdens unfairly. The reason why this arrangement is objectionable is that, by associating the state with a particular religion, it fails to express the equal standing of all citizens, including those who do not share that same religion.[32]

Equal standing is not the only egalitarian ideal that political institutions should instantiate and express. Equality as reciprocity is a further ideal, at least if we accept the conception of society—as many liberals do—as a scheme of mutual cooperation. Within this framework, equal citizenship itself can be conceptualized as "a relational ideal of reciprocity among those who support and maintain the state's capacity to provide the basic collective goods necessary to protect us from physical attack and to maintain and reproduce a stable system of property rights and entitlements."[33] We owe obligations of reciprocity to fellow citizens and residents who provide us with the basic conditions necessary to freely form and pursue our ends and conceptions of the good, and our fellow citizens owe the same to us.[34] Political institutions and arrangements must be designed so as to not only satisfy obligations of reciprocity through a just distribution of benefits and burdens, but also to visibly and publicly express this egalitarian idea of reciprocity to all citizens. This is what I refer to as the expressive function of political institutions.

In what follows I will suggest that the privatization of some public functions, including the provision of crucial welfare and human services, especially when systematic, prevents liberal-democratic institutions from *simultaneously* discharging the above three functions and thus from simultaneously realizing the corresponding values of equal freedom, value pluralism, and symbolic reciprocity. This is so regardless of the nature of the agent, for-profit or nonprofit, to whom public functions are delegated or contracted out.

## II. THE EQUAL FREEDOM ARGUMENT

We saw that Kant provides a clear and compelling explanation for why we need a state, understood as a unified and omnilateral system of rules. In order to be consistent with freedom, decisions that change the normative situation of others—define their entitlements or impose new obligations—must be made in the name of all those subjects to those choices. They must also determine the content of rights equally for all, with one unified interpretation.

In order to argue that privatization threatens this functional essence of political institutions, we would need to demonstrate that (1) within a system of widespread privatization, private actors, regardless of whether they are nonprofits or for-profit, unavoidably make presumptively authoritative decisions that do change the normative situation of citizens in a relevant sense, in the sense of *defining* their entitlements and/or obligations. We would then need to further show that (2) private actors' entitlements-defining decisions, even if authorized through government contracts, nevertheless fail to meet the relevant conditions of omnilaterality, thereby remaining unilateral acts of men and women, and thus incompatible with freedom.

Formally, while private actors are delegated the responsibility to implement or execute state programs (e.g., welfare programs) or functions (e.g., the delivery of healthcare services or the administration of prisons), the lawmaking power to decide and adjudicate what people are entitled to as a matter of right remains in the hands of government and the courts. It follows that while private actors can have significant impact on the wellbeing and welfare of those subject to their decisions, their decisions would not seem to qualify as entitlements-defining in any relevant sense. They, at most, restrict people's options for choice but do not restrict individuals' freedom as independence.

This picture of privatization is, however, far too idealized. As empirical scholars have abundantly shown, "Delegations of discretion [to private actors] are unavoidable because the power to implement and apply rules is inseparable from the power to set policy,"[35] that is to say, to set those rules. The transfer of governmental power to private agents in many instances of privatization is something that cannot be easily solved through regulatory monitoring and oversight. As legal scholar Gillian Metzger puts it, "Close government oversight or specification of policies and procedures can limit the extent of discretionary authority delegated to private actors, but cannot eliminate it."[36]

Consider the question of who determines what healthcare services an American citizen is entitled to. Under the US healthcare system, recipients of publicly provided healthcare services typically enroll in some private, often nonprofit, "managed care organizations" (MCOs). In many cases, given resources scarcity and the impossibility to cover all requests for treatment, MCOs must make decisions about what treatment to cover. This decision in turn determines whether a citizen is eligible for publicly funded health-care services.[37] However detailed the directives specified in the contract, the organization will necessarily remain with a significant degree of discretion about how to both (a) interpret the meaning of the directives, and (b) how to balance competing claims fairly. Even if the organization is fully committed to act both fairly and reasonably, and even if for-profit motives are absent, both fairness and reasonableness—and the public reasons these values support—may be in and of themselves indeterminate. This means that there can be multiple, equally fair and equally reasonable decisions and that the organization must pick one of them. This indeterminacy, I am assuming, is an ineliminable consequence of the fact that general principles of distributive justice are too indeterminate to provide determinate directives for particular cases.[38]

To illustrate this indeterminacy, consider the case of two patients, A and B, who claim access to different kinds of treatments, T1 and T2. Both patients advance reasonable claims and are *prima facie* owed the treatment; however, due to resource constraints only one treatment can be covered. The private organization must decide how to balance their claims. Now government could try to reduce to a minimum the organizational discretion by providing strict ethical guidance. First, it could require the MCO to either adopt a prioritarian position according to which priority ought to be given to those who are worst off in absolute terms. In this case however, the MCO would still unavoidably retain discretion in establishing whether A's needs count as more urgent than B's or vice versa. Alternatively, government could require the MCO to adopt a maximizing position, prioritizing the treatment with the highest chances of producing the greatest health net benefit per dollar spent. In which case the MCO would have to establish what counts as the greatest net benefit. Further, this guideline would provide unreasonable directives in some cases—e.g., in a case where A's claim is much more urgent and B would only benefit marginally more from the treatment. Government would then have to provide guidelines that specify, exactly, how much net health benefit, exactly, the MCO would have to be willing to sacrifice in order to give priority to worse-off patients. Providing this kind of specification in a way that leaves no discretion to the MCO is simply impossible. The result is that, in the absence of such specification, it will be up to the MCO to determine whether A or B should be entitled to be treated or, at least, who should be entitled to it as a matter of public right.

This, note, is not a decision that simply executes already-determined entitlements, or affects the way these entitlements can be exercised. The MCO's decision rather *determines the contours of the patient's entitlements.* Through their treatment decisions MCOs de facto establish what is mine and what is yours when it comes to healthcare resources. By doing so they change the normative situation of citizens in a relevant sense. They provide them with entitlements that they previously had only *prima facie* (there is a sense in which both A and B are *prima facie* entitled to be treated but, all things considered, only A turns out to be de jure entitled to the treatment). The MCO, simultaneously, determines that A's fellow citizens are under an obligation to pay for A's treatment but not for B's. The fact that, in a context of widespread privatization, private actors make entitlements-setting decisions is not surprising. What I have suggested is that this fact is an unavoidable feature that follows from the, also unavoidable, indeterminate nature of entitlements—an indeterminacy that remains even *after* a system of government is in place.

But is it not the case that, as long as courts retain the final authority to adjudicate disputes in accordance with the law, the decisions of private actors do not settle anyone's entitlement? For one thing citizens do not always have a private right of action against private providers of public entitlements, and private providers, at least insofar as they do not count for legal purposes as "state actors," are not subject to the same requirements of due process as public actors.[39] Second, and more importantly for our purposes, even when citizens are provided with a right to sue a private organization for violating a state-provider agreement—the standards or requirements specified in the privatization contract—our discussion has shown that it is precisely these standards and requirements that are necessarily underdetermined, in a way that leaves the private actor with lawful (because implied in the state-provider agreement itself) discretion to interpret them in certain ways, by choosing among alternative reasonable interpretations which cannot be fully specified *ex ante*. It would then seem to follow that, if there are multiple reasonable ways in which A's and B's healthcare entitlements could be assigned (who should get what treatment), the fact that an organization authorized to define those entitlements selects one of the other of available competing interpretations should provide us with a reason to accept that interpretation as final. We would then have no reason to sue the organization in the first place. In order to prove that this is not in fact the case one needs to further show that either (1) the institution or organization in question is not in fact *authorized* to make that interpretation (this, however, cannot be the case at least insofar as state contracts leave a margin of discretional choice to the organization), or that (2) even if authorized through contract, whatever interpretation the organization makes cannot count as "our" interpretation, for it necessarily remains a *unilateral* interpretation. In this case, were we forced to accept this decision, we would be subjected to the unilateral will of another. But in order to prove this is the case, we need to explain why the fact that a private organization is authorized by government, through contract, to make certain interpretative decisions is not sufficient to provide us with reasons to accept those decisions as omnilateral acts of law. I will now attempt to provide such explanation.

If the decisions of a state were simply reducible to the aggregation of decisions made by particular individuals *qua* individuals, these decisions would necessarily remain unilateral. They would consist in individuals' particular interpretation of the public interest or the nature of the public good, as seen from their own point of view. This is precisely why, for Kant, we must distinguish between, on the one hand, publicly constituted *offices*, and, on the other hand, the *individuals* occupying them who might have their own private purposes.[40] We can regard the actions and decisions of a state as omnilateral, consistent with the right of everyone, only because, and insofar as, even if concrete individuals ultimately do the ruling, it is the laws—a publicly authorized mandate created by their office and made consistent through a unified system of rules with the mandate of other offices—that rule, not the people who occupy those offices.

But what does it take for a decision to count as a decision of law rather than of people? As several legal theorists have pointed out, the law is a *collective social practice*—an instance of shared agency.[41] If this is correct, the question then becomes: how can a group of individuals create and apply laws in a way that displays the systematic unity necessary for their actions to count as omnilateral acts of law—as integral parts of the social practice of law-making? A full answer to this question would require a more extensive treatment than I can provide here. Here I will build on Christopher Kutz's theory of collective action insofar as, unlike other theories, his can be extended to cases of large forms of institutional shared agency.[42] Before doing so, let me clarify that by legal activity I refer not simply to the activities of lawyers and judges but, much more broadly, to all that activity of "governance" that changes the normative situation of citizens in a relevant sense.

Kutz points out that two conditions are necessary for an action to be attributable to an institution: (1) the members of the institution who perform the action can be regarded as part of a "collective." This condition is met when each member of the institution acts with a "participatory intention," namely an intention to contribute to a collective end. (2) A set of rules and procedures structuring the institution, which assign roles (offices) and mandates to each member, must be in place. Institutional rules define what an institution (e.g., a department) is and prescribes "mandates" for the members to play accordingly. They also establish a specific set of *relations* among the members of the collective—e.g., common procedures—as well as a space of unified, collective action.

It is not only the participatory intentions of individuals but also the institutionally framed relations among them that transform a group of people acting separately into a unified collective agent. In order for our acting to count as the acting of a particular institution, we must "orient our action within that institutional space," where this orientation consists of the (i) "agents' acceptance of the norms constitutive of the institution," their (ii) commitment to the overall project of the collective, as well as (iii) the way in which the agents are *related to the other members of the collective in a way that sustains that commitment.* Without a shared institutional space there is no unified collective action that can be attributed to an organization made of different offices and members.

Now, legal institutions consist of a set of individuals each having a participatory intention to contribute to the collective project of defining and applying norms in an appropriate way. The unity of the legal system is unity *through* the agents' orientation towards a collective goal. This orientation in turn consists of the agents' acceptance of the norms constitutive of the institution, including an acceptance of certain restraints with regards to what kind of reasons (public versus private) can be advanced in support of their decisions, as well as the project of determining law qua a collective project. But this orientation cannot exist without an institutional space and web of relations capable of directing the behavior of different officials through its constitutive norms. Without this space we cannot attribute separate actions of law-making to the collective social practice of law-making. As Kutz argues, "When judges do share an institutional orientation, no matter how they disagree in their decisions, their decisions count as conclusion of law, not of men. . . . *The normativity of the decisions consist in their being product of the collective project* . . . Law is grounded in an adjudicative community."[43]

This claim can be extended to all law-making activity, including those aspects of policymaking involved in the administration of justice. It is only when officials and administrators are part of a common institutional space that provides them with a shared orientation that their decisions can count as the results of law, rather than of particular men or women. The relevant question then becomes whether private actors, within political systems in which privatization is widespread, can inhabit the same institutional space of "official" members of the law-making political community. My contention is that they do not. They are not connected to official members through an appropriate web of relationships that serve to provide the necessary shared institutional orientation. It is because of *this* reason that their decisions, however well intentioned or even deferential, cannot be fully attributed to that law-making community that is responsible for making, interpreting, and applying norms on behalf of the entire political community.[44] They are not acts of law.

In practice this unitary institutional space which provides the possibility of collective agency oriented towards a common purpose—i.e., to define and implement norms in the name and from the point of view of the political community as a whole—is secured by the presence of appropriately deliberative administrative procedures and by the relationships between bureaucrats and elected officials that these procedures create. While the broader system of administrative rules secures a tight institutional and relational connection between the individual decisions of bureaucrats and the law-making community as a whole, so that we can see their actions as a part of a broader instance of shared agency, that system does not frame the institutional space within which private actors operate. This leaves these actors outside of the project of collective, shared political agency.

In a democracy, elected officials represent the public point of view. It is from this omnilateral point of view that the content of norms and the public interest must be articulated in a unitary way. It is thus the task of elected officials to orient the mode of operation of the social practice as a whole and to make sure the other participants in the law-making practice maintain the appropriate institutional orientation and commitment. Since the definitions and implementation of policies and norms are necessarily underspecified and always entail some discretion on the part of the people carrying them on, including unelected officials like bureaucrats, in order for these decisions to count as acts of the state they must be made within an institutional framework that constructs channels of public practical reasoning between the individual decision-maker and the political offices within the broader law-making community.[45] Members of the law-making community must all act with an institutional identity in mind, thus orienting their action towards a common purpose.

Through administrative procedures, elected officials retain control over the decisions and deliberations of unelected officials and administrative bureaucracies, so that the latter can *orient* their decisions according to the actions and decisions made by public officials. Administrative procedures should not be regarded and used merely as sanctioning and monitoring mechanisms of effective implementation and accountability through independently defined rules; they can rather constitute *channels of public practical reasoning* that contribute to the very definition and justification of those rules through a collective, shared practice. Beyond judicial review, as well as monitoring and sanctioning, an important, if neglected, function of administrative procedures is to create integrated deliberative relations between administrators and elected representatives.

This is one way to read common American practices of administrative law, including those in which administrative agencies solicit public comments on rulings and provide all interested parties with an opportunity to communicate their views—forms of participation in the administrative decision-making process.[46]

Through administrative procedures, therefore, it is not simply accountability that is achieved. These procedures create an *institutional space for collective public practical reasoning* on behalf of the democratic political community that would not exist in their absence. Democratically elected representatives can orient and structure the political environment in which an agency operates to adopt the political point of view and interlock her conduct with the conduct of political officials. This is the virtue of public bureaucracy.

Stand alone, ad hoc contractual agreements between government and private actors may include accountability requirements, but they necessarily fail to establish a systematic, continuous, and shared web of relationships between those actors and the law-making community of the kind necessary to produce a shared institutional space and orientation. Indeed, privatization contracts could be regarded as having the very purpose of separating private actors' decision-making from the institutional constraints of a community that brings together the political and the bureaucratic. Only in this way, defenders of privatization argue, can cost-effectiveness and innovation be achieved.

Because private actors are situated outside of that institutional space that brings together elected officials and administrators and allows them to share an institutional orientation through a system of institutionalized relationships of reciprocal responsiveness, no matter how well intentioned they are, their decisions cannot count as omnilateral acts of law. They necessarily remain unilateral conclusions of men. The decisions of private actors claim the authority that only legal institutions can claim. Their decisions do not count as something that the law-making community has done *together*, for there is no truly shared collective project in which private actors participate.

If I am correct that (1) private actors are often empowered to make decisions that change the normative situation of citizens, and if it is also true that (2) private actors, no matter how well intentioned to reason publicly and impartially, exercise their decision-making power in a way that remains unilateral, it follows that, for the very reasons pointed out by Kant in the *Metaphysics of Morals*, (3) privatization, especially when widespread, is incompatible with the establishment of a system of equal freedom. Privatization systematically subjects citizens to the unilateral will of others. This is true independent of the nature of the private actor, including whether they are a for-profit or nonprofit organization. If my argument is correct, the private decisions of charitable associations can be as unilateral and thus as freedom-undermining as the private decision of for-profit corporations.

### III. The Value Pluralism Argument

One obvious answer to the problem of unilateralism illustrated above would be to argue that private actors can and should be brought into the law-making community by extending to them relevant administrative procedures and constraints. If private actors were so included within the bureaucracy, the first function of political institutions and the value of equal freedom that underpins it would both be satisfied. This solution, however, would risk defeating the second function of political institutions—the externalization function—as I shall now turn to explain.[47]

Of course, under conditions of widespread privatization, it may be better, indeed required, to extend to private agents procedures and requirements generally limited to state actors. After all, if one agrees with Rawls that "it is the distinct purposes and roles of the parts of the social structure . . . that explains their being different principles for different kinds of subjects," then once private associations come to *share* with political institutions the role of securing justice, e.g., because they come to act as state contractors in welfare delivery, the claim that different normative principles should apply to them starts to lose force.[48] As privatization blurs the *institutional* division of labor between political institutions and private actors, it consequentially also blurs the *moral* division of labor between them. Yet, this blurring of institutional and moral boundaries between public and private comes with costs.

To understand the nature of these costs we must go back to the reasons that underpin the division of labor in the first place. As we saw, those reasons have to do with respect for value pluralism. It is because individuals have an interest to form and pursue, alone or through their associations, their particular ends and conceptions of the good, whatever these may be, that they need a non-public sphere of action, free from the burdensome demands of political morality. This, of course, neither means that this sphere should be free from interference nor that individuals and associations should be exempted from the requirements of just laws. All it means is that they should be granted the real freedom to form and pursue particular ends, in the knowledge that justice is *independently* secured. Yet, by blurring the division of institutional labor between the public and the private, privatization transfers demanding social and moral burdens to private associations. By doing so it simultaneously threatens the very conditions that make the free pursuit of different values possible.[49]

As a consequence of entering into state contracts, associations may be expected (and rightly so) to enlarge their community of interest so as to include those who might not have otherwise been a part of their intended sphere of action. They may be further expected to democratize their decision-making process and internal governance, and also to abandon their original ends, if in conflict with political purposes.[50] They may become legally accountable under public law norms and come to bear duties to act on political principles.[51] These demands may not arise from the simple fact that associations receive public money. Yet, they become morally binding when associations come to act as a part of the political structure. The resulting narrowing of a moral division of labor between state and civil society associations thus compromises the ability of the latter to act as channels through which individuals can freely originate and pursue particular ends and plural values (within the rightful boundaries of justice).

To provide some empirical support for this claim, it is worth considering actual instances of associations that have experienced a loss of integrity as a consequence of entering into close relationships of partnership with government. One such case is represented by US shelters for battered and sexually abused women, which have lamented the way in which their ideological commitment and relations with clients changed as a consequence of signing a contract with the state. These associations were independently founded and directed by non-professional feminist activists. The US government then started hiring them, through grants and contracts, to provide the above services on its behalf. As a consequence of this, it has increasingly required these associations to hire human service professionals as a condition of winning state support. This is in part because the private founders of these charitable organizations were regarded as too partial and ideologically oriented, and not sufficiently trained to meet the needs of shelter clients, according to public standards. If we take seriously the fact that these associations de facto come to act as arms of government, this request is fully justified. Yet, this does not make it costless. As a consequence of the change in staffing and governance, not only has the motivational commitment behind, and the mission of, the association changed, but so has the method of distributing services become more impersonal and less expressive of the original values of the association.[52]

This is just a cursory example of how privatization can, and often does, undermine the control that members and employees have upon the ends of their own association, by changing the modality of interactions among them, as well as the social role and responsibility of the associations themselves. Insofar as associations become the proxies through which a political society pursues its public goals and discharges its public responsibilities, civil society risks being co-opted by the state. When sixty-four percent of overall registered civil society associations perform critical service-delivery functions on behalf of government, as is currently the case in the US, this becomes a pressing concern.[53]

To sum up so far, either privatization is incompatible with equal freedom, or it can be (arguably) made compatible, by bringing private actors into the administrative structure of bureaucracy and making them subject to public principles and strict administrative procedures, but only at the cost of value pluralism. Importantly, from the perspective of value pluralism, privatization may be *more* problematic, rather than less, when it involves civil society (nonprofit) associations than when it involves market firms or business corporations. This is because, while the market is generally understood as the sphere of instrumental associations, civil society is often regarded as a privileged site of expressive, educational, religious, and cultural associations, as well as advocacy groups, the aims of which are to pursue and express a variety of comprehensive conceptions of the good and/or to voice marginalized interests—functions that could be directly compromised by the internal bureaucratization of these associations. While the distinction between for-profit and nonprofit actors is over-idealized, there is some truth to it. It follows that the costs, in terms of value pluralism, of co-opting civil society are arguably higher than the costs involved in the market being co-opted by government.

## IV. THE SYMBOLIC RECIPROCITY ARGUMENT

In this section I shall examine the way in which widespread privatization compromises a third, expressive function of political institutions, and does so regardless of whether it compromises the previous two functions.

Consider the case of a society—call it *Privatazia*—in which the state funds all justice-required goods but contracts out their management and provision to private actors *entirely*. No public (publicly owned and publicly managed) schools, public hospitals, public universities, or public police exist in this society. Suppose also that in this society private actors are efficient in delivering these services; they are also well-intentioned and embedded in tight administrative procedures and regulations that leave to them no discretion in decision-making. Further, there are plenty of alternative associations so that privatization does not compromise the ability of civil society to be a site of value pluralism. Would there be anything amiss in this society?

Whereas we might (arguably) not care much about having the delivery or provision of a few services privatized, we might find uncomfortable the idea of a society where only private actors, including charities, churches, nonprofits, and business corporations are entitled to deliver public goods and services to the public, no matter how good they are at performing these tasks. The question is whether this negative reaction is justified.

One notable difference between public and private actors—a difference that, by assumption, would remain in societies like Privatazia as well—is expressive. Private actors, unlike public ones, often exhibit visible signs of being privately managed or owned. These signs can range from religious symbols in the case of religious organizations delivering public services (e.g., crucifixes on the wall of nonprofit Catholic hospitals), to plaques in honor of donors or private persons who have significantly contributed to the organizations (think, e.g., about the plaques in honor of philanthropists outside the buildings of private universities). Further, in their own name private organizations often allude to particular private persons or families, conceptions of the goods, or ideological commitments. To use a real-world example, consider the names of some of the largest nonprofit hospitals in the US: *Jackson* Memorial Hospital in Miami; New York-*Presbyterian* Hospital; *Christiana* Hospital across the mid-Atlantic; or the name of the largest health and human services nonprofit in America (by total revenue), the *Lutheran* Services in America. These names express either special recognition for particular persons or the endorsement of particular religious affiliations.

Given the "symbolic parochialism" of private organizations, it could be tempting to argue that privatization is incompatible with liberal neutrality, no matter how efficient private actors are at delivering important goods. After all, it seems that when privatization encompasses the delegation of public functions (e.g., publicly funded services-delivery) to private associations, it unavoidably compromises *neutrality of treatment*. A state realizes neutrality of treatment between the rival conceptions of the good held by its citizens, when its policies are equally accommodating of all reasonable conceptions of the good, in the sense that they extend equivalent forms of assistance (e.g., subsidies) to each conception of the good and impose the same forms of hindrance (e.g., taxes) on each.[54]

In order to remain neutral in this sense, if government contracts out certain public functions to, say, Lutheran nonprofits or publicly fund their work, it should make sure that the same treatment (e.g., pro-rated funding) is extended to Muslim, Jewish, Buddhist, and nonreligious nonprofit associations. Since, given the endless number of conceptions of the good in large, liberal societies, it is impossible to secure full equality of treatment in this respect, neutrality of treatment would seem to provide liberal states with an at least pro tanto reason to avoid entangling themselves with particular private organizations or to use them as state contractors.

The problem, however, is that—as I have argued elsewhere— neutrality of treatment may not be a suitable conception of state neutrality.[55] Assuming that a liberal state should attempt to remain neutral in the first place, neutrality of justification would seem to be a more promising conception. In this second sense, however, there would be nothing wrong, not even pro tanto, with a state giving special funding to or using as contractors certain associations but not others, as long as the reasons for doing so are public in a relevant sense.

To illustrate, consider the case of a state that decides to run an empirical study to evaluate what organizations within its territory are the most effective in delivering social and human services. It turns out that Lutheran organizations are, statistically, much more effective in delivering this kind of assistance than non-Lutheran ones. On instrumental grounds, the government decides to provide special subsidies to Lutheran organizations, without extending the same benefits to non-Lutheran ones, so as to discharge its duties as effectively as possible.

Is this policy neutral? According to neutrality of treatment the policy is non-neutral since it provides religious organizations with special benefits. Note that to say that the policy is non-neutral is to say that it is biased in favor of a particular conception of the good and at least pro tanto unjust. But, in fact, the policy involves no preference for Lutheran conceptions of the good *as such*. The policy only involves an official preference for organizations that are most effective. The policy, therefore, is not biased towards particular conceptions of the good.

Second, the policy is neutral with respect to what seems to me the right kind of object of a conception of neutrality. Neutrality cannot be owed to conceptions of the good as such because these are not agents. A liberal state owes neutrality to people in their capacity as bearers of a conception of the good and as competent judges of how particular aspects of their conception of the good fit within a broader scheme of values, including shared social values. This implies that any appropriate conception of neutrality must prevent *people* from being treated differently on the basis of their conception of the good.[56] But the above policy does not treat people differently in this way. The policy is neutral with respect to the relevant object of neutrality insofar as, by assumption, even non-religious people have good reasons, internal to their own overall scheme of values (which contains but cannot be reduced to particular aspects of their conception of the good) to endorse that policy. The policy does not, therefore, treat people differently on the basis of their conception of the good, since those who may happen to be burdened by the unequal accommodation would themselves endorse, were they reasonable, that policy in light of reasons they themselves (by assumption) share. The policy is therefore neutral among different individuals' overall conceptions of the good defined, following Gaus, as "a scheme in which different values are weighted."[57]

Finally, the policy is not, even pro tanto, unjust, for it imposes no arbitrary obstacles to nonreligious people's ability to pursue their commitments. Even if the policy might impose some opportunity costs upon them, these costs would be justified from their own evaluative standpoint, taken as a whole. Neutrality cannot therefore explain what is morally objectionable with a society like Privatazia where public provision is entirely privatized, at least if we assume that privatization can be justified by appealing to neutral reasons. This explanation must be found elsewhere.

I believe that this explanation can be found in the way private associations, given their symbolic features, fail to *represent* and thus render visible the ideal of equality as reciprocity among citizens, regarded as participants in a shared scheme of social cooperation.

They do so in two ways. First, the *impersonality* of public organizations and, more generally, of bureaucracy—their exhibiting no religious or ideological symbols, their making no reference to particular missions and loyalties, or particular families and persons—allows them to visibly express and represent the equality of citizens, regardless of their particular affiliations, ideological orientations, or religious beliefs. This is because, of course, being impersonal means nothing else than lacking those features that define, characterize, or constitute the singular "personality" of a particular entity or individual as different from others. This, note, neither entails that the particularities of individuals should not matter at all in establishing what is owed to whom nor that there shouldn't be plenty of space in a society for the expression of particular allegiances and affiliations. Indeed, to create this space is precisely, we saw, the purpose of a moral and institutional division of labor between political institutions and civil society. However, when political institutions act entirely through private entities, all having their own distinctive personalities, their symbols, and their idiosyncratic commitments, these institutions progressively lose the ability to mirror and visibly represent in their own constitution the moral equality of their people, that is, what is equal among people *in spite of their different personalities*.[58] This is so even if private actors *treat* people as equals.

Second, and relatedly, when a good is delivered by a public agent, the very fact that the public agent delivers this good visibly expresses the nature of this good qua a public entitlement, as opposed to an associational good. This is so because public agents, unlike private associations, are meant to have no other ends than justice itself, or compliance with their democratic mandates. In the absence of particular ends, when I receive a good, say education, from a public school, I clearly receive it as something that I am entitled to as nothing else than as a matter of reciprocity—as a benefit of social cooperation to which I have a claim as a member of an impersonal and shared relationship of citizenship. When I receive it from a private school, whether a religious nonprofit or a for-profit institution, things change. Qua a private organization, the raison d'être of the school and its willingness to provide educational goods are inescapably bound to its particular mission and the way its members or employees interpret that mission—a mission that is often rendered visible in the symbolic edifice and name of the organization. Students of a private school are also members of a private association. Therefore, even if strictly regulated and funded by government, the private school unavoidably expresses the character of education as an associational good, rather than as a good to which I am entitled as nothing else than a public entitlement.

Since, in their daily lives, citizens "see" and experience the state mainly *through* "street-level" goods and service providers, it might become difficult to sustain a sense of citizenship understood as "a relational ideal of reciprocity among those who, through the state, provide each other basic collective goods"[59] in a condition in which the "face" of the state is entirely privatized. Even if the state funds the goods that I receive from private agents or provides me with a voucher to purchase those goods, I must become a participant in or a client of a particular association, whose overarching beliefs and commitments I may or may not share, in order to receive those goods, to which I should be entitled *simply* as a participant in a shared, impersonal scheme of cooperation. Since nonprofit associations, many of which are cultural or religious, tend to visibly express particular comprehensive conceptions of the good in their constitution, even more so than market actors, the argument from symbolic reciprocity applies with particular strength to the former kind of associations.

One could object that these expressive concerns can easily be solved by rendering private actors more impersonal. Nothing in principle prevents a government from making delegation contracts conditional on private actors' willingness to get rid of their particular symbols, or of names that make essential reference to particular families or persons or to ideological and religious commitments. But, then, once again, this would amount to nothing else than transforming private associations into impersonal bureaucratic actors, with a consequent loss in terms of their ability to express and pursue a variety of particular ends.

The argument developed in this essay thus leaves us with a *double dilemma.* We can support widespread privatization, conditionally on bureaucratizing private actors so as to render it compatible with equal freedom and symbolic reciprocity. This, however, comes at the cost of value pluralism. We can secure value pluralism by coupling privatization with lax forms of regulation and administrative control, but this comes at the cost of equal freedom and symbolic reciprocity. Finally, we can preserve value pluralism, equal freedom, and symbolic reciprocity by restoring a more radical institutional and normative division of labor between state and civil society, but this requires abandoning privatization, or at least significantly limiting its extent. The last solution seems to me preferable.

NOTES

1  Michael Walzer, *Spheres of Justice: A Defense of Pluralism and Equality* (New York: Basic Books, 1983); Michael J. Sandel, *What Money Can't Buy: The Moral Limits of Markets* (New York: Farrar, Straus and Giroux, 2012).

2  Debra Satz, "Markets, Privatization, and Corruption," *Social Research* 80, no. 4 (2013.): 993–1008.

3  Wendy Brown, *Undoing the Demos: Neoliberalism's Stealth Revolution* (Cambridge, MA: MIT Press, 2016).

4  For a discussion of this motivational argument, see James Pattison, "Deeper Objections to the Privatisation of Military Force," *Journal of Political Philosophy* 18, no. 4 (2010): 425–47.

5  To be fair, not all arguments advanced against privatization are market-centered in this way. For example, Avihay Dorfman and Alon Harel have recently argued that some instances of privatization are wrong because private actors, whether for-profit or nonprofit, necessarily fail to provide inherently public goods like, e.g., punishment. See their "The Case against Privatization," *Philosophy and Public Affairs* 41, no. 1 (2013): 67–102. Elsewhere (in an unpublished manuscript) I argue that their argument, even if compelling in many respects, ultimately fails to provide a fully satisfactory account of the wrong of privatization. Regardless, it is importantly limited to cases where the provision of intrinsically public goods is at stake. Their argument cannot therefore explain what is objectionable with the extensive privatization of other functions, e.g., the provision of welfare goods and services—functions in relation to which nonprofits tend to play a particular prominent role.

6  Michael Trebilcock and Edward Iacobucci, "Privatization and Accountability," *Harvard Law Review* 116, no. 5 (2003): 1422–53.

7  Peter Frumkin, "After Partnership: Rethinking Public-Nonprofit Relations," in *Who Will Provide? The Changing Role of Religion in American Social Welfare*, eds. M. J. Bane, B. Coffin and R. Thiemann (Boulder, CO: Westview Press, 2000): 198–218; Scott W. Allard, "Helping Hands for the Working Poor: The Role of Nonprofits in Today's Safety Net," paper presented at the 2008 American Political Science Association Annual Meeting.

8  The Urban Institute, "Human Service Nonprofit-Government Contracting," 2010, www.urban.org.

9  Gillian Metzger, "Privatization as Delegation," *Columbia Law Review* 103 (2003): 1367–502, at 1385.

10  Courtney Burke, "Medicaid Funding for Nonprofit Healthcare Organizations," presented at the Rockefeller Institute of Government for the Aspen Institute, Washington, D.C (2007).

11  Geo, Inc., "Corporate Annual Report," 2005, available at www.library.corporate-ir.net.

12  Saki Knafo, "Nonprofit Floats Unusual Alternative To Private Prison," *Huffington Post*, September 5, 2014, www.huffingtonpost.com.

13  Elsewhere (in an unpublished manuscript) I defend the use of a normative baseline against (1) economists' use of a baseline defined by reference to the idea of market failure, and (2) political scientists' use of a purely historical/descriptive baseline. For a philosophical defense of the

economic baseline, see Joseph Heath, "Three Normative Models of the Welfare State," *Public Reason* 3, no. 2 (2011): 13–44.

14 This assumption would need more extensive justification than I can provide here. Indeed, not only libertarians but also many "general" egalitarians have often argued against the provision of in-kind goods on grounds of efficiency, freedom, and anti-paternalism. See, e.g., Ronald Dworkin, *Sovereign Virtue* (Cambridge, MA: Harvard University Press, 2000). For an excellent critique of general egalitarianism, see Debra Satz, *Why Some Things Should Not Be for Sale: The Moral Limits of Markets* (New York: Oxford University Press, 2010).

15 Nonprofits can generally claim charitable status for tax purposes, which allows them generous tax exemptions.

16 Immanuel Kant, *The Metaphysics of Morals* (hereafter *MM*), trans. and ed. Mary Gregor (Cambridge: Cambridge University Press, 1996): 30 (6: 237). My interpretation of Kant is indebted to Arthur Ripstein's magistral reconstruction of Kant's political philosophy in his *Force and Freedom: Kant's Legal and Political Philosophy* (hereafter *FF*) (Cambridge, MA: Harvard University Press, 2009).

17 Kant, *MM*, 41 (6: 251).

18 Ibid., 52 (6: 264).

19 Ibid., 51 (6: 263).

20 Ibid., 26 (6: 233).

21 For an extensive discussion of the connection between indeterminancy and unfreedom, see Anna Stilz, *Liberal Loyalty: Freedom, Obligation, and the State* (Princeton, NJ: Princeton University Press, 2009), 45–51.

22 *MM*, 24–25 (6: 231); Ripstein, *FF*, 151.

23 *MM*, 26 (6: 233).

24 "Idea for a Universal History with a Cosmopolitan Purpose," in *Kant: Political Writings*, ed. H. S. Reiss (Cambridge: Cambridge University Press, 1991), 47 (8: 24).

25 By value pluralism I mean the existence of irreducibly different conceptions of the good and comprehensive conceptions of what makes a life worth living.

26 I defend this interpretation in Chiara Cordelli, "The Institutional Division of Labor and the Egalitarian Obligations of Nonprofits," *Journal of Political Philosophy* 20, no. 2 (2012): 131–55. A similar interpretation of Rawls's division of labor is provided by Samuel Scheffler in his "Egalitarian Liberalism as Moral Pluralism," *Proceedings of the Aristotelian Society* 78, no. 1 (2005): 229–53.

27 John Rawls, *Political Liberalism* (New York: Columbia University Press, 1993): 269.

28 Will Kymlicka, "Civil Society and Government: A Liberal Egalitarian Perspective," in *Civil Society and Government*, eds. Nancy Rosenblum and Robert Post (Princeton, NJ: Princeton University Press, 2002): 79–110.

29 Rawls, *Political Liberalism*, 262.

30 Thomas Nagel also supports a moral division of labor when he argues that "the aim is to externalize through social institutions the most impartial requirements of the impersonal standpoint." See his *Equality and Partiality* (Oxford: Oxford University Press, 1985): 53.

31 Joshua Cohen, "For a Democratic Society," in *The Cambridge Companion to Rawls*, ed. Samuel Freeman (Cambridge: Cambridge University Press, 2003), 86–138.

32 Cécile Laborde, "Political Liberalism and Religion: On Separation and Establishment," *Journal of Political Philosophy* 21, no. 1 (2013): 67–86; Chiara Cordelli, "Neutrality of What?," *Critical Review of International Social and Political Philosophy* 20, no. 1 (2017): 36–48.

33 Andrea Sangiovanni, "Global Justice, Reciprocity and the State," *Philosophy and Public Affairs* 35, no. 1 (2007): 3–39, at 19.

34 This is not to say that there are no obligations of justice beyond the state. For one thing, reciprocity may not be the only ground of such obligations. Further, the level of socio-economic interdependence currently existing between countries may be sufficient to ground reciprocity-based obligations of justice across countries. See Charles Beitz, *Political Theory and International Relations* (Princeton, NJ: Princeton University Press, 1979).

35 Metzger, "Privatization as Delegation," 1395.

36 Ibid.

37 For an overview of the role of private actors in healthcare delivery, see Jody Freeman, "Extending Public Law Norms Through Privatization" *Harvard Law Review* 116 (2003): 1285–300.

38 Norman Daniels extensively discusses the normative relevance of indeterminacy in MCO's coverage decisions in "Limits to Health Care: Fair Procedures, Democratic Deliberation, and the Legitimacy Problem for Insurers," *Philosophy and Public Affairs* 26, no. 4 (1997): 303–50.

39 For example, in *Blum v. Yeretsky* the US Supreme Court concluded that "privately made decisions which affect individuals' eligibility for government benefits" do not qualify as state action for legal purposes and cannot therefore be subject to judicial review (*Blum v. Yaretsky*, 457 U.S. 991, [1982]: 102).

40 Kant, *MM*, 112 (6: 341). See also discussion in Ripstein, *FF*, 192–3.

41 Christopher Kutz, "The Judicial Community," *Philosophical Issues* 11 (2001): 442–69; Scott Shapiro, "Laws, Plans, and Practical Reason," *Legal Theory* 8 (2002): 387–441; Jules Coleman, *Practice of Principle: In Defense*

of a *Pragmatist Approach to Legal Theory* (Oxford: Oxford University Press, 2001); Michael Bratman, *Faces of Intention: Selected Essays on Intention and Agency* (Cambridge: Cambridge University Press,1999): chs. 5–8. For a skeptical view, see Matthew Noah Smith, "The Law as Social Practice," *Legal Theory* 12 (2006): 265–92.

42 Christopher Kutz, "Acting Together," *Philosophy and Phenomenological Research* 61, no. 1 (July 2000), 1–31.

43 Kutz, "The Judicial Community."

44 Dorfman and Harel also emphasize the importance of an integrated "community of practice" between the political and the bureaucratic. While they regard this practice as a necessary condition for fidelity of deference I take it to be a necessary condition for the possibility of shared agency, which does not necessarily require full deference. Dorfman and Harel, "The Case against Privatization."

45 See Dorfman and Harel, "The Case against Privatization."

46 See Mathew McCubbins, Roger Noll, and Barry Weingast, "Administrative Procedures as Instruments of Political Control," *Journal of Law, Economics, and Organization* 3, no. 2 (1987): 243–77.

47 This solution would also defeat the primary purpose of privatization, which is precisely to bring certain decisions outside of the bureaucratic structure, so as to foster innovation and efficiency.

48 See Chiara Cordelli, "Justice Below the State: Civil Society as a Site of Justice," *British Journal of Political Science* 46, no. 4 (2016): 915–36, and Cordelli, "The Institutional Division of Labor."

49 I advance a similar version of this argument in Chiara Cordelli, "How Privatisation Threatens the Private," *Critical Review of International Social and Political Philosophy* 16, no. 1 (2013): 65–87.

50 Cordelli, "Justice Below the State."

51 Martha Minow, "Public and Private Partnerships: Accounting for the New Religion," *Harvard Law Review* 116 (2003): 1229–70; Freeman, "Extending Public Law Norms"; Metzger, "Privatization as Delegation."

52 Steven Smith and Michael Lipsky, "Nonprofit Organizations, Government, and the Welfare State," *Political Science Quarterly* 104, no. 4 (1989): 625–48, at 638. See also Cordelli, "How Privatisation Threatens the Private."

53 Lester Salamon and Helmut Anheier, "The Nonprofit Sector in Comparative Perspective," in *The Nonprofit Sector: A Research Handbook*, 2nd ed., eds. Woody Powell and Richard Steinberg (New Haven, CT: Yale University Press, 2006): 97.

54 Alan Patten supports this conception of neutrality in his *Equal Recognition: The Moral Foundations of Minority Rights* (Princeton, NJ: Princeton University Press, 2014): ch. 4.

55 I develop this criticism in "Neutrality of What?"

56 Gerald Gaus, "The Moral Foundations of Liberal Neutrality," in *Contemporary Debates in Political Philosophy*, eds. T. Christiano and J.P. Christman (Oxford: Wiley-Blackwell, 2009): 79–98.

57 Ibid., 93.

58 For a similar interpretation of the idea of moral equality, see Bernard Williams, "The Idea of Equality," in *Philosophy, Politics and Society*, series II, ed. P. Laslett and W. G. Runciman (Oxford: Blackwell, 1962), 110–31.

59 Sangiovanni, "Global Justice, Reciprocity and the State," 19.

# 6

## COERCION AND PRIVATIZATION

### JESSICA FLANIGAN

Should goods and services be provided by private actors and consumers or by public officials and taxpayers? Avihay Dorfman and Alon Harel argue that at least some publicly provided services are inherently public goods, which can only be realized if government officials perform them.[1] Chiara Cordelli and Samuel Freemen develop non-instrumentalist cases against privatization too.[2] Dorfman and Harel frame their argument against instrumentalist arguments for or against privatization, such as Debra Satz's suggestion that in principle, services may be provided either by public or private actors and that the normative merits of either institutional approach should ultimately be assessed with reference to the benefits they bring—such as overall welfare, the common good, a reduction in inequality, efficiency, or accountability.[3] Jason Brennan also defends a broadly instrumentalist approach.[4]

In this essay, I develop a non-instrumentalist defense of privatization that justifies a moral presumption against the governmental provision of services, including law enforcement, national defense, and potentially even the establishment of property rules. My thesis contrasts with non-instrumentalist defenses of the governmental provision of services and instrumentalist arguments in favor of governmental or private provision of services. Though I agree with Dorfman and Harel that normative debates about public and private provision amount to more than empirical disputes, I contend that non-instrumental normative considerations favor privatization for two reasons. First, people cannot consent to the governmental provision of services and, all else equal, it is morally better if people consent to provide and receive services. Without citizens' consent, governments do not have the authority to tax citizens in order to provide services. Second, in most circumstances citizens do not have enforceable duties to provide public goods to their compatriots.

I begin in section I with an analysis of instrumentalist arguments against privatization. Instrumentalist defenses of the public provision of services rely on empirical assumptions that it is feasible for public officials to effectively provide services in ways that are insulated from the corrupting effects of the marketplace. Yet in political contexts where the boundaries between industry and the public are blurry and contested, many of the problems that proponents of the governmental provision of services cite against private provision apply with equal force against public provision. And many of the benefits of privatization that instrumentalist defenders of the market emphasize are compromised when private actors enlist public officials to protect or promote their economic interests. I conclude that when we hold instrumentalist arguments for and against privatization to the same standards of empirical support, we should not support a presumption in favor of either on instrumentalist grounds.

In section II, I lay the foundation for the case for privatization on non-instrumental grounds by disputing several non-instrumental arguments against privatization. I first argue, against Dorfman and Harel, that inherently public goods needn't be provided by public officials or through governments at all. The claim that public officials and governments must provide inherently public goods is false as an empirical matter and is not conceptually necessary. I then consider and reply to the claim that public officials and governments ought to provide services in order to treat people as equals or recognize people's entitlements to the services. Last, I address Samuel Freeman's claim that it is morally significant whether goods are provided through institutions that are backed by public power.

I then develop a positive argument in favor of the private provision of services in section III. It goes like this: all else equal, it is better if a good or service is provided without coercion. That is, it is morally better if the people who consented to provide a service provide it to people who consented to receive it. When public officials provide services, those who finance the services through taxation and the citizens who receive the services do not consent to their provision. So if it is not necessary for governments to provide particular services, meaning that people are not morally required to provide the service in the first place or that private actors could provide the service in the absence of government, then governments ought not provide those services.

In section IV, I address the possibility that people have positive duties to provide some security services to their compatriots, such as the rule of law, clean air, and national defense. I present an argument against the claim that people have enforceable duties to provide even these public goods. But even if it were true that people had enforceable positive duties to promote public safety, for example, it would not follow that public officials must provide those security services or that security services ought to be publicly financed. For example, private actors currently provide security services without coercing people who are not liable to be coerced in some cases.

I consider several implications of this argument in section V, such as the claim that full privatization is impossible and that even anarchic communities are governed by some state-like common rules. However, this argument does not undermine the case in favor of privatization as a moral ideal, since proponents of privatization may allow that some public rules are good while maintaining that they ought to be enforced with citizens' consent. And to the extent that proponents of the public provision of services only mean to advocate for institutions in which some rules are public and universal, then they do not disagree with proponents of privatization after all.

## I. Instrumental Arguments against Privatization

One way to assess the merits of privatization relative to the public provision of goods and services is by comparing the effects of each approach. The effects of each institutional arrangement vary depending on the nature of the good or service in question. As Satz points out, the privatization of the steel industry in Brazil was socially beneficial, whereas the privatization of public transportation in Britain was not.[5] Still, there may be some reliable features of privatization and public provision that justify one approach to providing particular goods over the other.

However, instrumentalist justifications for either institutional arrangement face three challenges. First, any instrumentalist justification must appeal to a potentially controversial conception of wellbeing, and in this way instrumentalist defenses of institutional arrangements are more controversial than they may initially appear. Second, critics of privatization should not cite concerns about the feasibility of effectively privatizing an industry or people's failure to comply with their contractual duties, without holding the public provision of services to the same standard. Third, in many cases it is difficult to know whether the problems associated with an industry are due to market forces or government interference, and this makes it difficult to know whether instrumentalist defenses of either arrangement succeed.

Debra Satz identifies several "consequentialist concerns" about privatization and advances a broadly instrumentalist defense of the public provision of essential services on the grounds that "moving a good or service out of the public sector and into the private sector can sometimes change the structure of governance in ways that worsen inequality and both distort and fragment important public goals."[6] Satz's framing of this concern presumes that goods within the public sector are governed in a way that promotes public goals and establishes the burden of proof for proponents of privatization to show that moving goods from the public sector to the private sector does not sometimes change the structure of governance in ways that distort public goals. Yet consequentialist proponents of privatization may deploy a similar strategy, arguing that moving a good from the private sector into the public sector can sometimes change the structure of governance in ways that worsen efficiency and distort incentives. For any industry, consequentialist proponents of each institutional arrangement may agree about the effects of privatization and public provision but disagree about which consequences matter or which approach is justified by the balance of consequentialist considerations.

Satz's instrumentalist objection to privatization is that it will contribute to inequality. This is an empirical objection to the privatization of government functions that is founded in a potentially controversial normative commitment to the value of equality.[7] Even if we accept that inequality is one important consequence to consider, people may disagree about the weight of moral reasons to promote equality relative to other moral reasons. Satz rightly points out that efficiency is not necessarily a morally important goal, and that it would require further argument (to say the least) to establish that gains in efficiency were always justified, even if they contributed to inequality or some other injustice. But the same can be said about gains in equality or transparency.

Moreover, instrumentalist assessments of institutional arrangements must also clarify the *scope* of wellbeing that they are concerned with. When Satz argues that an advantage of the public provision of goods and services is that it more reliably promotes public goals, presumably she is referring to the goals of a political community. But consequentialists should also consider the effects of an institutional arrangement more broadly, to include future generations and foreigners.[8] And if the relevant consequences are understood in this way, then even if the value of equality were given a great deal of weight, the public provision of goods and services could be worse on balance because public officials tend to focus on the wellbeing of their existing populations and not future generations or foreigners.[9]

One other reason to be skeptical about instrumentalist arguments against privatization that appeal to a conception of individual wellbeing is that people are generally in the best position to judge whether a good or a service will promote their wellbeing.[10] Public officials lack the information that is necessary to efficiently distribute resources in accordance with each person's needs and values, whereas prices in a private market are more capable of reflecting the value that each individual person derives from a good or service. This is not true in all cases. People may be genuinely wrong about what is good for them, and in some cases people may lack the means to effectively promote their wellbeing. But officials' relative ignorance about people's values and wellbeing poses greater challenges to instrumentalist justifications for public provision than for privatization.

Though it is necessary to clarify the axiological assumptions of instrumentalist assessments of privatization, it is not sufficient for an instrumentalist assessment, because whether privatization or public provision is better for people also depends on context and the nature of the industry. Privatizing a state monopoly will not always promote efficiency and freedom, nor will nationalizing an industry always promote equality and the common good. At this point, evaluating a particular institutional arrangement becomes an exercise in non-ideal theory, where the merits of privatization or public provision will depend on whether an arrangement achieves the desired effects.

In this spirit, critics of privatization warn that privatizing government functions effectively is often infeasible due to the corrupting effects of the marketplace. This is a non-ideal consideration, meaning that even if *in principle* privatization would be better, *in practice* it rarely is because effective privatization is not feasible.[11] Yet non-ideal assessments of institutions should hold all agents to the same standards, meaning that if critics of privatization assume that private actors are easily swayed by pecuniary incentives in ways that have bad effects, they should also assume that public officials are similarly subject to pecuniary incentives or explain why public officials are different.

One may reply that public officials are motivated by electoral incentives, rather than pecuniary incentives, and that they are therefore more accountable to the public's interest. But this reply assumes that the profit motive is necessarily worse than an electoral incentive. And this assumption isn't obvious, given the reliable biases and irrationalities of voters, especially when they organize into groups such as public employee unions.[12] To the extent that this reply assumes that there is an epistemic justification for using democratic procedures to allocate resources, markets are also democratic in the sense that prices are responsive to people's revealed preferences, just as representatives are responsive to people's votes.

Instrumentalist assessments of privatization should therefore consider not only the corrupting effects of the market but also the corrupting effects of electoral incentives. Both forms of corruption contribute to the problem of crony capitalism, which blurs the line between private and public provision. Consider for example the Fly America Act, which requires that all flights funded by the US government use "US flag airlines." Or certificate of need requirements that prohibit businesses in industries such as hospitals or housing from expanding into jurisdictions without first obtaining authorization from public officials, or private actors in the industry who are empowered by public officials, to effectively limit competition within their jurisdictions. Or consider the mayor of Chicago's decision to sell the city's parking meters to a private company, but to still require the police and courts to enforce parking tickets. More generally, policies that combine public and private provisions of goods and services risk causing rent-seeking behavior that results in an inefficient distribution of resources, often at consumers' expense.

In these circumstances, it is difficult to know whether the poor outcomes of an institutional arrangement can be attributed to the public's influence or to private actors. As Satz notes, privatization of an industry is sometimes associated with more regulation or non-competitive government contracts, which is even less efficient than the straightforward public provision of services.[13] Proponents of privatization will agree that this is a problem but disagree that this is a solution. While it may be more politically feasible to combine public funding and regulations with private companies in order to provide services, such an approach inherits the inefficiencies of public provision and introduces new inefficiencies as well.

I do not mean to suggest that instrumentalist arguments will never favor the public provision of goods and services. While not all cases of market failure require governmental solutions, governmental solutions can be a promising way to avoid genuine tragedies of the commons such as climate change or antibiotic resistance.[14] As Satz writes, "bureaucratic red tape sometimes beats out the invisible hand."[15] Not all markets are efficient; monopolies develop and firms create negative externalities.[16] For this reason, instrumentalist arguments will probably not take on a universal presumption in favor of or against privatization. Yet there are other values at stake, such as the value of respecting people by avoiding coercion, which supports a presumption in favor of privatization. I will spend the rest of this essay defending this claim.

## II. NON-INSTRUMENTAL ARGUMENTS AGAINST PRIVATIZATION

Instrumentalist arguments do not clearly favor privatization or the public provision of goods and services as a general matter. And as Dorfman and Harel argue, instrumentalist considerations are not decisive when weighing the merits of privatization against the public provision of services.[17] Instead, moral assessments of privatization must consider non-instrumentalist considerations. It may be that even if privatization has better consequences and is more efficient, there are nevertheless decisive non-instrumental moral reasons to oppose it. In this section, I will consider arguments in favor of this claim. Or it may be that even if the public provision of goods and services has better consequences and is more efficient, there are nevertheless decisive non-instrumental moral reasons to oppose it. I will argue for this claim in the next section.

Dorfman and Harel develop a two-step non-instrumental argument against the privatization of government services. First, they argue that some government functions provide inherently public goods that can only be realized if the government employs public officials to provide them. They write, "Some decisions must be executed by public officials and should not be privatized since private actors would inevitably fail in performing these tasks."[18] Specifically, private actors fail to provide "inherently public goods" that necessarily require that a person with a public role perform them. They focus on practices such as punishment and war, the ends of which can only be realized by public agents. Second, they argue that it is good that someone perform the kinds of tasks that require performance by someone speaking and acting on behalf of citizens.

Taking each step in turn, Dorfman and Harel's argument relies on the claim that "the success of performing a task sometimes hinges (conceptually) on the identity of the agent performing it," because tasks like punishment and war, which aim to provide deterrence and security, can only realize these desirable ends if they are provided by public agents.[19] As a first pass, it seems false that only public agents can provide deterrence through punishment or security through war. As I argue elsewhere, private actors can permissibly use private means of enforcement to effectively punish and deter fraud and theft as long as they interfere with wrongdoers in ways that are proportionate to the crime, even though they do act in a public role.[20] In weak states, private military organizations may provide peace and security for people when official state actors cannot.[21] The difference, according to Dorfman and Harel, is that "punishment is distinguished from mere violence by the fact that the state is a legitimate authority not only for the purpose of judging the wrongfulness of our action but also for inflicting the punishment for the right reasons."[22]

But as critics have pointed out elsewhere, private actors may also legitimately inflict punishment for the right reasons, and there is no guarantee that public actors will.[23] Legal scholar John Pfaff illustrates this point with reference to private prisons in the United States. Pfaff writes, "The critique of private prison groups actually misses the real source of the problem. Public prison officials, when given the same basic incentives that privates often contractually face act exactly the same way as the privates. Conversely, private actors with 'better' contracts . . . may well outperform public prisons."[24]

The same can be said of military contractors. And if not as an empirical matter, then at least as a theoretical matter public officials do not have a monopoly on the ability to use violence or coercion for the right reasons, nor are they immune from acting for the wrong ones.

If Dorfman and Harel maintain that it is conceptually necessary that only public actors provide certain goods, their argument is potentially question-begging. It is true that only public actors can provide a good if the good is defined as a good that is provided by public actors, but this strategy assumes the conclusion it is intended to establish. Even those goods that Dorfman and Harel argue are inherently political goods needn't necessarily be provided by public officials. For example, law enforcement is plausibly an inherently political good and there are laws against assault, but this does not entail that only public officers may defend and deter assault. If a private citizen intervenes to stop a fight, his action could be legitimate even if he was not authorized or required to intervene in virtue of his public role. Even if some practices were inherently political, the identity of the person acting may not matter as much as the legitimacy of the cause.

Dorfman and Harel claim that such a view would turn soldiers into mercenaries by implying that all citizens are equally entitled to use violence on behalf of a cause and that an official political role is not normatively significant.[25] But it is not conceptually necessary that we therefore accept that only public actors can provide certain important goods. Rather, the claim relies on a controversial normative commitment that some actions, such as those involving violence, are only permissible if carried out by public actors on behalf of legitimate states.

In other words, their argument assumes that public officials are morally entitled to use coercion where private actors are not in order to establish that it is morally better if public officials use coercion. This argument is valid, but as I argue in the next section, even if coercion by public officials is not as morally objectionable as coercion by private actors, it is still morally risky and there are reasons to avoid it if possible. Dorfman and Harel implicitly assume that the coercive provision of some services, such as punishment, is necessary and that private actors cannot permissibly achieve this good. But if it is possible to provide goods without coercing people who are not liable to be coerced, then such a system would still be preferable to the coercive provision of a good that requires performance by a public official.

Chiara Cordelli also develops a non-instrumental argument against privatization. Cordelli imagines a society, Privatazia, where the state finances all goods and services that are required by justice through private providers.[26] In such a society, Cordelli also imagines that private providers, selected on the basis of whether they efficiently provided services, would use certain symbols, such as family names and religious icons, as they do today. For this reason, they would "fail to represent and thus render visible the ideal of equality as reciprocity among citizens, regarded as participants in a shared scheme of cooperation."[27] A moral advantage of public providers, in her view, is that they are impersonal and they therefore mirror and visibly represent the moral equality of people by failing to mirror or visibly represent any particular group. Another advantage of public provision is that "public agents, unlike private associations, are meant to have no other ends than justice" so those who receive services from them can more easily see those benefits as public entitlements rather than associational goods.[28]

Proponents of privatization may reply that the use of personalized symbols is not a necessary feature of privatization. Privatazia may require that providers avoid the use of these symbols when they accept public funds, for example. In any case, public agencies also use personalized symbols, names, and icons, such as official state flags, agency seals and logos, and public buildings and bridges that are named after public officials. Nor do public institutions visibly represent the moral equality of citizens any more than private agencies. Consider the demographic composition of most

representative bodies, where women and economically marginalized citizens are vastly underrepresented.[29] It is also false that members of public associations have no other ends than justice. Elected
officials act on behalf of their constituents, to protect their legacy,
to win reelection, and sometimes to enrich themselves. Moreover,
a voucher system or a property system providing each citizen with
a basic income could also convey a sense that the benefits citizens
receive are a matter of entitlement even if citizens access those
benefits by buying goods and services through public providers.[30]

Samuel Freeman develops a similar case against privatizing
seemingly political functions on the grounds that "political power
is a public power, to be impartially exercised for the common
good."[31] And even if existing political institutions are far from
impartial and do not promote the common good, their fundamental purpose is to promote the public good, whereas private institutions fundamentally aim to promote more specific ends. Yet both
of these claims could be false, so it is not the case that political
institutions necessarily aim to promote the public good, nor is it
true that private companies necessarily do not. Some public political institutions, such as state and local governments, fundamentally aim to promote the interests of particular geographic groups
in ways that may set back the public good. And some private institutions, such as nonprofits, fundamentally aim to promote the
public good.[32] Here again, in theory the private provision of goods
and services can meet the same normative desiderata that are cited
as justifications for the public provision of goods and services, and
public institutions encounter the same practical challenges that
face private institutions in their efforts to meet these normative
desiderata. Freeman's non-instrumental defense of public institutions therefore amounts to an instrumental defense, but as I
argued in the previous section, instrumental considerations do not
favor either institutional arrangement as a general matter.

### III. Public Provision and Coercion

Inherently public goods needn't be provided by public officials,
either as a conceptual matter or as an empirical matter. Anything
that a person can provide out of a sense of public spiritedness
and duty, they can also provide in exchange for money. And many

people who act on behalf of the state do act for money. Many people who act on behalf of a corporation are also public spirited. So when non-instrumental critics of privatization argue that private actors "inevitably" will fail to provide inherently public goods, whatever reasons they may cite as evidence of this inevitability are either question-begging or also reasons to doubt that public officials can provide those goods as well.

Instead, non-instrumentalist arguments against privatization are better understood as the claim that some public goods *ought* to be provided by public officials, even if they could be provided privately. In the previous section, I suggested that these arguments appeal to a contentious conception of political authority. In this section, I will present an alternative account of political authority, according to which privatization is non-instrumentally better than the public provision of goods and services all else equal. I will also argue that whatever one's conception of political authority, there are non-instrumental reasons to favor privatization because private providers generally avoid the moral risks associated with using coercion to provide goods and services. My argument goes like this:

(1)  All else equal, it is morally worse to use force or coercion to provide a good than to use voluntary mechanisms (e.g., incentives, persuasion).

(2)  When public officials provide goods and services, they generally coerce people who do not consent to receive or contribute to the provision of the goods and services.

(3)  Therefore, all else equal, it is morally worse for public officials to provide goods and services.

In the next section, I will address the possibility that voluntary mechanisms may be inadequate for the provision of goods and services that are required by justice.

The first premise of my argument is that it is morally worse to use force or coercion to provide goods when voluntary mechanisms are available. Force is pro tanto wrong because it consists in the violation of a person's bodily rights. Imprisonment is an act of force. It involves limiting a person's use of her body while she is incarcerated. If a person did not forfeit her rights against imprisonment by committing a crime, then forcing her to remain in prison is wrong, all things considered. Coercion is wrong for similar reasons. In paradigm cases, coercion consists in the threat to violate a person's right. When a mugger says, "Your money or your life," he is issuing a threat to violate his victim's property rights or her right to life. Just as it is wrong to disrespect a person's authority to make decisions about her body and property, it is also wrong to threaten to.[33] In contrast, if a person authorized others to use her property (e.g., by issuing a loan) or to commit acts of violence against her (e.g., by joining a boxing match), then her consent would make an act that would otherwise be wrong permissible.

In general, the provision of services through taxation involves coercion. People do not typically consent to live in political communities that use force to collect taxes. But in all political communities officials collect taxes by using threats of violence and imprisonment in order to publicly provide goods and services.[34] If people have rights to keep their property and bodily rights, then public officials act wrongly by enforcing taxes. This is Michael Huemer's argument in favor of political anarchism. Huemer argues that people are entitled to retain their property and that taxation violates these rights.[35] Dan Moeller makes a similar argument on the grounds that the justifications for people's entitlement to retain their property are seemingly stronger in advanced service economies, so the case for taxation is weaker.[36]

One may object that this argument is question-begging because proponents of taxation assert that people do not have entitlements to keep their property or to be protected from violence, and so the theory of entitlements that is implicit in this account of coercion is controversial. It is less controversial that people have rights to their bodies, but perhaps people forfeit those rights when they attempt to retain property that the public has a right to. I share this skepticism about whether seeming violations of property rights always constitute wrongful force or coercion.[37] Property rights are partly conventional and proponents of the public provision of services may argue that a more just convention would allow for taxation. Nevertheless, to the extent that people have rights against some level of taxation, then this argument would still tell against some level of public provision if not all public provision of services through taxation.

Furthermore, since the enforcement of taxation always involves threats against people's bodily rights, one needn't commit to political anarchism or a controversial theory of property rights in order to establish that *all else equal* it is better that goods and services be provided and received in ways that people consent to. Laws that compel citizens to contribute to the public provision of goods and services are effective because they use enforcement mechanisms, threats of violence and imprisonment, in order to achieve their goals. Using violence is pro tanto morally worse than not using violence, even if public officials would be authorized to use violence in order to provide a good. Consider this point in light of recent discussions of moral risk.[38] In general, it is more morally risky to kill, injure, imprison, threaten, or intimidate a person than to not kill, injure, imprison, threaten, or intimidate her.

For this reason, if it is not *necessary* that governments provide particular goods and services, given that it is morally risky for governments to do so, public officials should favor private provision. By *necessary* I mean that (a) members of political communities are morally required to provide the good or service to citizens, and (b) private actors cannot effectively or efficiently provide the service in the absence of public provision. Whether any particular good meets conditions (a) or (b) will require further argument.

For example, some argue that members of the political community are morally required to provide their compatriots with health care and education, so the provision of health care and education satisfy condition (a). One might argue for this claim on the grounds that people should adopt fair and impartial institutions, which would provide all citizens with equal opportunities to participate as equals in society.[39] Or members of the political community could have duties of beneficence that require that they provide at least a minimum standard of health care and protection from illness for all citizens.[40] But if people could efficiently provide these services for themselves and their children in the absence of public provision, at least as a general matter, then education and healthcare would not meet condition (b).

On the other hand, one might argue that the provision of health care and education would satisfy conditions (a) and (b) for the worst-off members of a society if not for everyone. If so, then according to the foregoing argument, the moral risks of coercion may be justified in order to publicly provide access to education and health care for the worst off. But officials should still take care to use the minimal necessary coercion to achieve this goal. So unless members of a political community were morally required to ensure that even those who could afford to pay for health coverage and education had access to a public option, or universal coverage and education were required necessary to ensure the provision of education and healthcare to the worst off, such an argument still would not justify expanding publicly financed health coverage and education to all citizens.

Other goods clearly do not meet conditions (a) and (b). For example, members of political communities probably are not morally required to provide public television, art, or public playgrounds to their fellow citizens and these goods could be (and are) provided privately. Even if such goods are valuable and beneficial to all who use them, their value is not sufficient to justify using coercion in order to publicly provide them. There may be other compelling reasons against the private provision of some goods that do not meet conditions (a) and (b), but whatever the reasons in favor of public provision of these kinds of goods there remain strong moral reasons against using coercion to provide them.

## IV. COERCION AND PUBLIC GOODS

One may reply to the foregoing argument against the public provision of goods and services by arguing that some goods do meet conditions (a) and (b), meaning that members of political communities are morally required to provide citizens with these goods and services, and private actors cannot efficiently provide the services in the absence of public provision. Consider two arguments to this effect, in defense of the claim that citizens have enforceable duties to contribute to certain public programs and that public officials have the authority to provide them. First, one may argue that a principle of fairness and reciprocity authorizes states to compel citizens to contribute to the public provision of certain goods. Second, one may argue that members of a political community have Samaritan obligations to support the public provision of some goods and services. Though these arguments do address the pro tanto wrongfulness of coercion in defense of the public provision of some goods and services, they may not justify the public provision of goods and services all things considered and they also do not justify the public provision of much.

George Klosko's argument may be used to justify the public provision of goods and services in the following way. Klosko begins with the claim that people have duties of fairness to contribute to certain mutually advantageous ventures, such as the provision of presumptively beneficial, non-excludable public goods such as clean air, the rule of law, and national defense.[41] These are goods and services that everyone has reason to want, but in the absence of enforcement, people will not contribute to these ventures, even though they are obligated to, because they can receive the benefits by free riding on the efforts of others.[42] Yet according to Klosko, "the obligations generated by a principle of fairness are moral requirements that can be supported by the use of force."[43] This argument therefore speaks directly to the aforementioned concern about the wrongfulness of using force and coercion to provide goods and services, because in Klosko's view those who fail to contribute to the provision of certain public goods when public provision is necessary forfeit their rights against being coerced.

Christopher Wellman arrives at a similar conclusion via a different route. Though Wellman agrees with many of the concerns raised in the previous section, he argues that people have enforceable duties of Samaritanism that authorize public officials to use coercion in some circumstances.[44] Wellman argues that people have enforceable duties to obey the laws of just states because legal obedience is required as part of doing one's fair share of rescuing people who would otherwise be imperiled by the absence of political society that protects their basic moral rights and secured peace.[45]

Both arguments appeal to the idea that people have enforceable duties to contribute to the public provision of some goods, and in this way they potentially challenge the arguments against the public provision of goods and services that I developed in the previous section because people do not have rights against being coerced when coercion is necessary to compel them to comply with their moral obligations. For example, the fact that people have presumptive rights against force and coercion does not require that bystanders refrain from coercing a person who would otherwise commit assault. Yet whereas negative duties, such as the duty to refrain from coercion, are clearly enforceable, it is less clear whether and to what extent positive duties are enforceable. Unlike negative duties, positive duties, such as the duty to contribute to a beneficial scheme or Samaritan duties, are sensitive to costs.[46] And the costs associated with the pro tanto wrongfulness of coercing a person can outweigh the benefits provided. If so, then even if a proposal to publicly provide a good otherwise meets conditions (a) and (b), meaning that citizens have a duty to provide a good and public provision is necessary, they may not have a duty to provide the good at any price, and in light of the pro tanto wrongfulness of coercion, even if people do have a duty to provide a good it may not be an enforceable duty.[47]

Furthermore, if these arguments for the public provision of some services only apply when public provision is *necessary*, then such a defense of public provision is unlikely to apply in many cases. The mere theoretical risk of free riders does not establish that using coercion to publicly provide security services and other beneficial non-excludable goods is necessary. After all, small-scale societies in some contexts develop informal private mechanisms to govern common resources and provide public goods while discouraging free riders.[48] In theory, larger voluntary cooperative anarchic communities can provide security services without public financing or provision.[49] And if a voluntary society that provided the same benefits that enforcing duties of fairness or Samaritan duties provided were feasible, it would be morally preferable to these coercive alternatives. One may reply that a large-scale voluntary society that protects people's rights without the use of coercion is politically infeasible at this point, so there are good reasons to support institutions that publicly provide people with beneficial, non-excludable public goods, secure peace, and protect people's rights. But even if the public provision of this limited range of goods is necessary at present, such goods should be provided with minimal coercion and this argument would not justify the public provision of most of the goods that proponents of public provision support, such as public education or a postal service.

As Wellman writes,

> For each potential state function, we should ask whether the goods secured are important enough to justify the nonconsensual

coercion that inevitably accompanies political coordination. And even if the function is important enough, we must be sure that non-coercive extragovernmental means could not satisfactorily secure the benefits . . . in most cases, the forced imposition of any nonessential state function is not only inefficient, it is unjust.[50]

In other words, the best case for the public provision of goods and services is that in some cases coercion is necessary in order to provide important benefits, such as the protection of people's rights. But this case only justifies the public provision of a relatively minimal state.[51] Beyond that, the public provision of other goods and services is difficult to justify in light of the wrongfulness of coercion.

This may sound like a fairly libertarian conclusion, but as I mentioned in the previous section, one's definition of coercion ultimately presupposes a theory of rights and it is not clear that a libertarian theory of natural property rights is justifiable. If not, then the public enforcement of a capitalist system of private property may be one of the goods that, according to my argument, it is very morally risky (and perhaps impermissible) for public officials to provide. Like the other goods that I discussed in this section, officials may justify the public enforcement of a property system by an appeal to the substantial benefits of capitalism, but nevertheless, a private, voluntary, non-coercive property system would be morally better than any state-backed property intuitions, including existing forms of capitalism.

## V. CONCLUSION

Whether goods and services should be provided through public or private means will depend on whether institutions should be assessed primarily in terms of their effects or whether non-instrumental considerations bear on the ethics of public and private provision as well. If institutions should be assessed primarily in terms of their effects, then the case for or against privatization will depend on which effects are morally relevant—equality, freedom, an objective list of things that are good for people, efficiency? It will also depend on the scope of consequentialist considerations. The case for the public provision of resources is stronger if assessments of institutions only consider their effects on existing citizens, since public officials have strong incentives to prioritize the wellbeing of their constituents. In any case, any instrumental case for privatization or public provision should hold actors to the same standards, meaning that concerns about corruption or the infeasibility of effective regulation apply equally to private actors and public officials.

Turning to non-instrumental considerations, I argue that non-instrumental arguments against privatization often rely on conceptual claims that some goods, by their very nature, cannot be provided by private means. These arguments are potentially question-begging. If the goods in question are defined as goods that must be publicly provided, then critics of privatization do not establish that public provision is preferable to privatization without a further argument that the provision of inherently public goods is preferable to the provision of their privately provided counterparts. If the goods in question are not defined in a way that makes reference to how they are provided, then critics of privatization must show why it is nevertheless true that the public provision of such goods is non-instrumentally better than private provision, all else equal.

In contrast, I argue that non-instrumental considerations favor privatization because, all else equal, it is worse to coerce people, and the public provision of goods and services is generally coercion, so it is generally worse or at least more morally risky. This is not to say that the public provision of goods and services is never permissible. But if it is, it is only justified in limited cases. And even then, public provision is still in some sense morally worse than its private counterpart would be.

One may reply to the foregoing arguments by re-framing the private provision of goods and services as public practice to the extent that it is also adopted by a political community and in the public interest. But even if privatization is itself a kind of voluntary public practice, blurring the line between privatization and public provision in this way does not undermine the case in favor of privatization because the relevant moral consideration in debates about privatization should not be the distinction between private profit motives and public humanitarian motives.[52] Rather, the relevant moral consideration in debates about privatization is whether and when coercion is permissible. Privatization as a moral ideal reflects the ideal of voluntarily providing goods and services. The problem with public provision is that citizens do not consent to it. If public officials could provide goods and services in ways that did not impermissibly coerce people, then the public provision of goods and services would not be morally worse than privatization. Proponents of privatization may even allow that some public-spirited norms are valuable, as long as citizens adopt them voluntarily, just as proponents of the public provision of services grant that markets are valuable when they are in the public interest. The case in favor of privatization is not a denial of the moral significance of the public interest; it a denial of the moral permissibility of coercing people for the sake of public ends.

## ACKNOWLEDGMENTS

I would like to thank Javier Hidalgo and Melissa Schwartzberg for reading an earlier draft of this essay and for providing very helpful comments and suggestions.

## NOTES

1  Avihay Dorfman and Alon Harel, "The Case against Privatization," *Philosophy & Public Affairs* 41, no. 1 (2013): 67–102.

2  Chiara Cordelli, "Privatization without Profit?," in this volume.

3  Debra Satz, "Markets, Privatization, and Corruption," *Social Research: An International Quarterly* 80, no. 4 (April 30, 2014): 993–1008; Debra Satz, "Some (Largely) Ignored Problems with Privatization," in this volume.

4  Jason Brennan, "Consequences Matter More: In Defense of Instrumentalism on Private Versus Public Prisons," *Criminal Law and Philosophy*, November 4, 2015: 1–15, doi:10.1007/s11572-015-9385-y.

5  Satz, "Some (Largely) Ignored Problems with Privatization."

6  Ibid.

7  Critics of privatization may be concerned about distributive inequality because markets allocate resources to people in ways that can entrench unjust initial distributions of resources or because markets cause some people to have a lot more resources than others. Or they may be concerned about relational inequality because markets can change social relationships between people and cause some citizens to feel dominated or stigmatized by others. Whether instrumentalist egalitarian arguments

against privatization succeed will therefore depend on the somewhat controversial assumptions that a just society should promote a more equal distribution of resources or equal status among citizens, which sufficientarians, libertarians, and utilitarians may dispute. It will also depend on the controversial claim that private patterns of relational inequality are more objectionable than the inequality between public officials and the people who are subject to their laws.

8 David Schmidtz, "A Place for Cost-Benefit Analysis," *Noûs* 35 (October 1, 2001): 148–71, doi:10.1111/0029–4624.35.s1.6.

9 For example, public officials may enforce policies that fund social security programs that disadvantage future generations, or they may incur debts or enforce environmental policies that prioritize the interests of existing citizens over future citizens. Or public officials may enforce immigration restrictions or wage wars that prioritize the interests of citizens over non-citizens. Public officials make these choices either because they are influenced by electoral incentives, because they are subject to cognitive biases such as anti-foreign bias or short-sightedness, or because they adopt an ethical theory that gives much greater moral consideration to existing compatriots than future generations and foreigners.

10 John Stuart Mill, *On Liberty and Other Essays*, ed. John Gray (Oxford: Oxford University Press, 2008).

11 Laura Valentini, "Ideal vs. Non-Ideal Theory: A Conceptual Map," *Philosophy Compass* 7, no. 9 (September 1, 2012): 654–64, doi:10.1111/j.1747–9991.2012.00500.x.

12 Bryan Caplan, *The Myth of the Rational Voter: Why Democracies Choose Bad Policies* (Princeton, NJ: Princeton University Press, 2008); Jason Brennan, *The Ethics of Voting* (Princeton, NJ: Princeton University Press, 2012); John Pfaff, *Locked In: The True Causes of Mass Incarceration—and How to Achieve Real Reform* (New York: Basic Books, 2017).

13 Debra Satz, "Some (Largely) Ignored Problems with Privatization," in this volume.

14 For example, problems such as the under-provision of scientific research, climate change, vaccine refusal, and antibiotic resistance may require governmental solutions.

15 Satz, "Some (Largely) Ignored Problems with Privatization," in this volume.

16 Jonathan Anomaly, "Public Goods and Government Action," *Politics, Philosophy & Economics* 14, no. 2 (2015): 109–28, doi:10.177/1470594X13505414.

17 Dorfman and Harel, "The Case against Privatization."

18 Ibid., 68.

19 Ibid., 102.

20 Jessica Flanigan, "Rethinking Freedom of Contract," *Philosophical Studies* 174, no. 2 (May 17, 2016): 1–21, doi:10.1007/s11098-016-0691-6.

21 This practice is controversial, but for instrumental reasons. Some critics worry that private firms do not promote the public good as well as public officials could, but in weak states public officials cannot effectively secure peace and security without the use of private military organizations. For a discussion of the costs and benefits of these arrangements, see William Reno, "How Sovereignty Matters: International Markets and the Political Economy of Local Politics in Weak States," in *Intervention and Transnationalism in Africa: Global-Local Networks of Power*, ed. Thomas Callaghy, Ronald Kassimir, and Robert Latham (Cambridge: Cambridge University Press, 2002): 210–11.

22 Dorfman and Harel, "The Case against Privatization," 93.

23 Brennan, "Consequences Matter More."

24 Pfaff, *Locked In*, ch. 3, at 2.

25 Dorfman and Harel, "The Case against Privatization," 100. In this sense they are critical of Jeff McMahan's view that the "deep morality of war" does not hold soldiers to different moral standards regarding rights to kill or to act in self-defense. Jeff McMahan, *Killing in War* (New York: Oxford University Press, 2011).

26 Chiara Cordelli, "Privatization without Profit?"

27 Ibid.

28 Ibid.

29 Anne Phillips, "Democracy and Representation: Or, Why Should It Matter Who Our Representatives Are?," in *Feminism and Politics*, ed. Anne Phillips (Oxford: Oxford University Press, 1998): 224–40; Nicholas Carnes, "Does the Numerical Underrepresentation of the Working Class in Congress Matter?," *Legislative Studies Quarterly* 37, no. 1 (February 1, 2012): 5–34, doi:10.1111/j.1939–9162.2011.00033.x.

30 Philippe Van Parijs, "Competing Justifications of Basic Income," in *Arguing for Basic Income*, ed. Philippe Van Parijs (London: Verso, 1992): 1–43.

31 Samuel Freeman, "Illiberal Libertarians: Why Libertarianism Is Not a Liberal View," *Philosophy & Public Affairs* 30, no. 2 (April 1, 2001): 105–51, 107, doi:10.1111/j.1088–4963.2001.00105.x.

32 Cordelli's essay in this volume provides a more detailed discussion of the role that nonprofits should play in assessing the merits of privatization. Cordelli, "Privatization without Profit?"

33 For a further defense of this account of coercion, see Japa Pallikkathayil, "The Possibility of Choice: Three Accounts of the Problem with Coercion," 2011, www.philpapers.org.

34 This isn't necessarily true, however. States also finance goods and services in other ways, such as through voluntary fees or by investments. See John Simmons's work for a further discussion of taxation and consent. A. John Simmons, "Justification and Legitimacy," *Ethics* 109, no. 4 (1999): 739–71, doi:10.1086/233944.

35 Michael Huemer, *The Problem of Political Authority: An Examination of the Right to Coerce and the Duty to Obey* (Houndmills, Basingstoke, Hampshire: Palgrave Macmillan, 2012).

36 Dan Moller, "Property and the Creation of Value," *Economics & Philosophy* 33, no. 1 (November 2015): 1–23, doi:10.1017/S0266267115000395.

37 G. A. Cohen, for example, argues that all property systems are systems that distribute rights of interference, so one cannot critique a particular property system on the grounds that it violates people's rights of interference. I am assuming that people have some rights against interference, e.g., bodily rights, that do independently constrain property systems. For a critique of this assumption, see Cecile Fabre's arguments against "body exceptionalism." G. A. Cohen, *Self-Ownership, Freedom, and Equality* (Cambridge: Cambridge University Press, 1995); G. A. Cohen, "Once More into the Breach of Self-Ownership: Reply to Narveson and Brenkert," *Journal of Ethics* 2, no. 1 (1998): 57–96; G. A. Cohen, "Freedom and Money," *Filosoficky Casopis* 48, no. 1 (2000): 89–114; Cécile Fabre, *Whose Body Is It Anyway?: Justice and the Integrity of the Person* (Oxford: Oxford University Press, 2006); Cécile Fabre, "Against Body Exceptionalism: A Reply to Eyal," *Utilitas* 21, no. 2 (June 2009): 246–8, doi:10.1017/S0953820809003525.

38 Alexander A. Guerrero, "Don't Know, Don't Kill: Moral Ignorance, Culpability, and Caution," *Philosophical Studies* 136, no. 1 (2007): 59–97.

39 Norman Daniels, "Health-Care Needs and Distributive Justice," *Philosophy & Public Affairs* 10, no. 2 (1981): 146–79; Harry Brighouse and Adam Swift, "Educational Equality versus Educational Adequacy: A Critique of Anderson and Satz," *Journal of Applied Philosophy* 26, no. 2 (May 1, 2009): 117–28, doi:10.1111/j.1468-5930.2009.00438.x; Debra Satz, "Equality, Adequacy, and Education for Citizenship," *Ethics* 117, no. 4 (July 1, 2007): 623–48, doi:10.1086/518805.

40 J. Paul Kelleher, "Beneficence, Justice, and Health Care," *Kennedy Institute of Ethics Journal* 24, no. 1 (2014): 27–49; Elmar H. Frangenberg, "A Good Samaritan Inspired Foundation for a Fair Health Care System," *Medicine, Health Care and Philosophy* 14, no. 1 (2011): 73–9.

41 This argument applies only as long as it is worth the effort to contribute to providing the good and the burdens of contributing are fairly distributed. George Klosko, "Presumptive Benefit, Fairness, and Political Obligation," *Philosophy & Public Affairs* 16, no. 3 (1987): 241–59.

42 Robert Nozick famously objects to this argument on the grounds that people do not have duties of fairness to contribute when they receive benefits, but that even if they did, these duties would not be enforceable. Klosko replies that Nozick mistakenly focuses on goods that are not presumptively beneficial or worth people's efforts in providing them. Robert Nozick, *Anarchy, State, and Utopia*, 2nd ed. (New York: Basic Books, 2013).

43 George Klosko, *The Principle of Fairness and Political Obligation* (Lanham, MD: Rowman & Littlefield, 2004), 48.

44 Christopher Wellman and John Simmons, *Is There a Duty to Obey the Law?* (Cambridge: Cambridge University Press, 2005), 30.

45 Ibid., 45.

46 Christian Barry and Gerhard Øverland, "How Much for the Child?," *Ethical Theory and Moral Practice* 16, no. 1 (December 21, 2011): 189–204, doi:10.1007/s10677-011-9325-4.

47 For example, conscription may be unjustifiably coercive even if people have Samaritan duties to join the military for the sake of humanitarian intervention, and providing the good of humanitarian intervention requires that people participate in the military.

48 For example, see Elinor Ostrom's work on this topic. Elinor Ostrom, *Governing the Commons* (Cambridge: Cambridge University Press, 2015).

49 One may object that such arrangements are practically unavailable, but so too is a state that limits the public provision of resources only to Samaritanism or the provision of public goods. In any case, this point is merely meant to show that in some sense, even these arguments in favor of the public provision of goods depend on the assumption that a noncoercive alternative is unavailable. Jason Brennan, *Why Not Capitalism*, 1st ed. (New York: Routledge, 2014).

50 Wellman and Simmons, *Is There a Duty to Obey the Law?*, 73.

51 Nozick, *Anarchy, State, and Utopia*.

52 Scanlon defends this claim about the irrelevance of a person's intention to the permissibility of her actions. T. M. Scanlon, *Moral Dimensions* (Cambridge, MA: Harvard University Press, 2009).

# PART II

# PRIVATIZATION AND THE STATE

# 7

# PRIVATIZATION AS STATE TRANSFORMATION

## HENRY FARRELL

### I. INTRODUCTION

Privatization is an ambiguous term covering many loosely related phenomena. In this essay, I focus on one specific aspect of privatization—the privatization of governance. This sidesteps arguments about the presumed efficiency gains of, e.g., turning state-owned entities into for-profit corporations, and highlights the *political* consequences of privatization—how it takes decisions which had once been within the remit of democratic politics and hands them over to regulated private actors. Considered in this light, privatizing governance surely includes privatization in its narrow economic sense, especially given that the current trend towards privatized governance had its beginnings in economic privatization.

Yet it also involves broader transformations. The key point, and key argument, of this essay is that privatization does not so much involve the shrinking of the state as its transformation. State control exercised through direct ownership (with associated relations of influence) is replaced by state control exercised through regulation (with associated relations of influence). In a very important sense, privatized entities typically remain imbricated with and embedded within the state. They are not abandoned to the vagaries of competitive markets. However, the politics of the state is transformed from one of ownership relations to one of politics mediated through regulators, which in part seek to turn privatized entities' activities towards the purposes of the state, and in part look to protect these entities against external pressures.

The privatization of state-owned entities helped transform the state's relationship with the economy, so that it sought to shape economic outcomes externally through regulation rather than ownership while internally shifting its mode of operation to more closely resemble contractual relations. The turn to regulation has had international consequences, as national regulations clashed with each other, sometimes leading to some regulators winning, but often leading states that could not reach agreement among themselves to either limit the scope of regulation (through treaties intended to protect private actors) or to turn to private actors as governors themselves. Finally, the serpent is beginning to bite its own tail as private actors have sought to take advantage of international regimes to reshape the domestic reach of the state, defining inconvenient regulations as a kind of "taking" of their property and demanding compensation for them.

In short then, the privatization of governance involves three different aspects—national privatization strategies, the conversion of state structures, and international responses to regulatory clashes that sometimes allow private actors to reach down and further re-engineer the form of the state. I deliberately present a stylized schema here, emphasizing the ways in which these different levels reinforce each other, rather than the frictions that often arise between them. This has the obvious disadvantage of over-simplifying a very complex set of relationships, but the advantage of isolating plausibly important causal interconnections, which are typically obscured in political science accounts that tend to focus on national or international politics rather than the complicated interactions between them. When I look at specific national experiences, I focus primarily on the US and UK for ease of exposition. These are not typical cases, but they do illustrate the possible consequences of privatization in especially pungent ways.

This account helps explain not only why key parts of the state have become privatized or semi-privatized, being put out to private operators, but why states are increasingly relying on private systems of ordering. It shows how the privatization of governance spans the international sphere as well as domestic politics, since international and cross-national forms of regulation have sometimes been partly privatized, and sometimes structured so as to provide private entities with new opportunities to challenge government decisions. Finally, it provides the basis for a specific normative critique of privatization. Here, I do not try to evaluate whether the economy works worse, or better, after privatization than it did in an era when the state exercised control through ownership rather than regulation. Instead, more simply, I show that privatization did not work as its enthusiasts argued and believed that it would, looking to evaluate it in terms of its own promises. Rather than pushing back the state, and replacing political inefficiency with the competitive disciplines of the market, it has replaced one form of political control with another.

First, I examine the origins of the most recent wave of privatization: in simple or "economic" privatization, the processes through which aspects of the economy that used to be under state control have been privatized, either being transformed into, or bought by, profit-oriented market entities. This wave of privatization has lasted from the 1980s to today (e.g., the UK government's recent privatization of the Royal Mail and current proposals to privatize the land registry) and has profoundly changed politics. Today, states seek to avoid direct ownership of large firms, and even when states have taken over businesses (as when the UK government took over the Royal Bank of Scotland to prevent its collapse), they have usually sought to return these businesses to profit and the private sector as quickly as possible. Functions that were previously seen as core to the state—such as education and healthcare in the UK, and intelligence and military operations in the US—have increasingly been put out to private industry.

Next, I examine how states have renounced ownership stakes in business: they have moved from a paradigm of direct control, to one in which their instruments consist primarily of independent regulatory agencies (for businesses with which the state has an arms-length relationship) or contracts (for businesses that the state relies on directly). However, it has often turned out to be difficult to regulate businesses effectively or to craft contracts that provide real accountability, especially when the businesses have much greater expertise or resources than the regulators. This means that states are increasingly reliant on private actors with their own pecuniary interests for resources and information, replacing traditional forms of public influence (such as political parties) with intimate patterns of exchange between political and economic elites, which often engage in elaborate forms of *pantou-flage* in which private sector personnel move into government for a period or vice versa. Not only have states privatized state-owned companies, but they have also put out many of their own internal operations to the market, becoming increasingly reliant on private actors to understand how best to regulate, and sometimes to implement, their regulations.

Third, I address the question of cross-national and international forms of regulation. As privatization has led to a renewed focus on regulation, it has led both to greater opportunities for private actors to escape the reach of regulators by shifting jurisdiction, and to greater potential for conflict as regulators seek to limit international exit opportunities so as to retain their control. This creates a new arena for politics, in which the increased prominence of national regulators makes clashes between countries with different regulatory approaches more likely, empowering actors who can influence the processes through which these disputes are resolved, and weakening actors who do not have such influence.[1] It also strengthens the hand of multinational firms vis-a-vis regulators, since they now have greater opportunity to move their activities to locations with friendly regulators, as well as multiple access points for influence on international policy discussions.

This has led to a *partial privatization* of international regulatory processes,[2] as states increasingly turn to private standards or private regulators to resolve conflicts, or alternatively find themselves subject to international dispute resolution mechanisms that have allowed private actors to challenge and seek redress for regulatory actions that they believe impinge upon their rights. These new cross-national arrangements help private actors to reach down into domestic political systems, making it much more difficult for regulators to impose costly regulations, and hence expanding the space for purely privatized governance. For example, ISDS (Investor State Dispute Settlement) resolution mechanisms, incorporated into bilateral and multilateral investment and trade treaties, effectively provide businesses with an opportunity to challenge public regulations that is not available to ordinary members of the public, and to win substantial damages when private arbitrators find in the interests of the plaintiffs.

These different aspects of privatization often tend to reinforce each other. As more aspects of the economy are privatized, it becomes easier for actors who might benefit from privatization to press the state to make further concessions. As states become more reliant on the private sector for information and resources, they become more inclined to acquiesce to the demands of private actors who see potential profits from privatization. As international regulatory processes are privatized or opened up to the influence of private actors, it becomes easier for private actors with access to the relevant international forums to press for concessions and limits in regulatory powers that advantage them and further reshape the role of the state. By keeping the state at the heart of analysis, one can see how the kinds of feedback loops between interest groups and state entities identified by historical institutionalists can thrive in an environment of privatization.[3]

They also have important consequences for power relations. As noted, advocates of privatization tend to stress the economic advantages of liberalization. They tend not to focus very much on the ensuing politics. There is evidence that the privatization of governance tends to benefit particular interests rather than the general public. Many traditional privatizations were carried out on favorable terms for buyers or managers, who sometimes went from poorly paid government servants to very well paid executive officers, often with significant stakes in the new profit-making enterprise.

Hence, as privatization has advanced towards the core competences of the state, rather than creating free markets, it makes and reproduces patterns of diffused and complex chains of authority and semi-invisible forms of interchange and mutual advantage between economic and political elites. The privatization of core state functions makes it hard for specialists—let alone members of the public—to keep track of who is responsible for what, as chains of authority and obligation become ever longer and ever more tangled with each other. Finally, international private regulatory processes are usually heavily skewed in favor of specialist actors and against members of the general public.

The account of privatization that I present is at heart a story of changing power relations, building on both skeptical rationalist[4] and historical institutionalist[5] accounts. It is thus at odds with, e.g., some public choice accounts[6] that see privatization as, essentially, a set of managerial innovations and improvements aimed at remedying deficiencies in the state-managed economy, and hence tend to present a narrative of privatization as a series of ever-continuing improvements brought through by benignly intentioned bureaucrats and policymakers. As per Knight's arguments,[7] self-interested actors are only likely to seek Pareto-improving institutional changes under relatively unusual circumstances. This skepticism may be overstated (actors are not always simply self-seeking), but provides a clearer and more consistent account than alternatives. It does, however, underestimate the role of ideas, which also plausibly played an important role in the relevant transformations.

## II. ECONOMIC PRIVATIZATION

The current wave of economic privatization began in the late 1970s and early 1980s. The word itself was popularized in Margaret Thatcher's Britain, and used to refer to processes that had previously been dubbed "denationalization." However, there is disagreement about *where* the turn towards privatization came from.

Some scholarship highlights the collapse of Keynesian patterns of demand management, and points towards partisanship and government composition as key factors.[8] For example, Carles Boix argues that the wretched economic conditions of the 1970s led different governments to behave in different ways.[9] All governments faced difficult economic conditions and the need to generate new economic revenues without raising taxes. Right wing governments, which had previously gingerly embraced Keynesianism, abandoned it in favor of economic reform programs that were aimed at promoting the market and raising money through sales of state companies, while left wingers continued to favor the state.

Others point to public opinion (and the personal experiences of individuals),[10] noting that public service employees are less likely to favor privatization than other citizens. Others still highlight the power of ideas,[11] showing how variation in ideas held by governing elites, as well as variation in the ability of the state to shape policy debate, led to sharp variation in outcomes. Finally, a EU-centric literature examines privatization as one manifestation of "Europeanization"—the replacement of national markets with protections for incumbents by a more liberalized "Single Market" under pressure from the European Commission and the European Court of Justice.[12] The International Monetary Fund and other international actors similarly pressed for privatization in countries under their tutelage.[13]

Over time, privatization has escaped its conditions of origin. Schneider, Fink, and Tenbucken find that there was a statistical relationship between right wing rule and privatization in the 1980s, but that the relationship disappeared in the 1990s, when, in their pithy description, "the motto became 'Everyone privatizes.'"[14] While right-wing parties were more enthusiastic to privatize than parties on the left,[15] privatization had become part of the accepted policy repertoire, shaping both public opinion and the scope of politically acceptable ideas, while also helping international bodies such as the European Commission and International Monetary Fund to press for further privatization in states under their sway.

Privatization escaped via diffusion processes. Once it had become sufficiently established in a number of core states, it spread to other states that wanted to imitate and emulate them.[16] Diffusion of privatization policies was more likely to occur between countries that were geographically close to each other.[17] It also snowballed over time—as more countries adopted privatization policies in areas such as telecommunications, the perceived legitimacy of the policy (and hence the likelihood that other countries would adopt it) increased too.[18]

The diffusion of privatization policy has had sweeping—and varied—consequences. It has not led states to converge in any simple and straightforward way on a single model of economic policymaking. Instead, it has been taken up in different ways by different national states.[19] States were quicker to take up privatization in some sectors than in others, often looking to pick low-hanging fruit in the privatization of telecommunications, before moving to more difficult and less lucrative targets such as electricity.[20] While ideas have spread, they have been taken up in different ways in different national contexts. Marion Fourcade and Sarah Babb find that perceived economic failures and sharp social conflicts led dissident coalitions in the UK and Chile to take up liberalization and privatization policies in a struggle to take over control of the state.[21] In contrast, liberalization and privatization had a far less dramatic immediate import in countries such as Mexico and France, where they were integrated into more long-lasting state projects of modernization.

This has led to variegated outcomes across (at least) three dimensions. First, there is variation across sectors. Some sectors have been much more likely to be privatized than others. Second, there is variation across countries. Some countries have gone further in privatizing certain sectors than others. Finally, there is variation in the form of privatization. Very often, economists think of privatization as a simple process in which economic activities that were under the direct control of the government are given over to profit-maximizing actors who vigorously compete with each other in a minimally regulated market. This is rarely (and perhaps almost never) the case. Privatization typically comes with strings attached, and the kinds of string vary across countries. Privatization has not meant that the state has become uninvolved in the economy (a point to which I return below), or that the retreat of the state has led to corresponding advances for free markets. Rather, the involvement of the state now takes different forms.

## III. Privatization and Regulation

Privatization has not led to a retreat of the state so much as its transformation. First, advanced industrialized states typically no longer own large swathes of the economy. Instead, they have adopted the US model—they seek to control outcomes through regulation rather than ownership. This goes far beyond privatized industries; states now regularly resort to regulation across a wide variety of topics and issue areas, delegating regulation to specialized agencies, or even self-regulatory bodies. Second, states have transformed themselves internally too. States have not only privatized state-owned firms, but have "privatized" essential aspects of their own internal operation. Some parts of the functions of states, which were traditionally managed with internal resources, are now subcontracted out to for-profit entities. Others are handled within the state, but through mechanisms that seek to simulate some of the aspects of free markets (e.g., through putting different units of the state in direct competition with each other).

Very often, people see privatization and deregulation as two sides of the same coin. However, there is a strong scholarly consensus that this generalization is wrong. As privatization has proceeded, states have often tended to increase rather than decrease their reliance on regulation. In Christopher Hood and Colin Scott's description, "[the] privatization of utilities has meant government has shifted from owner regulator to . . . regulator alone for many key industries."[22] Giandomenico Majone documents how privatization meant both that the government often had to regulate the prices of the newly profit-oriented firms and to prevent some of these firms from abusing their dominant position to deter competitors.[23] Steven Vogel finds that privatization has been associated with re-regulation rather than deregulation.[24] Levi-Faur claims that "a new division of labor between state and society (e.g., privatization) is accompanied by an increase in delegation, proliferation of new technologies of regulation, formalization of interinstitutional and intrainstitutional relations, and the proliferation of mechanisms of self-regulation in the shadow of the state."[25]

European states now rely far more on regulation than in the past.[26] In the UK, even while the numbers of traditional civil servants fell sharply, the numbers of employees working for regulators rose quite dramatically. As Hood and Scott note, the state used to be able to exercise authority by means of direct ownership.[27] Now, it uses a different toolkit. Regulators typically have the authority to make and interpret rules within a broader legislative mandate, and to interpret these rules in ways that bind private actors. In the US, for example, law courts are usually quite deferential to regulators' interpretation of their own rules, under the *Chevron* standard. Some regulators—such as the Securities and Exchange Commission—even have their own internal administrative judges, who both work for the regulator and issue binding rulings on how the regulator's rules should be understood and enforced. Sometimes, state regulators may work at one remove, effectively outsourcing much of the implementation of regulations to self-regulatory bodies, and acting only as a final backstop.

However, there are important differences in the level of regulation across economic sectors. Braithwaite and Drahos find that "regulation of the environment, safety and financial security have

ratcheted up more than they have been driven down by globalization,"[28] and that ratcheting up is in general more common than a
regulatory race to the bottom, but that there has been a ratcheting down of economic regulation of issues such as bank capital
adequacy.

Why has privatization been so often associated with an increase
rather than a decrease in regulation? There are two main theories.
One sees regulation or re-regulation as a reassertion of the public
interest.[29] Here, regulations are designed by states to restrain private actors in ways that conduct towards the general interest, perhaps in response to public pressure. As important economic activities have moved from the public to the private sector, the public
sector has needed to keep new private interests in check and, ideally, harness them for public benefit. Regulation provides one way
to achieve this. A second approach sees regulation as an assertion
of state interest, without necessarily assuming that it is normatively
attractive. Vogel sees both privatization and re-regulation as state-
led processes, and examines how different states with different
interests end up with very different combinations of regulation
and private sector activity.[30] Braithwaite and Drahos and Mattli and
Woods show how power relations (and in particular the role of the
US, as most powerful state in the international system) shape regulation at the global level.[31]

As an extensive literature discusses, the intimate relationship
between the regulators and regulated is often likely to lead to
regulatory capture, in which the regulator identifies the interests
of the regulated sector (or its biggest firms) with its own institutional interest, and seeks to protect these interests.[32] Public choice
accounts[33] tend to claim that independent firms identify how they
can harness the regulatory power of government to their benefit,
to control entry to their market and hence limit competition. The
problem, according to this analysis, is that government has the
power to coerce and that some businesses are politically influential enough to bend government to their will.

In actuality, as economic sociologists have observed, the relationship between the state and domestic markets is actually rather
more intimate than Stigler suggests, especially in sectors that have
been privatized.[34] It is not so much that the state is interfering with
markets that otherwise would be naturally inclined to gravitate

towards competitive relations, as that state rules originally constituted the market and continue to constitute it and remake it,
creating an intimate—but two-way—relationship between the state
and market actors.

This highlights aspects of privatization that are obscured
by standard economic theory. The change from control-via-
ownership to control-via-regulation is not a retreat of the state and
encroachment of the market, but a reshaping of the relationship
between them so that they blur together in different ways, creating new hybrid political relations that are neither traditional state
hierarchy, nor state ownership of partially independent firms, nor
yet market competition.

Indeed, privatization has consequences too for the inner workings of the state. Hood and Scott document how the external
regulation of firms has gone in lockstep with increased internal
reliance on internal contracts (rather than bureaucratic hierarchy) within the British state, rightly predicting in the 1990s that
"bureaucratic regulation [the ways in which some parts of the state
oversee and regulate the operation of others] is likely to become
more similar to business regulation in style and operation."[35] Civil
service units are now more like service providers than traditionally
secure and specialized bureaucratic institutions. These changes
mean that government becomes a kind of ersatz market in which
units compete (or, sometimes, pretend to compete) with each
other and with external service providers for contracts. The government both tries to become more like a market in how its own
units deal with each other, and to put out as many of its activities as
it can to external providers.

As Colin Crouch has documented in a pair of important books
building on the experience of the United Kingdom, states have
not only sold off their stakes in key economic sectors, but have
begun increasingly to rely on market-like arrangements for their
own core functions.[36] On the one hand, they directly integrate subcontracting relations with private entities within the core functions
of the state. On the other, state or state-funded entities seek to
compete with each other internally in designed schemes that ape
the logic of markets with greater or lesser verisimilitude.

Most obviously, states now subcontract out many aspects of
their core functioning to private subcontractors. In a series of

publications, Deborah Avant and her colleagues have documented how key aspects of the US military have been privatized,
in a process that accelerated dramatically during the Iraq War.[37]
Many traditional security functions are now performed by private subcontractors. The same is true of intelligence, where, e.g.,
Edward Snowden concluded that he would be more easily able
to get access to government secrets as an employee of the private
firm Booz Allen Hamilton than as an employee of the NSA. This
reflects both a more general trend of putting out key intelligence
technical and research tasks to private enterprise, and the specific
dynamics of the cybersecurity sector, where the US state has been
particularly dependent on specialized help.

The United Kingdom too has seen a sharp increase in privatization of government services, both under Labour and Conser-
vative administrations. While the National Health Service remains
heavily regulated, the UK government has tried to encourage the
development of national chains of hospitals to achieve efficiencies,
with mixed results. It has also sought to move schools from the
state sector into the non-profit sector, allowing a variety of experi-
mental governance arrangements, which again have led to significant controversy.[38] None of these subcontracting arrangements
are properly competitive, either because they require compliance
with complex mandates (which makes it hard for many potential
providers of the service to compete for them), or because they
require specific and unusual technical knowledge, or knowledge
of how government processes work, or because they are mediated
through close personal or political connections with key decision-
makers. Hence, they are more pseudo-market than market.

Other pseudo-markets can be seen in those aspects of government that have not been put out to sale. Units in the UK government compete with each other as though they were independent
entities in a market, rather than bureaucratic entities linked in a
common hierarchy.[39] Common metrics such as the Research Assessment Framework for higher education in the UK[40] and the testing
provisions associated with the No Child Left Behind Act in the US[41]
are intended to provide many of the benefits of markets through
obliging units to compete for resources in a transparent framework.

The evidence on the overall success of these efforts to build
pseudo-markets within the state is murky enough that both their

enthusiasts and detractors can claim that the facts support them. What *is* clear is that, like all schemes that seek to substitute metric-based incentives for actual market efficiencies,[42] they can be, and are, gamed by sufficiently ingenious actors, who may look to maximize benefits in perverse ways. For example, universities looking to do well in the Research Assessment Exercise can pay foreign academics to affiliate themselves in more or less nominal ways, so that their work is "counted" as part of the university's research output. Schools looking to do well under No Child Left Behind have incentives to "teach to the test" (even when this does not help the child learn) or even to encourage systematic cheating.

The efficiency benefits of putting government services out to for-profit contractors are difficult to measure. Many of the goods provided by the state are difficult to price. State services are furthermore typically bound up with complex bureaucratic practices that are difficult for outsiders to understand, let alone adapt their own practices to. Either state authorities seek to impose their own practices on external market providers, not creating markets so much as pseudo-markets with little real competition, or they embrace the logic of markets with possible damage to their own legitimacy.

Crouch discusses the negative consequences of the first path— pseudo-markets for external contracting—arguing that they have created new kinds of firms, which specialize not in providing any particular service, but rather in leveraging their knowledge of how government works and their privileged relations with government employees. Such firms interface with government across a wide set of contracting activities. These firms need very high levels of resources, expertise, and contacts to operate, limiting the number of market players and hence limiting the benefits of competitive bidding.

Katzenstein and Waller document some of the dangers associated with the other path. US states increasingly contract out major aspects of running prisons and probation services to the private sector.[43] Often, this is done on the basis of contracts which effectively turn private sector businesses into tax farmers, providing them with a monopoly, e.g., on phone calls, financial transfers, commissary sales, or similar services that prisoners and their families need, in return for a kickback. The state of Florida, for example, mandates that financial transfers to prisoners be subcontracted to "the responsive, responsible bidder submitting the highest percentage commission" [to the state].[44] In such contracting arrangements, government and the private sector join forces to extract the highest rates possible from what is, quite literally, a captive market, combining the coercive power of the state (without any obvious mechanisms of legitimacy) with the extractive power of business monopoly.

Notably, this can create a self-reinforcing cycle of the kind identified by Paul Pierson for interest groups.[45] The state generates a policy, which in turn creates an interest among those actors whom the policy benefits. These actors then have an incentive to organize themselves, so as to protect the interest that they have, and to demand an expansion of the policy, with more benefits. The bureaucrats or other officials charged with administering this policy benefit from the support of an outside interest group in their own struggles over resources. Hence, a tacit alliance forms between interest group and officials, and moreover a feedback loop, in which the growth of a policy area benefits those (whether outside interest groups or officials) who are involved in it, and have greater resources to press for still more growth.

Just such a mechanism appears to have underpinned the privatization of much of the US incarceration system. Initially, privatization was driven by the belief that private industry could incarcerate prisoners more cheaply and efficiently than the state. Rapid privatization led to a rapidly growing private correctional industry, with firms like the Corrections Corporation of America (CCA), which is currently the largest firm in the sector in the US, running sixty-one facilities with approximately 90,000 beds and $1.7 billion in revenue in 2011.[46] This firm enjoyed strong political connections—a co-founder is former chairman of the Tennessee State Republican Party and many senior officials held stock in the company.[47] It was also well connected to the public prison system. A senior official at the company was former head of the American Correctional Association and Commissioner of Corrections departments in Virginia and Arkansas.[48] As the industry has burgeoned, large firms like CCA and their senior management have donated large amounts of money to the Republican Party and to individual legislators, while lobbying for more privatization of prisons. More recently, these corporations have pressed quietly for an enforcement-heavy approach to immigration reform, which provides much of their profits (nearly half of undocumented immigrants in custody are held in privately owned facilities).[49] Hence, the policy of prison privatization has generated new interest groups, which are using their resources to press for privatization, which is likely to benefit them given their political clout and contacts.

Privatization is not then generating free market competition so much as it is changing the nature of the state. The state often (and likely typically) needs to remain involved in managing these economic activities, either through regulation or through contract. The creation of a zone of specialized intersection between the public and private sector plausibly corrodes both. Profit-making entities are typically able to pay much better than the government. This, at a minimum, results in a continual drainage of expertise from the public into the private sector. At its worst, it encourages corrupt relations between the two, ranging from implicit cozy arrangements, in which government officials overseeing contracts know that complaisant behavior will likely eventually be rewarded with a well-paid private sector job, to more direct forms of exchange and peculation. For many managers, the status of government employee and government contractor are different phases in the same life cycle.

Furthermore, visibility and accountability are occluded by a dense cobweb of relationships. It is difficult for anyone who is not directly involved to be certain what is going on in complex webs of contractual arrangements between the government and private sector. It is even more difficult to establish who should take the blame when things go wrong. When a contractor fails to deliver the promised benefits, it is often not clear whether it, or the government which employed it, should be held accountable.

Finally, as the state hives off core competences, it begins to lose the capacity to make independent judgments about how to regulate, or even which goals to pursue, again making it more dependent on intimate and long-term relationships with private interests, whether they be regulated firms, telling the state how it should craft its regulatory policies to achieve appropriate goals; sub-contractors, telling the state how it should manage its relations; or businesses, lobbying under-resourced legislators. Over the last few decades, the analytic capacity of the US state has withered away, as, for example, Congress has lost the Office of Technology Assessment, and seen the starvation of legislative staff and institutions such as the Congressional Research Service that are intended to provide it with independent capacity to analyze policies. This has made it ever more dependent on lobbyists to provide information and often even to draft bills. The situation is replicated in statehouse legislatures, which often rely on business-dominated organizations such as ALEC, the American Legislative Exchange Council, for model legislation.

All this leads to a new kind of semi-privatized state, most eloquently described by Crouch, who sees the state as having been transformed from an independent and authoritative actor in society to a nexus in a web of contracting and regulatory relationships. He argues that the capacity of the state to recognize and act upon a clear sense of the public interest has radically diminished:

> As government contracts out an increasing range of its activities, its employees really do lose competence in the areas being covered by the contractors, areas within which public servants have until now had unrivaled expertise. As they become mere brokers between public principals and private agents, so professional and technical knowledge pass to the latter . . . In the process of trying to make themselves as similar as possible to private firms, public authorities also have to divest themselves of an intrinsic aspect of their role: the fact that they are authorities. It should be noted that this loss does not extend to the political center of national government itself. In fact, far from achieving the disappearance of state power dreamed of by libertarians, the privatizing state concentrates political power into . . . a tight central nucleus, which deals predominantly with its peer elites in private business.[50]

Crouch's remarks are aimed at the UK (and to a lesser extent the mainland European and US) experience, and draw a strong general conclusion that some may contest. Even so, they describe a very important tendency in the privatization of the state. His arguments are bolstered by those of Peter Mair, who finds that traditional democratic relations, in which parties play a key mediating role between public and elites, are being replaced by intense intra-elite relationships of resource exchange.[51]

## IV. Privatization of Rule-Making on the World Stage

Privatization is remaking the state in different ways in different countries. This has important consequences for global politics too. Privatization and regulation are not creating a more homogenous world, but one in which different styles of regulating are more likely to lead to disputes than before. Clashes between different regulators from different countries provide new opportunities for private actors to influence or implement policy, and even to reach down again into domestic politics.

If states are more prone to governance-by-regulation than in the past, they also face new difficulties regulating in a complex international system.[52] The more willing states are to regulate, the greater the risk of rule clash between different regulatory jurisdictions, each with their own regulators and rules. If privatization and regulation are two legs of the stool, globalization is the third. National markets are no longer separate from each other, to the extent that they ever were. They interpenetrate each other. We have moved from a world where markets for many commodities (especially network commodities) were national, and were governed by state-owned entities, to one in which markets are not limited by national borders, and are governed by different regulators, who often disagree with each other. In the description of Abraham Newman and Elliot Posner, there is very often a "mismatch" between the jurisdiction of regulators and the extent of the market.[53] The state has been transformed from a hierarchical actor at the "commanding heights" of the economy to a regulator of market actors, who increasingly work on a regional or global, rather than a national, scale.

This has important implications for the privatization of governance. Most obviously, it often provides firms with increased bargaining opportunity vis-à-vis the state. Many businesses are relatively mobile, and hence capable of relocating their assets from one jurisdiction to another. This provides them with "structural power" vis-à-vis state regulators, which have to pay attention to their interests, lest they decide to relocate.[54] Some businesses can often pick and choose across different regulatory regimes. The structural power of business may vary by sector or country, so that some firms, in some states, are more influential than others.[55] Yet in many situations, we may expect that businesses will be able to use their bargaining power to re-tilt their relationship with regulators in their favor, so that they favor firms more and the other actors to whom governments are responsible less.

It also sometimes allows businesses to replace formal state regulation with what might be described as a tacit privatization of rules. For example, for a significant period of time, US rules banning online gambling and the rules of other states that sought to regulate gambling were effectively undermined by the activities of a small group of gambling businesses, which set up offshore on the island of Antigua, a country which imposed no very strenuous limits on these businesses' activities. It is difficult to retain the force of national regulations when businesses can systematically evade them. Under such circumstances, the relevant rules will be those set by the businesses themselves to try to ensure customer confidence (e.g., by persuading potential customers that the gambling companies will not create a secret house advantage, and will pay up on winnings).

States may, of course, respond to this by seeking to extend their jurisdictional reach so as to better grasp slippery firms that are seeking to evade it (or that might be in a better bargaining position if they were credibly able to threaten to evade it).[56] Regulators are increasingly willing to work extraterritorially, either by cooperating with other regulators in other states, or by using other businesses as proxies, or by coercing other regulators to change local standards, or by simply barring firms from relocating sensitive activities overseas. For example, the US managed to cripple the Antiguan gambling industry by pressing the financial industry into service as its enforcers, obliging them to block payments that appeared to be directed to or from offshore gambling concerns.[57] The European Union (EU) has sought to prevent private actors from escaping EU privacy rules by barring them from exporting the personal data of Europeans overseas, unless the receiving country has an "adequate" privacy system.[58] This has strengthened the EU against demands from large firms that it weaken their privacy rules, while allowing EU regulators to shape the privacy laws of other countries to better reflect EU standards.

Yet efforts by regulators to apply their rules extraterritorially are likely to result in renewed clashes with the regulators of other states, which may have different rules or no rules. This provides a new set of opportunities for well-situated private actors to propose or influence solutions to regulatory disputes, very often in ways that involve a greater privatization of governance.

For example, when the EU sought to get the US to change its rules on privacy, the US balked, first proposing that the EU should accept US self-regulatory schemes as providing adequate privacy protection, and then, in consultation with major US firms, coming up with an arrangement in which self-regulation would be embedded in a system with minimal government oversight.[59] Large businesses in the pharmaceutical, software, and entertainment industries created an ad-hoc Intellectual Property Committee that succeeded in setting the agenda for divisive inter-state negotiations over WTO (World Trade Organization) intellectual property rules where the US had previously engaged in extraterritorial pressure against countries that it believed had insufficient intellectual property protections,[60] providing businesses with new abilities to take action against governments that were perceived as recalcitrant. Private creditors played a key role in shaping contentious cross-national discussions over sovereign debt, opposing proposals for a far-reaching mechanism for restructuring sovereign debt, and acting as "private entrepreneurs" to promote their own model international code of conduct, backed by a body of senior financial sector executives and government officials, in which the former have majority representation on the board.[61]

Such opportunities have arguably transformed the relationship between private and state-led governance in the international arena. Arguably, private governance arrangements no longer fall under "the shadow of the state," or consist primarily of self-regulatory arrangements intended to forestall more far-reaching government rules.[62] As different regulatory approaches have come into conflict with each other, generating the need for solutions, the private actors who dominate various cross-national self-regulatory arrangements have been able to take advantage of new opportunities. Some specific examples illustrate a much more general trend.

First, alliances of cross-national actors have often been able to *influence* proposed solutions to regulatory clash by, for example, proposing standards that benefit themselves, perhaps at the cost of others. In particular, private sector entities that are easily able to cooperate across the borders of the relevant jurisdictions are likely to be better capable of affecting standards, since they can mobilize across both or many jurisdictions, offering cross-jurisdictional support for the solutions that they favor. In general, this has tended to favor businesses vis-à-vis other social actors that are less easily able to work across borders, and has favored some businesses (those involved in the relevant cross-national networks) over others.[63] For example, EU and US clashes over accounting standards led both to accord a crucial role to standards created by the International Accounting Standards Board, a private organization set up by a variety of cross-national accounting and financial firms to influence European debates.[64] Businesses have, however, found their cross-national influence substantially limited in situations of significant public controversy.[65]

Second, they have sometimes been able to *implement* solutions that have the formal or informal blessing of the states in question, being delegated by states individually or collectively to solve a problem that states lack the resources or expertise to solve themselves. For example, Buthe and Mattli show how producer groups have come together in international standard-setting bodies to play a key role in shaping national rules, e.g., about product standards. Organizations such as the International Organization for Standardization (ISO) and the International Electrotechnical Commission (IEC) specifically exclude states and governments from membership.[66] They provide specifications for products that are implemented in the national regulations of the WTO. The WTO agreement requires all member states to "use international standards as the technical basis of domestic laws and regulations *unless* international standards are 'inefficient or inappropriate' for achieving the specified public policy objective."[67] Non-conforming standards can be treated as violations of international trade law.

Third, they have sometimes *substituted* for more traditional means of regulation, regulating some area that states have been either unwilling or incapable of regulating themselves. For example, there are several international self-regulatory bodies that certify forest management. States were themselves incapable of agreeing to sign a convention on forestry at the Earth Summit in 1993,[68] leading the World Wildlife Fund and other organizations with a strong cross-national presence to set up the Forestry Stewardship Council in order to create and certify standards for timber producers. This council is purely voluntary and depends on consumer willingness to accept its certification as a sign of better production practices. However, it has been incapable of preventing industry led groups from creating their own competing standards, generating confusion among consumers who are unlikely to understand the differences between groups.

These efforts are primarily international in scope, although they may have domestic consequences. More recently, however, private actors have begun to use cross-national or international arrangements in order to reshape domestic regulation. Most simply, actors with privileged access can use the transposition of international agreements into domestic law either to strengthen or weaken rules. Sell documents how businesses used the transposition of an international treaty on intellectual property into US law to impose rules that they might have had difficulty introducing otherwise.[69] Here, businesses were able both to organize internationally as private interests to shape international rules, and then use these rules to reshape domestic institutions. Similarly, firms from both the US and European financial industries have a privileged voice in negotiations between the US and EU over trade and standards. US firms would like to weaken domestic financial regulations by introducing common and watered down rules.[70]

Such efforts resemble traditional lobbying, albeit through the back door provided by the international system. However, international processes sometimes give businesses more direct means of private action. For example, international businesses have begun to use the international investment regime to try to push back domestic regulations that are not in their interest. Over the last half-century, there has been an extraordinary proliferation of Bilateral Investment Treaties (BITs) worldwide.[71] These treaties allow investors from one signatory state to take state authorities in the other to international arbitration for measures or policies that affect their investments. These treaties both reinforce the regime of privatization and extend it.

They reinforce the regime by making it highly expensive for states to reverse course on privatization by renationalizing businesses that have been sold in full or in part to investors from countries with relevant treaties. BITs are designed precisely to make state expropriation expensive, and thus to discourage it. Only countries such as Venezuela, Bolivia, and Ecuador that are strongly disaffected from the existing international economic system have sought systematically to renationalize aspects of energy or infrastructure. Unsurprisingly, such countries have found themselves being sued in arbitral tribunals.

Second, the regime of privatization is being extended, as relevant "investments" under BITs are redefined in increasingly broad ways.[72] For example, an energy company is currently suing India for making a retrospective tax assessment, which it claims substantially hurt its share price, thus causing it substantial economic damage. Notoriously, the US tobacco giant Philip Morris sued Uruguay, Norway, and Australia for introducing legislation requiring that cigarettes be sold in plain packages or packages graphically depicting the consequences of smoking, claiming that this represented a regulatory expropriation of Philip Morris's intellectual property. Although these suits failed, the prominent New York law firm Skadden, noting the "novel" ways in which BIT clauses are being reinterpreted, has effectively invited potential clients to consider suing, e.g., European governments that have forcibly bailed out financial entities during the global economic crisis. As Haley Edwards notes,

> In July 2014, a group of 120 professors of law and legal theory wrote a letter to the U.S. Trade Representative's office complaining that phrases were often so vague that tribunals could feasibly interpret all kinds of legitimate regulatory actions as a treaty violation demanding compensation.[73]

Julia Gray further argues that BITs allow multinationals to forum shop across states, so as to find the treaty with the clauses most likely to support an action; for example, the Philip Morris case against Australia was filed by Philip Morris's Hong Kong subsidiary to take advantage of an especially lax treaty.[74] She finds evidence that businesses have actually set up paper subsidiaries in countries such as the Netherlands so as to be able to sue particular jurisdictions.

Thus, BITs complete the circuit from the national to the international and back to the national, providing an internationally based means of private action that can then be used to reshape the state's domestic regulatory capacity. Their consequences off the equilibrium path are likely more important than their direct deployment. Investment professionals believe that a previous threat of action under NAFTA's investor dispute resolution mechanism restrained Canada from introducing anti-smoking legislation, while the action against Uruguay is widely perceived as a shot across the bows of other states that might be contemplating similar action. States that are considering regulations are likely to be nervous if they fear these regulations might see them hauled before arbitral tribunals.[75] In part as a result of privatization, states have turned towards regulation, but they are finding that their capacity to regulate is being significantly constrained.

## V. The Three Aspects of Privatization

In this essay, I have tried to show how the wave of privatizations that began in the late 1970s or early 1980s has had profound political consequences. Specifically, it has reshaped the state, so that it increasingly relates to the economy as a regulator, and to increasingly use market-like mechanisms in its own workings. The move towards regulation at the domestic level had international consequences, as globalization created a mismatch between cross-national markets and national regulatory systems. This helped private actors to evade regulatory power, leading some jurisdictions to seek to extend their grasp extraterritorially. This in turn led to greater clashes between regulators over whose rules, if any, should prevail, providing new opportunities to private actors that had organized cross-nationally to propose, influence, or shape solutions to regulatory clash. Most recently, we have seen private actors use international agreements to reach back within the state, using ISDS provisions to undermine state regulations that are not in their economic self-interest.

The purpose of this essay is to disentangle a complex skein of causation between markets, states, international regulatory processes, and back again, rather than to provide a complete account of how privatization works nationally and on the global level. The latter would be an Augean labor. Thus, the account presented here is necessarily simplified. Specifically, it emphasizes the ways in which these different levels of activity reinforce each other rather than (as they sometimes do) rub against each other. It presents the impression of a seamless totality, rather than the complex, ambiguous, and ever-shifting network of relationships that is present in actuality. One could emphasize different causal chains between the national and global, and by so doing arrive at quite different stories.

Nonetheless, even partial accounts like this one are potentially valuable. Political science has great difficulty in thinking clearly about the political relationship between national and global processes of regulation and privatization. The same is true of cognate disciplines such as economics (to the extent that it concerns itself with politics) and economic sociology. The scholarly literature tends to focus either on purely national patterns, or on international patterns of regulation, or, to the extent that it is interested in the relationship between the two, to focus on processes such as diffusion, that tend to discount or pass over the political relations through which one set of ideas diffuses, while another withers on the vine. Equally, those who are practically concerned with regulation and privatization tend to neglect such relationships, exactly because they are complicated, and involve interactions that usually extend far past the issues and relations that any individual or organization can easily concern themselves with.

Mapping out these relationships is a crucially important task for the social sciences, together with legal scholarship (which has begun to think more explicitly about these relationships but could surely do more) and political theory and philosophy (which has, e.g., important accounts of responsibility at both the global and national levels, but relatively little about the interaction between them). This essay should be read as one—partial and imperfect— effort to start mapping out one key chain of causation as a step towards this broader agenda.

Notes

1 Henry Farrell and Abraham L. Newman, "Domestic Institutions Beyond the Nation-State: Charting the New Interdependence Approach," *World Politics* 66, no. 2 (2014): 331–63.

2 Tim Büthe and Walter Mattli, *The New Global Rulers: The Privatization of Regulation in the World Economy* (Princeton, NJ: Princeton University Press, 2011).

3 Paul Pierson, "When Effect Becomes Cause: Policy Feedback and Political Change," *World Politics* 45, no. 4 (1993): 595–628.

4 Jack Knight, *Institutions and Social Conflict* (New York: Cambridge University Press, 1992).

5 Jacob Hacker and Paul Pierson, *American Amnesia: How the War on Government Led Us to Forget What Made America Rich* (New York: Simon and Schuster, 2016); Peter Hall and Kathleen Thelen, "Institutional Change in Varieties of Capitalism," *Socio-Economic Review* 7 no. 1 (2009): 7–34.

6 E.g., Joseph Heath, "Three Normative Models of the Welfare State," *Public Reason* 3 (2012): 13–44.

7 Knight, *Institutions and Social Conflict.*

8 Carles Boix, "Privatizing the Public Business Sector in the Eighties: Economic Performance, Partisan Responses and Divided Governments," *British Journal of Political Science* 27, no. 4 (1997): 473–96; Bernardo Bortolotti, Marcella Fantini, and Domenico Siniscalco, "Privatisation Around the World: Evidence From Panel Data," *Journal of Public Economics* 88, no. 1 (2004): 305–32; Reimut Zohlnhöfer, Herbert Obinger, and Frieder Wolf, "Partisan Politics, Globalization, and the Determinants of Privatization Processes in Advanced Democracies (1990–2000)," *Governance* 21, no. 1 (2008): 95–121.

9 Boix, "Privatizing the Public Business Sector in the Eighties."

10 R. Paul Battaglio and Jerome S. Legge, "Self-Interest, Ideological/Symbolic Politics, and Citizen Characteristics: A Cross-National Analysis of Support for Privatization," *Public Administration Review* 69, no. 4 (2009): 697–709.

11 Ian Bartle, "When Institutions No Longer Matter: Reform of Telecommunications and Electricity in Germany, France and Britain," *Journal of Public Policy* 22, no. 1 (2002): 1–27; Marion Fourcade-Gourinchas and Sarah L. Babb, "The Rebirth of the Liberal Creed: Paths to Neoliberalism in Four Countries," *American Journal of Sociology* 108, no. 3 (2002): 533–79; Bruce Kogut and J. Muir Macpherson, "The Decision to Privatize: Economists and the Construction of Ideas and Policies," *Global Diffusion of Markets and Democracy* (2008): 104–40.

12 Christoph Knill and Dirk Lehmkuhl, "How Europe Matters: Different Mechanisms of Europeanization," *European Integration Online Papers (EIoP)* 3, no. 7 (1999); Rainer Eising and Nicolas Jabko, "Moving Targets, National Interests, and Electricity Liberalization in the European Union," *Comparative Political Studies* 34, no. 7 (2001): 742–67; Volker Schneider and Frank M. Hage, "Europeanization and the Retreat of the State," *Journal of European Public Policy* 15, no. 1 (2008): 1–19.

13 Sarah Babb and Ariel Buira, "Mission Creep, Mission Push and Discretion: The Case of IMF Conditionality," ed. Ariel Buira, *The IMF and the World Bank at Sixty* (London: Anthem Press, 2005): 59–84; Witold J. Henisz, Bennet A. Zelner, and Mauro F. Guillen, "The Worldwide Diffusion of Market-Oriented Infrastructure Reform, 1977–1999," *American Sociological Review* 70, no. 6 (2005): 871–97.

14 Volker Schneider, Simon Fink, and Marc Tenbucken, "Buying Out the State: A Comparative Perspective on the Privatization of Infrastructures," *Comparative Political Studies* 38, no. 6 (2005): 720.

15 Zohlnhöfer, Obinger, and Wolf, "Partisan Politics."

16 Henisz, Zelner, and Guillen, "Worldwide Diffusion."

17 Carina Schmitt, "What Drives the Diffusion of Privatization Policy? Evidence From the Telecommunications Sector," *Journal of Public Policy* 31, no. 1 (2011): 95–117.

18 Simon Fink, "A Contagious Concept: Explaining the Spread of Privatization in the Telecommunications Sector," *Governance* 24, no. 1 (2011): 111–39.

19 Steven Kent Vogel, *Freer Markets, More Rules: Regulatory Reform in Advanced Industrial Countries* (Ithaca, NY: Cornell University Press, 1996).

20 David Levi-Faur, "The Politics of Liberalisation: Privatisation and Regulation-for-Competition in Europe's and Latin America's Telecoms and Electricity Industries," *European Journal of Political Research* 42, no. 5 (2003): 705–40.

21 Fourcade-Gourinchas and Babb, "The Rebirth of the Liberal Creed."

22 Christopher Hood and Colin Scott, *Regulating Government in a Managerial Age: Towards a Cross-National Perspective* (London: Centre for Analysis of Risk and Regulation, London School of Economics and Political Science, 2000): 2.

23 Giandomenico Majone, "The Rise of the Regulatory State in Europe," *West European Politics* 17, no. 3 (1994): 77–101.

24 Vogel, *Freer Markets, More Rules.*

25 David Levi-Faur, "The Global Diffusion of Regulatory Capitalism," *Annals of the American Academy of Political and Social Science* 498, no. 1 (2005): 12–32, at 12.

26 Majone, "The Rise of the Regulatory State in Europe"; Giandomenico Majone, "From the Positive to the Regulatory State: Causes and Consequences of Changes in the Mode of Governance," *Journal of Public Policy* 17, no. 2 (1997): 139–67.

27 Hood and Scott, *Regulating Government.*

28 John Braithwaite and Peter Drahos, *Global Business Regulation* (Cambridge: Cambridge University Press, 2000): 5.

29 David Levi-Faur, "Regulatory Capitalism and the Reassertion of the Public Interest," *Policy and Society* 27, no. 3 (2009): 181–91.

30 Vogel, *Freer Markets, More Rules.*

31 Braithwaite and Drahos, *Global Business Regulation*; Walter Mattli and Ngaire Woods, eds., *The Politics of Global Regulation* (Princeton, NJ: Princeton University Press, 2009).

32 Jean-Jacques Laffont and Jean Tirole, "The Politics of Government Decision-Making: A Theory of Regulatory Capture," *Quarterly Journal of Economics* (1991): 1089–127; for an overview, see Ernesto Dal Bó, "Regulatory Capture: A Review," *Oxford Review of Economic Policy* 22, no. 2 (2006): 203–25.

33 E.g., George J. Stigler, "The Theory of Economic Regulation," *Bell Journal of Economics and Management Science* 2, no. 1 (1971): 3–21.

34 Neil Fligstein and Doug McAdam, *A Theory of Fields* (New York: Oxford University Press, 2012).

35 Christopher Hood and Colin Scott, "Bureaucratic Regulation and New Public Management in the United Kingdom: Mirror-Image Developments?," *Journal of Law and Society* 23, no. 3 (1996): 322.

36 Colin Crouch, *Post-Democracy* (Cambridge: Polity, 2004); Colin Crouch, *The Strange Non-Death of Neo-Liberalism* (Cambridge: Polity, 2011).

37 Deborah D. Avant, "The Privatization of Security: Lessons From Iraq," *Orbis* 50, no. 2 (2006): 327–42; Deborah D. Avant and Renee de Nevers, "Military Contractors and the American Way of War," *Daedalus* 140, no. 3 (2011): 88–99.

38 Dawn Foster, "Free Schools," *London Review of Books* 37, no. 9 (2015): 8–9.

39 Crouch, *Post-Democracy.*

40 Simon Smith, Vicky Ward, and Allan House, "'Impact' in the Proposals for the UK's Research Excellence Framework: Shifting the Boundaries of Academic Autonomy," *Research Policy* 40, no. 10 (2011): 1369–79.

41 James E. Ryan, "The Perverse Incentives of the No Child Left Behind Act," *New York University Law Review* 79 (2004): 932.

42 See, e.g., Gary J. Miller, "Monitoring, Rules, and the Control Paradox: Can the Good Soldier Svejk be Trusted?," eds. Roderick M. Kramer and Karen S. Cook, *Trust and Distrust in Organizations: Dilemmas and Approaches* (2004): 99–126.

43 Mary Fainsod Katzenstein and Maureen R. Waller, "Taxing the Poor: Incarceration, Poverty Governance, and the Seizure of Family Resources," *Perspectives on Politics* 13, no. 3 (2015): 638–56.

44 Mary Feinsod Katzenstein and Maureen Waller, "Phone Calls Won't Cost Up to $14 a Minute Anymore but Here's How Prisoners' Families Are Still Being Fleeced," *Washington Post*, October 26, 2015, www.washingtonpost.com.

45 Paul Pierson, "When Effect Becomes Cause: Policy Feedback and Political Change," *World Politics* 45 (1993): 595–628.

46 Suevon Lee, "Here's What You Need to Know About the Two Companies Dominating the Private Prison Industry," *Business Insider*, June 22, 2013.

47 Tracy F. H. Chang and Douglas E. Thompkins, "Corporations Go To Prisons: The Expansion of Corporate Power in the Correctional Industry," *Labor Studies Journal* 27, no. 1 (2002): 45–69.

48 Ibid.

49 Lee Fang, "How Private Prisons Game the Immigration System," *Nation*, February 27, 2013.

50 Crouch, *Post-Democracy*, 100.

51 Peter Mair, *Ruling the Void: The Hollowing of Western Democracy* (New York: Verso Books, 2013).

52 Mattli and Woods, *The Politics of Global Regulation.*

53 Abraham L. Newman and Elliot Posner, "International Interdependence and Regulatory Power: Authority, Mobility, and Markets," *European Journal of International Relations* 17, no. 4 (2011): 589–610.

54 Charles E. Lindblom, *Politics and Markets* (New York: Basic Books, 1982).

55 Pepper D. Culpepper and Raphael Reinke, "Structural Power and Bank Bailouts in the United Kingdom and the United States," *Politics & Society* (2014): 0032329214547342; Pepper D. Culpepper, "Structural Power and Political Science in the Post-Crisis Era," *Business and Politics* 17, no. 3 (2015): 391–409.

56 Henry Farrell and Abraham L. Newman, "Structuring Power: Business and Authority Beyond the Nation State," *Business and Politics* 17, no. 3 (2015): 527–52.

57 Henry Farrell, "Regulating Information Flows: States, Private Actors and E-Commerce," *Annual Review of Political Science* 6 (2006): 353–74.

58 Henry Farrell and Abraham Newman, *Of Privacy and Power: The Transatlantic Fight over Freedom and Security* (Princeton, NJ: Princeton University Press, 2019).

59 Henry Farrell, "Constructing the International Foundations of E-Commerce: The EU-US Safe Harbor Arrangement," *International Organization* 57, no. 2 (2003): 277–306.

60 Susan K. Sell, *Private Power, Public Law: The Globalization of Intellectual Property Rights* (Cambridge: Cambridge University Press, 2003).

61 Eric Helleiner, "Filling a Hole in Global Financial Governance? The Politics of Regulating Sovereign Bond Restructuring," in Mattli and Woods, eds., *The Politics of Global Regulation.*

62 Christoph Knill and Dirk Lehmkuhl, "Private Actors and the State," *Global Governance: Critical Concepts in Political Science* 3, no. 1 (2004): 412.

63 Farrell and Newman, "Structuring Power."

64 Ibid.

65 Pepper D. Culpepper, *Quiet Politics and Business Power: Corporate Control in Europe and Japan* (New York: Cambridge University Press, 2010); Abraham Newman and Nikhil Kalanpur, "Mobilizing Market Power: Jurisdictional Expansion and Economic Statecraft," *International Organization* (forthcoming 2019).

66 Büthe and Mattli, *The New Global Rulers.*

67 Ibid., 6.

68 Benjamin Cashore, "Legitimacy and the Privatization of Environmental Governance: How Non State Market-Driven (NSMD) Governance Systems Gain Rule Making Authority," *Governance* 15, no. 4 (2002): 503–29; Tim Bartley, "Institutional Emergence in an Era of Globalization: The Rise of Transnational Private Regulation of Labor and Environmental Conditions," *American Journal of Sociology* 113, no. 2 (2007): 297–351.

69 Sell, *Private Power, Public Law.*

70 See Christian Oliver and Shawn Donnan, "Brussels Wants Finance Rules Back in US Trade Pact," *Financial Times,* January 27, 2014.

71 Zachary Elkins, Andrew T. Guzman, and Beth A. Simmons, "Competing for Capital: The Diffusion of Bilateral Investment Treaties, 1960–2000," *International Organization* 60, no. 4 (2006): 811–46.

72 Haley Sweetland Edwards, *Shadow Courts: The Tribunals that Rule Global Trade* (New York: Columbia Global Reports, 2016).

73 Ibid., 65.

74 Julia Gray, "Jumping Someone Else's Treaty: Treaty Shopping, Shell Companies and Investor State Disputes," (unpublished paper, 2015).

75 Edwards, *Shadow Courts.*

# 8

# PUBLIC-SECTOR MANAGEMENT
# IS COMPLICATED

## COMMENT ON FARRELL

### JOSEPH HEATH

I was born in the Canadian province of Saskatchewan in 1967, towards the end of what was undoubtedly the high-water mark of socialist experimentation in North America. When I was young, our provincial government was very much committed not just to the ownership of natural monopolies and the creation of a social safety net, but to public ownership of the means of production. Thus not only were water, gas, electricity, telecommunications, education, and health care under public ownership, but so was the entire mining industry, as well as intercity bus transportation, automobile insurance, alcohol sales, and various other odds and ends. More significantly, the province was laying the groundwork for the nationalization of agriculture. Meanwhile, the banking sector, grocery stores, retail gasoline sales, farm supply and insurance, and of course grain marketing were dominated by cooperatives. Finally, the Canadian federal state owned and operated an airline, an oil company, both freight and passenger rail companies, a hotel chain, a steamship and telegraph company, as well as radio and television broadcast firms in both official languages.

Since that time, there has been—perhaps needless to say—a fundamental restructuring of the economy, not just in Saskatchewan, but in Canada more generally, and throughout the Western world. The most visible face of this has been the wave of privatization of state-owned enterprises (SOEs) that began in the 1980s and has continued into the twenty-first century. It will surprise no one to learn, for instance, that mining in Saskatchewan is no longer under state monopoly, or that if one wants to buy a new telephone, there is no longer any obligation to order it from the government (as a result of which they are now available in colors other than black). The story, however, is complicated, first by the fact that the privatization was not wholesale, but rather selective, and second, that no simple ideological story can capture the full range of concerns that were in play, or that determined which SOEs were sold off.

The great merit of Henry Farrell's paper is that it shifts attention away from the focus on ownership, which is typically the flashpoint of ideological disagreement about privatization, towards a discussion of governance, which is a more nuanced and, in my view, far more interesting topic. Whether it be in the public or the private sector, the separation of ownership and control in large organizations has progressed to the point where governance questions are, in general, far more consequential than ownership ones in determining whether, or to what extent, "the public interest" will be served. The history of governance reform of state-owned enterprises in the West is a fascinating one, not least because it is central to the fortunes of the socialist project in its more ambitious forms. Unfortunately, I think the most interesting segment of that history is the one that occurred *prior* to the wave of privatizations that began in the 1980s, which serves as the focus of Farrell's discussion. Of particular interest is the phase of "corporatization" of these enterprises that began in the late 1960s and '70s, and was undertaken in most cases by centrist or left-wing governments. Farrell, however, says nothing about this institutional pre-history. This would be fine, except that he goes on to treat as effects of privatization several governance reforms—such as increased reliance on contracting—that had in fact been enacted long before the change of ownership occurred. Thus the focus of my critical remarks will be to show how and why many of the reforms that Farrell identifies with privatization were actually undertaken prior, during the corporatization phase. I will end with a few thoughts about what consequences this perspective might have for our thinking about the final issue that he discusses, pertaining to globalization.

## I. The Control Mentality

Before I begin, I would like to flag a common fallacy, which Farrell may or may not be committing, but which his phrasing at several points certainly encourages the reader to commit. This is the assumption that a system that imposes "direct control" over an individual or organization necessarily, or perhaps even presumptively, provides a higher level of effective control than one that relies upon merely "indirect control." One need only dip one's toe into the waters of principal-agency theory to see how problematic such an assumption is. My concern is aroused, however, when Farrell describes his analysis using contrasts like the following:

> Next, I examine how states have renounced ownership stakes in business: they have moved from a paradigm of direct control, to one in which their instruments consist primarily of independent regulatory agencies (for businesses with which the state has an arms-length relationship) or contracts (for businesses that the state relies on directly). However, it has often turned out to be difficult to regulate businesses effectively or to craft contracts that provide real accountability, especially when the businesses have much greater expertise or resources than the regulators.[1]

Although it is not stated explicitly, the assumption seems to be that, prior to renouncing ownership, the systems of "direct control" that were in place actually did achieve "real accountability," or that regulation was in some sense unnecessary when these firms were in the public sector. If this is indeed the assumption, then it seems to me a clear instance of what Joseph Stiglitz has described as the "control mentality," which he takes to be based on two conjoined fallacies: "It overestimates the power of direct control and it underestimates the powers of indirect control."[2]

Far too many political theorists treat the state as though it were an ideal Weberian bureaucracy, staffed by loyal agents, who accept instructions from their superiors—in particular, from elected officials—and carry them out with diligence and dispatch. The enormous focus on "democracy" in the literature encourages this, insofar as it appears to accept the suggestion that politicians exercise effective control of the policymaking process within the state (as opposed to, say, having input into it, or exercising a veto over it). And yet it is also widely recognized that the state is hypercomplex, and government agencies can be extremely opaque. Thus the public sector manager, not to mention the elected official, is confronted with organizations exhibiting the characteristic that Oliver Williamson referred to as "information impactedness."[3] This dramatically reduces the effectiveness of systems of direct control. As Stiglitz put it, "For direct control to be effective, the controller has to have an enormous amount of information at his disposal. He must not only have the information to decide what should be done; he has to have the capacity to monitor that it in fact gets done. Those in positions of centralized control seldom have the requisite information."[4]

Apart from information asymmetries, which reduce the power of direct control in all large organizations, there are limitations that are specific to the public sector, which have been the subject of considerable discussion over the years. Again, just to focus on Stiglitz's remarks, even when public officials are able to adequately monitor their agents, they have fewer "carrots and sticks" at their disposal to motivate compliance, or to punish and reward employees after the fact. For instance, pay structures in the public sector are generally "inverted"—while most low-level employees receive a wage premium relative to their private sector counterparts, as one ascends the organizational hierarchy, salaries become less competitive, to the point where most senior public managers are foregoing far more lucrative opportunities in the private sector. The state is also unable to offer equity-based compensation, which limits its flexibility when designing performance pay systems. Regardless of what one thinks about the trends in private sector compensation, the fact remains that escalating private sector salaries for people with managerial skills create serious retention issues in the public sector. As a result, when orders are issued, backed by the implicit threat, "Do this, or else," the answer that comes back is sometimes "Or else what?" When the major consequence of being fired is that one goes on to make two or three times more money working as a consultant in the private sector, the threat of dismissal loses much of its anxiety-provoking quality.

As a result of these and other issues, public sector managers can be notoriously difficult to control. Indeed, the weakness of direct control systems generated substantial reflection and reform during the '70s, especially after the oil shock, when many politicians in Europe found themselves unable to exercise any influence on the decisions made by SOEs in key sectors—with state-owned petroleum firms either refusing outright, or circumventing requests to protect domestic consumers from shortages, and SOEs in other sectors, including banking, either refusing or failing to support government efforts to combat inflation. Here, for instance, is an account of BP's (British Petroleum's) unhelpful demeanor during the oil crisis:

> Just as CFP [Compagnie Française de Petroles] had refused to divert deliveries from foreign customers during the 1973–74 oil embargo, so did BP. Supplies were cut to Britain despite requests of the Conservative government. The ensuing Labour government had no better luck controlling the corporation. Anthony Wedgewood Benn, then energy minister, complained of a rather cavalier attitude on the part of the 51 percent state-owned company, which had given its administrative overseer only twenty-four hours notice of a deal to take over VEBA's interests in Germany and gave the same limited notice of its deal with the French on the Southwest Approaches. The company also made surreptitious payments to Italian politicians, undermined the British position on European Economic Community (EEC) refinery policy, and secretly violated British economic sanctions against Rhodesia.[5]

Perhaps the best-known example of the agency problems that can afflict the public sector is the problem of the "soft budget constraint"—as a result of which it is very difficult to get public sector managers to stop running deficits. Since the 2008 financial crisis, everyone is familiar with the moral hazard problem that can be created in the private sector when banks become "too big to fail." The issue is that, once they become large enough that their bankruptcy would threaten the stability of the financial system, they thereby acquire an implicit government guarantee of solvency. This encourages various forms of irresponsible behavior, including excessive borrowing and leverage. And yet this problem is obviously going to be even more severe in the public sector proper, where firms enjoy an *explicit* state guarantee against bankruptcy.

SOEs are not "too big to fail," but rather "structurally incapable of failing." If they are also given the capacity for autonomous financing—to borrow money, or issue bonds, which for various reasons one might want an SOE to do—then it is very difficult to prevent excessive debt. This can lead to overcapitalization in the firms, but perhaps more importantly, can make it hard to prevent managers from running operating deficits, because they can just issue debt to cover any shortfall or, more commonly, call upon the public treasury to cover the losses.

Politicians have also encountered great difficulty imposing cost-cutting measures or budget reductions on these firms. Managers often deploy what is known within the civil service in Canada as the "musical ride" strategy, named after the suggestion that whenever the government demands cutbacks from the Royal Canadian Mounted Police (RCMP), the force offers to cancel the musical ride, which is one of the nation's most beloved institutions, and yet is also rather expensive and clearly of no operational value. To bolster its position, the RCMP also manages to ensure that the musical ride performs at least once per year in the riding of each member of cabinet. (The American equivalent of this, I am told, is the "Washington Monument" strategy, where whenever the U.S. National Park Service is threatened with budget cuts, they offer to close the Washington Monument.) Although this circulates as a joke, it is only a slight exaggeration of a genuine phenomenon, which is that elected officials typically lack the information to determine where cuts can be made, or lack the authority to make decisions at that level. As a result, they are subject to something resembling blackmail, from managers threatening to make politically injurious cuts if their budgets are not expanded. (This is a phenomenon that I witnessed while a student at McGill University, which at the time was running a large deficit, in part as a way of pressuring the provincial government to increase its funding. When the government insisted that McGill accept its existing funding level, and make cuts to eliminate the deficit, the university announced its plans to cut the Faculty of Dentistry, on the grounds that it was the most expensive program. Such a cut, however, would have left the province with no English-language dentistry program, a prospect that generated an immediate outcry within the Anglophone community, and quickly led the government to reconsider its position.)

Also, it is important not to overestimate how much "direct control" there is, even when managers are not being insubordinate. Farrell claims that "the state used to be able to exercise authority by means of direct ownership," but that now, because of privatization, the state must seek "to shape economic outcomes externally through regulation rather than ownership." This is, I think, highly misleading. The sense in which the state "owns" most SOEs very much resembles the sense in which shareholders "own" a large publicly traded corporation (and in some cases is the same sense, in that the SOE is just a standard business corporation, in which the state is a majority shareholder). As a result, "ownership" accomplishes surprisingly little. Elected officials are certainly not in a position to be giving anyone orders, at least in the standard run of cases. The type of ownership they exercise is a very formal type of control, primarily the power to appoint a supervisory board, and perhaps be consulted on high-level personnel decisions.

It is because of this extremely attenuated ownership relation that the state typically seeks to control the behavior of its own SOEs, not "internally" through the ownership relation, but "externally" through regulation.[6] For instance, when the agency responsible for health and safety in the workplace, or environmental regulation, wants to make changes in a publicly owned power plant, it does not approach the minister in the department with supervisory authority over the facility. On the contrary, it exercises its regulatory authority, "externally" as it were—issuing directives, sending in inspectors, imposing fines, and so forth.[7] This has always been the case, and privatization did absolutely nothing to change it. (This is particularly apparent in federal states, where different orders of government tend to guard their jurisdictions rather jealously, and governments are formed by different political parties, who are often non-cooperative and sometimes overtly antagonistic toward one another. In Canada, for instance, health, education, and natural resources are controlled at a provincial level, while a great deal of regulatory authority is federal. As a result, there are a large number of provincially owned SOEs, which often maintain a stance of overt hostility toward the Canadian government, typically with the support of provincial politicians, who benefit from the perception that they are defending regional interests. The history of asbestos mining in Quebec offers a striking example of this—the reason that Canada has never succeeded in banning the substance is not because private interests interfered, but rather due to a history of resistance from a lower order of government, acting in part to defend the interests of its own SOE—the *Société nationale de l'amiante* in Quebec.

## II. Corporatization

I have spoken of there being a "separation of ownership and control" in the public sector in the management of SOEs, but this has not always been the case. In some countries, the U.K. in particular, it has always been more or less the norm, with most SOEs historically having been set up as Crown corporations under the supervision of a particular ministry, but enjoying a largely arms-length relationship to the minister. Many other countries, however, began with a model that involved more direct supervision, where the activities of the SOE were integrated into one or more government departments, elected officials were actively involved in operational decision-making, and there was no separation between the budget of the "firm" and the department in which it was embedded (with the implication that operating losses were simply absorbed by departmental budgets). "Capital investment by state enterprises was, alongside road building, current expenditure on police and so on, part of public expenditure programmes, whilst their operating surpluses were, along with taxes, social security payments and so on, part of government income."[8]

We might think of this as the "democratic" model of SOE management because, on paper at least, it promises much greater "direct control" of the firm by elected officials. Beginning in the late '60s, however, a large-scale shift began, with countries moving away from the democratic model toward an arrangement that involved: (1) greater managerial autonomy, (2) creation of a board of directors to mediate relations between elected officials and managers, (3) partitioning of assets and liabilities between the SOE and line departments, (4) the demand for self-financing of capital investment by the SOE, (5) increased focus on economic efficiency (i.e., break-even, or profitability) as a managerial objective, and finally, (6) the use of contracting to implement the "social responsibility" mandate of the firm. Many of these reforms were pioneered in France, following the release of the Nora Report in 1967, and were imitated by other countries, such as Canada, during the 1970s. This overall period is often described as the "corporatization" phase of SOEs.

What is important to understand—and what gets overlooked in Farrell's paper—is that these governance reforms, which had as their major objective the removal of SOE decision-making from "the remit of politics," occurred long before privatization was on the agenda. Indeed, they were undertaken by politicians who consistently articulated a commitment to keeping these firms in the public sector. In many ways, of course, the reforms paved the way for privatization, because they changed the governance structure of these firms to such a degree that they were no longer operating in a way that was discernably different from the way that private firms would act. Once they had become independently managed profit-seeking corporations under public ownership, the question of why the public should retain ownership became more difficult to answer. But that is a later part of the story.

The reason that the reforms were undertaken had a great deal to do with agency problems, including some of the ones described in the previous section, that can arise in hierarchical organizations. The most conspicuous symptom of these agency problems was that SOEs lost a great deal of money.[9] The Nora Report, for instance, was commissioned after the annual operating losses being absorbed by the French state from its SOEs more than doubled over a period of only four years, from 2.3 billion francs in 1961 to 5.2 billion in 1965.[10] The 1967 U.K. white paper *Nationalised Industries: A Review of Financial and Economic Objectives* was motivated by similar concerns, and arrived at nearly identical conclusions.[11] The underlying problem was a breakdown of managerial discipline, resulting from the combination of what we would now refer to as "multiprincipal" and "multitask" agency problems.[12]

To provide a concrete example, which illustrates the general problem, consider Canada's national airline (Trans-Canada Airlines, subsequently renamed Air Canada). It was initially established with a clear public-interest mandate (as C.D. Howe, the minister responsible, described it in 1937, "the company will be protected against loss, but its profits will be very strictly limited. In other words, it is organized to perform a certain national service, and it is expected that the service will be performed at or near cost"[13]). It was created with a board of directors, but one that exercised very little authority. Key management decisions were made by the Department of Transportation, the Department of Finance, the Treasury Board Secretariat, and in some cases cabinet as a whole. Most dramatically, the purchase of new aircraft was, over the years, almost always a political decision, made by the minister or cabinet, sometimes over the opposite of airline management.[14] Key route decisions, both international and domestic, were also made by cabinet, with a number of so-called "social routes" to remote regions—routes that were too uneconomical to be serviced by a private carrier—imposed on "national interest" grounds. (These were not always imposed; the airline sometimes took the initiative and created "social routes" on its own, with direct flights to the ridings of powerful cabinet ministers from remote regions.[15]) And finally, the location of the airline's major maintenance operations was decided politically, as part of a regional-development strategy (most controversially, to maintain employment in Winnipeg, instead of consolidating operations in Montreal, as the airline's management had proposed).[16]

I think it is fairly easy to see the problems that this organizational structure can create. How can anyone tell whether the airline is being well managed or not? Naturally, Air Canada lost a great deal of money, and passengers were constantly complaining about the quality of service. But was this justifiable or not? The problem is that, when managers are given two contradictory objectives, they are essentially being freed from the obligation to achieve either. When asked to explain their failure to achieve one objective, they can point to the constraints imposed by the other. In particular, if the government is forcing an airline to fly money-losing "social routes," or to maintain uneconomical maintenance facilities, *and* it wants fares to be kept low, then it cannot really complain when the airline loses money. The question of whether the loss is larger than it necessarily had to be becomes effectively unanswerable.

This is the conclusion that was arrived at in the Nora Report, on similar grounds, particularly in its discussion of SNCF (the French national railway operator). On the one hand, SNCF managers were supposed to run their operations efficiently, but on the other hand, they were expected to keep fares low, to maintain service to low-population areas, to create employment in depressed regions, and so on. This made it impossible to determine whether the organization was being effective in its pursuit of *any* of these ends:

> Faute de bien distinguer la rentabilité propre de l'activité économique et le coût spécifique des contraintes d'intérêt public, il n'y a plus pour ces entreprises, ni critère de bonne gestion, ni incitation à la meilleure gestion, ni sanction pour la mauvaise. Comment dès lors attendre d'elles un financement équilibré, et le comportement inventif, autonome et responsable qui en constitue la garantie?

> [Absent the ability to distinguish the profitability of the economic activity from the specific cost of the public interest contraints, there is no longer, for these enterprises, any standard of good management, nor any incentive to improve, nor any punishment for failure. How then can one expect from them balanced financing, much less the innovative, autonomous, and responsible behavior that alone constitutes its guarantee?][17]

Nora's enormously influential recommendation was that the various objectives imposed upon the firm be disaggregated and separately costed. In other words, the firm should adopt a standard business model—choosing routes, for instance, where passenger revenue is sufficient to cover expenses, including capital outlays—as its baseline strategy. It should then take any deviations from the strategy—running "social routes," for instance, to underserviced regions—and determine how much it costs to achieve those particular objectives. The state should, in turn, determine how much it is willing to pay to achieve the various public interest objectives it would like to see the SOE pursue. The two parties should then negotiate, and work out an explicit contract, with the state essentially paying the SOE an agreed amount for each public interest objective it imposes on the firm.[18] In return, it can demand that the firm show an overall operating surplus, and that it maintain its own balance sheet, carrying its own losses. This arrangement makes it possible to impose a standard auditing regime upon SOEs, and to hold managers accountable to a single objective.[19]

It is a fairly natural consequence of this arrangement that, once the state begins to cost out how much it is paying to achieve particular public interest objectives, the question whether *le jeu en vaut la chandelle* can be posed much more sharply. The other question that arises, however, is whether the same objective might be achieved in some other way at lower cost. For example, if the state discovers that it has implicitly been paying SNCF to maintain employment in some depressed region, it can easily calculate how much it costs per job, then consider whether the same results could be achieved by subsidizing some other SOE, or perhaps by making direct investments in the region. Furthermore, if the state is now paying its own SOE to achieve regional employment goals, there is no longer any obvious reason why the entire operation must remain within the public sector. If a privately owned firm can accomplish the same objective at lower cost, then why not award the contract to it? Thus intra-governmental competition for "business," along with the eventual inclusion of outside contractors, is very much a consequence of the reforms proposed in the Nora Report.

I am delving into these details in order to make the point that several of the changes Farrell takes to be insidious consequences of privatization are actually public sector innovations that had little to do with privatization, and in some cases predated it by a decade or more. Most importantly the trend toward the state "internally shifting its mode of operation to more closely resemble contractual relations" was first proposed in France during the late '60s, and institutionalized during the '70s and early '80s (before the first wave of privatization, which did not begin in France until 1986).[20] Furthermore, I think that Farrell's suspicion of private markets leads him to misunderstand the motivation for many of these changes. For instance, when he claims that "visibility and accountability are occluded" by the "complex webs of contractual arrangements between the government and private sector," it is important to keep in mind what the alternatives are. The old hierarchical relationships were entirely opaque, and were reformed precisely because they were thought to undermine accountability. For example, the *Report of the Royal Commission on Financial Management and Accountability* (or "Lambert report") released in 1979 in Canada described the older system in the following terms: "After two years of careful study and consideration, we have reached the deeply held conviction that the serious malaise pervading the management of government stems fundamentally from a grave weakening and in some cases an almost total breakdown, in the chain of accountability, first within government, and second in the accountability of government to parliament and ultimately to the Canadian people."[21]

In order to understand the problem with the older systems of accountability, it is important to recognize not just that important information was not disclosed, or made explicit (the Access to Information Act having come into force only in 1983), but that in many cases it didn't exist. For example, at the time when the Canadian prime minister could simply order Air Canada to fly a particular route, at a particular fare, the question "How much is this costing the taxpayer?" did not have an answer. Contracting was intended to change this. Although it does not go all the way to achieving visibility and accountability, it puts into place at least some of the necessary conditions (e.g., it generates paper records that are, in principle, publicly available).

Furthermore, while the actual sale of SOEs to private investors may have been strongly influenced by political ideology, corporatization most definitely was not. The management problems afflicting SOEs were obvious to everyone—in many cases the economic losses they incurred were massive, sufficiently large to threaten the fiscal integrity of the state. Thus the major wave of corporatizing reform in Canada was undertaken by the center-left government of Pierre Trudeau, just as the government of François Mitterand in France was heavily involved in SOE reform. Indeed, it is precisely because corporatizing reforms were by and large successful that the question of ownership often wound up being settled by ideological preference. SOEs came to resemble standard business corporations in so many aspects of their management and behavior that it made very little economic difference whether they were owned publicly or privately. This is also one of the reasons that privatization in most cases appears to have achieved very little, in terms of increased efficiency—because it changed very little in the governance of firms.[22] Once SOEs were fully corporatized, the only significant economic argument for privatization was that, with its stock being freely traded, managers would become subject to the discipline of the "market for control." In practice, however, the difference between being owned by the state and being owned by a collection of large pension and mutual funds turned out to be not that significant.

Meanwhile, the problems that inspired corporatization have by no means gone away. Consider, for example, the case of British Columbia Ferries, an SOE that somehow slipped through the cracks during the first wave of corporatization, remaining under direct control of elected officials. It became engulfed in scandal during the '90s, for having commissioned construction of three aluminum "fast ferries." After failing to find a private firm willing to undertake the project (a red flag if there ever was one), the BC government decided to go it alone, partly as a way of aiding the province's ailing shipbuilding industry. Although the project was initially estimated to cost $210 million, the government wound up spending $460 million, only to end up with boats that did not come close to meeting specifications. The three ferries were taken out of service after only a few years, and sold for $19.4 million. The report of a commission of inquiry called in 2001 to investigate the scandal reads like something straight out of the 1970s:

> BC Ferries is entangled in a web of formal and informal account-ability to various government agencies, ministry personnel and politicians that it is powerless to change. Its enabling legislation provides that the Province, not BC Ferries' board, make all significant decisions. As a result the Province's policy imperatives can, at times, conflict with BC Ferries' primary goal of serving its customers. This was most notably the case when the public policy priority to rejuvenate BC's shipbuilding industry, through the export of aluminum ferries, overrode BC Ferries' objective to provide cost effective, customer-focused ferry service. But political interference is not limited to such a high profile example. It pervades every important decision whether it involves service levels, tariffs, labour negotiations or the purchase of new vessels.[23]

The solution recommended was corporatization, and most importantly that effective control be shifted to an "independent board of directors with responsibility for governing, exempt from political and bureaucratic interference."[24] No specific recommendation was made about whether the service should be privatized. In the end, the government wound up transforming BC Ferries into an independent corporation, with a single share owned by the newly created BC Ferry Authority, which describes itself as an "independent, no-share capital corporation."[25] This gave rise to an ongoing, metaphysically rich debate over whether the ferry service had actually been privatized or not. For our purposes, the interesting point is that it was possible to address the major problem while leaving ownership in such an ambiguous state. The overriding imperative was to remove decision-making at the firm from (what Farrell refers to as) "the remit of politics," so that it could focus on serving the public interest.

## III. Globalization

There is a view out there, which Farrell at times sounds not entirely unsympathetic to, that regards privatization as essentially the culmination of a conspiracy against the public, carried out by political parties that were little more than ideological front groups for the plutocracy. Indeed, the relationship of mutual reinforcement that Farrell sees between the various aspects of privatization ("the serpent is beginning to bite its own tail") seems to regard the essential dynamic as a contest between the public interest, served by state ownership, and private interests, served by privatization. The boundary between state and market is determined by the relative strength of the two parties, so that as "private interests" become stronger, they are able to achieve greater privatization of state functions, which in turn makes them stronger, and so on. Farrell does include the necessary caveats about the complexity of real world causal relations. Nevertheless, the essential picture strikes me as one in which the dynamic of privatization is driven by the power of the state relative to that of, let us say, "capital."

The central problem with this view, I have suggested, is that it fails to acknowledge a range of serious problems that arose within the public sector during the '60s and '70s, which were the subject of deep discussion and significant reform effort, in an environment that was not nearly as ideologically polarized as it became during the Thatcher-Reagan years. One of the many discoveries that was made during this period is that the state does some things very well, but other things quite poorly. This became particularly obvious in businesses that had a "customer service" dimension and where there was no natural monopoly, so that private operators could arise that could compete directly with an SOE. This allowed the public to compare directly the service it was receiving from the government and from the private sector—a comparison that seldom worked out favorably for the government. This is, for instance, what happened with intercity bus service in Canada, and it is the reason that Canadian provincial governments have largely withdrawn from that market (although not in Saskatchewan!). Governments were simply never very good at running these services, while private companies proved better at every level (most obviously with respect to customer service and pricing, but in the background, at achieving optimal levels of capital investment[26]). The fact that the public firms so often lost money was the final nail in the coffin. What is the point of owning the means of production if the profits disappear the moment the firm comes under public ownership? The only thing that the state really contributed was the capacity to cross-subsidize between routes, in order to benefit underpopulated (especially northern) regions. Eventually it became obvious to everyone that the state did not need to own and operate the bus company in order to do this. If the objective is truly valued, it can be achieved by paying subsidies to private companies to run the routes.

These observations lend support to the "transaction cost" approach to the analysis of public ownership and privatization. On this view, the question of whether a particular economic activity should be undertaken in the public or the private sector is *primarily* determined by the comparative advantage of different institutional forms. This is a widely held view, and I will not repeat the arguments for it.[27] Instead, I would like to show how the adoption of a transaction cost perspective suggests a very different reading of the developments that Farrell describes under the rubric of a "third aspect" of privatization.

While private rent-seeking has no doubt played a role, over the years, in the privatizations that have occurred, there has also been a great deal of pragmatism informing the decisions taken by politicians and public administrators, whether to produce a good or provide a service "in house," or to contract it out. The "make or buy" question, which transaction cost theorists take to guide determination of the boundaries of the firm, can also be seen to inform the decisions in the public sector, in determining the boundaries of the state. For example, the really obvious privatizations that occurred in the '80s—the ones that no one makes any noises about reversing—were the ones in which the state was involved in sectors where there was no obstacle to the creation of a reasonably competitive market, such as airlines, mining, or hotels. In these areas, one is tempted to say, there was never any good reason for the state to have been involved in the first place. In other sectors, circumstances changed in such a way as to undermine the case for state involvement. Because transaction costs are sensitive to a number of different factors, including the state of technology, they are likely to change over time, resulting in changes in the relative efficiency of different organizational forms. Computerization, for instance, made it much less expensive to track consumption and to bill customers, which in turn made it feasible to deliver services through one-on-one contracting that had previously been, in effect, club goods provided by the state.

From this perspective, I think that we can isolate at least three non-nefarious factors that drove a great deal of privatization:

1. Technological change made it possible to create competitive markets in areas that were previously natural monopolies. For example, while "land line" telephone service is a natural monopoly, technological innovation made it possible, in the '90s, to create a competitive market for long-distance carrier service, and later, for local service. This led to widespread "privatization" of one portion of the traditional telecom business. A similar bifurcation became possible between electricity distribution and electricity generation, or natural gas distribution and natural gas supply, with competitive markets being created in the latter domains. Almost all of this was driven by digital technology that made it less expensive to track individual usage and to bill customers.

2. The "traditional public sector model" involves a particular good or service being "free" at the point of delivery, provided or produced by public sector employees, paid for out of general tax revenue.[28] This model remains appropriate in cases where there is a serious market failure on both sides of the transaction, but in

cases where the market failure is only on the supply side, or the demand side, there may be no need for the state to take over the entire transaction. This has led to the development of "purchaser-provider splits," where the public sector model is applied only on one side. For example, with the installation of water meters in homes, consumers now purchase water by volume, the same way that they purchase many other commodities; it is just that the state continues to act as a monopoly supplier. Garbage removal services, by contrast, are often now provided by commercial suppliers, with the state acting as a monopsonist, purchasing the service on behalf of all residents.

3. Corporatization generated a certain harmonization of the governance structures between SOEs and standard business corporations. As a result, it became possible to have mixed public-private ownership structures, with the state as either minority or majority shareholder. Indeed, one World Bank study recommended that developing countries wanting to develop SOEs should incorporate them as business corporations, then have the state assume majority, or even exclusive, ownership.[29] (Ironically, the major reason for this recommendation is that publicly traded business corporations are subject to more demanding reporting requirements than traditional SOEs, and so incorporation as a private firm is recommended as a way of increasing transparency.) In fact, many of the headline "privatizations" of the '80s were not total, but only partial. (The "privatization" of PetroCanada in 1990, for instance, was not total. The government retained a 19% ownership stake, with rules that restricted any private shareholder from acquiring more than 10% of the company, thereby ensuring that the state remained in control.)

In many of these cases, privatization has been relatively unproblematic. Where it has acquired a bad name is in areas in which the state actually was the better provider, because of the persistence of market failure in the sector, which made the relevant "government failures" seem less problematic by comparison. It is important to recognize, however, that in many such cases—where anti-government ideology was put ahead of efficiency considerations—privatization has subsequently been reversed. Water services in particular have been the focus of many reversals, in jurisdictions where enthusiasm for private sector solutions led politicians to overlook the fact that water and sewer services remain a natural monopoly. (It is notable that with the bottled water industry, where there is no difficulty creating a competitive market, there is no pressure for state ownership. It is only water that is delivered through *pipes* that constitutes a public good. This suggests that it is actually the pipes that are at issue, not the water.)

Privatizations, however, tend to attract more attention than reversals, for the same reason that layoffs and outsourcing at private firms tends to eclipse hiring and acquisitions. In order to see the dynamic of privatization and reverse privatization, as well as what drives it, it is helpful to look at the behavior of municipal governments (where data sets are larger, and interesting cross-jurisdictional comparisons are possible). For example, a survey of 628 municipal governments across the United States found that in every year between 1992 and 1997, 93% of governments reported having contracted out at least one service, while 81% contracted back in at least one service (with almost 75% doing both).[30] One can see there the general trend towards increased privatization, and yet also a significant amount of movement back and forth, suggesting a degree of flexibility and pragmatism that runs contrary to the dominant tone of the literature, with its "singular focus on contracting out."[31] It also suggests that, whatever barriers private actors have been able to create against reversal, they cannot be too serious, as there has obviously been a great deal of "insourcing." If one examines the forces that are driving this, they are consistent with the transaction cost theory. According to the survey authors, Amir Hefetz and Mildred Warner, "contracting back in" is closely related to the government's inability to effectively monitor and control the external provider:

> Government managers who are successful users of contracts for service delivery understand the importance of monitoring systems that assess cost, quality, and citizen satisfaction. Governments with lower levels of monitoring are more likely to bring services back in-house. For these governments, contracting back-in appears to be a substitute for monitoring. This may reflect limited government capacity to monitor in general or selection of services for contracting that were inappropriate candidates for market delivery in that locale.[32]

Farrell argues that, thanks to certain dynamics that have shown up at the international level, states "are finding that their capacity to regulate is being significantly constrained." From a public-interest perspective, one would be inclined to regard this as a bad thing, insofar as it weakens the state. From a transaction cost perspective, however, it may not be a bad thing at all, in that it may strengthen the hand of the state. Not only does it weaken the case for privatization, but it makes state control look better, increasing its comparative advantage relative to market contracting. Thus, to the extent that private actors have been undermining the capacity of the state to regulate, their actions may prove to be self-defeating, as they are helping to build the case for more direct state involvement in the economy.

## IV. CONCLUSION

Farrell is certainly right in observing that there have been significant changes in public sector governance over the past few decades. Indeed, one of the most common complaints within the civil service has been the incessant demand for "reform."[33] Furthermore, it is also the case that many of these reforms have had the effect of reducing the distinctiveness of public administration, transforming management practices and governance structures in such a way as to increase their similarity to those in the private sector. This is often described as a shift away from "public administration" toward "managerialism."[34]

There are, however, at least three quite distinct aspects to the major reforms that were undertaken. The first, which I have spent a great deal of time discussing, is corporatization. The second is new public management, the signature feature of which was the "hiving off" of agencies from traditional line departments, and the creation of alternative incentive and accountability structures to motivate agency administrators (including pseudo-competition). The third is privatization, which can be understood broadly, to include not just the sell-off of SOEs, but also penumbral phenomena such as contracting out, public-private partnerships, and purchaser-provider splits.

I think it is important to observe that these initiatives are all quite different. This is often obscured, in the British case, because the Thatcher government was an early adopter, and pursued all three of the reforms simultaneously. This makes it rather tempting to run them together, and to imagine that they are part of a unified "neoliberal" agenda. This is, however, quite misleading, something that can be seen by looking at other countries, where the different initiatives were undertaken at quite different times, by governments of varying ideological complexions. One can also see that privatization was in many cases an extra gear, or the end result of a reform process that was in fact undertaken with quite different ends in mind. This is why, in my view, Farrell's emphasis on privatization does not cast much light upon the broader trends in public-sector governance over the past half-century, and risks obscuring the considerations that actually drove many of the reforms.

## Notes

1  Henry Farrell, "Privatization as State Transformation," in this volume. All quotations by Farrell in this chapter are from this source.

2  Joseph E. Stiglitz, *The Economic Role of the State*, ed. Arnold Heertje (Oxford: Oxford University Press, 1989): 34.

3  Oliver Williamson, "Markets and Hierarchies: Some Elementary Considerations," *American  Economic Review* 63, no. 2 (1973): 316–25, at 318.

4  Ibid.

5  Harvey B. Feigenbaum, "Public Enterprise in Comparative Perspective," *Comparative Politics* 15, no. 1 (1982): 101–22, at 111.

6  Christopher Hood, Oliver James, George Jones, Colin Scott, and Tony Travers, *Regulation Inside Government* (Oxford: Oxford University Press, 1999).

7  A recent study has also confirmed the widespread impression that regulators find it more difficult to secure compliance from publicly owned firms than private ones. See David M. Konisky and Manuel P. Teodoro, "When Governments Regulate Governments," *American Journal of Political Science* (forthcoming).

8  Robert Milward, *Private and Public Enterprise in Europe* (Cambridge: Cambridge University Press, 2005), 261.

9  Or to put it in more precise language: "The inability of state enterprises to reconcile the break-even target with the non-commercial obligations of state enterprises manifested itself in a consistently large shortfall of earnings below operating costs and capital charges" (Milward, *Private and Public Enterprise in Europe*, 296).

10 "Groupe de travail du comité interministeriel des entreprises publiques" (Nora Report), *Rapport sur les entreprises publiques* (Paris: La Documentation Française, Editions de Sécretariat Général de Gouvernement, 1967), 45. Hereafter referred to as Nora Report.

11 H. M. Treasury, *Nationalised Industries: A Review of Financial and Economic Objectives*, Cmd. 3437 (London: HMSO, 1967).

12 For discussion, see Joseph Heath and Wayne Norman, "Stakeholder Theory, Corporate Governance, and Public Management," *Journal of Business Ethics* 53, no. 3 (2004): 247–65.

13 John Langford and Ken Huffman, "Air Canada," in *Privatization, Public Policy and Public Corporations in Canada*, eds. Allan Tupper and G. Bruce Doern (Montreal: Institute for Research on Public Policy, 1988): 93–150, at 99.

14 Ibid., 116.

15 John Langford, "Air Canada," in *Public Corporations and Public Policy in Canada*, eds. Allan Tupper and G. Bruce Doern (Montreal: Institute for Research on Public Policy, 1981): 251–84, at 267.

16 Langford and Huffman, "Air Canada," 116.

17 Nora Report, 28.

18 Nora Report, 37–39.

19 On the importance of a single objective, see Michael Jensen, "Value Maximization, Stakeholder Theory, and the Corporate Objective Function," *Business Ethics Quarterly* 12, no. 2 (2002): 235–56.

20 Maria Vagliasindi, "Governance Arrangements for State Owned Enterprises," *Policy Research Working Paper 4542* (Washington, DC: World Bank, 2008): 18.

21 *The Report of the Royal Commission on Financial Management and Accountability* (Hull: Canadian Government Publishing Centre, 1979): 21.

22 Saul Estrin and Virginie Pérotin, "Does Ownership Always Matter?," *International Journal of Industrial Organization* 9, no. 1 (1991): 55–72.

23 Fred R. Wright, *Review of BC Ferry Corporation and Alternative Uses for the Fast Ferries* (Victoria: BC Government, 2001): 1.

24 Wright, *Review of BC Ferry Corporation*, 2.

25 BC Ferry Authority (website), accessed April 22, 2018, www.bcferryauthority.com.

26 John Palmer, John Quinn, and Ray Resende, "A Case Study of Public Enterprise: Gray Coach Lines Ltd," in *Crown Corporations in Canada*, ed. Robert Prichard (Toronto: Butterworth, 1983).

27 For those interested, see Joseph Heath, "Three Normative Models of the Welfare State," *Public Reason* 3, no. 2 (2011): 13–43, or Stiglitz, *The Economic Role of the State*.

28 Evan Davis, *Public Spending* (London: Penguin, 1998).

29 Vagliasindi, "Governance Arrangements for State Owned Enterprises," 8.

30 Amir Hefetz and Mildred Warner, "Privatization and Its Reverse: Explaining the Dynamics of the Government Contracting Process," *Journal of Public Administration Research and Theory* 14, no. 2 (2004): 171–90, at 172.

31 Ibid.

32 Ibid., 184.

33 See B. Guy Peters and Donald J. Savoie, *Taking Stock: Assessing Public Sector Reforms* (Montreal: McGill-Queen's University Press, 1998): 3–4.

34 Keith Dowding, *The Civil Service* (London: Routledge, 1995): 92–99.

# 9

# FREEDOM, RESPONSIBILITY, AND PRIVATIZATION

## ERIC MACGILVRAY

### I. Privatization and Freedom

Any discussion of "privatization" presupposes the existence of a modern state which, to use Max Weber's terms, successfully asserts a monopoly over the legitimate use of force within a given territory.[1] Before the modern state came into being, there was no clear line to be drawn between the public and private domains— between the king's private estate and his public office, for example.[2] And when we enter a realm in which the modern state's monopoly on force is incomplete or nonexistent—the realm of international trade, for instance—then it becomes difficult once again to draw a clear distinction between public and private actors.[3] Even within a modern state it would seem to be an open question whether anything is, properly speaking, "private," since the existence of a private sphere depends on the will, or at least the forbearance, of whomever controls that state. This at least was Thomas Hobbes's view of the matter; he writes that "in cases where the Soveraign has prescribed no rule, there the Subject hath the Liberty to do, or forbeare, according to his own discretion," and "such Liberty is in some places more, and in some lesse; and in some times more, in other times lesse, according as they that have the Soveraignty shall think most convenient."[4]

If a discussion about the boundary between public and private presupposes the existence of a modern state, a discussion about how the boundary *should* be drawn presupposes the existence of a liberal state. That is, while all modern states recognize a de facto distinction between public and private, the idea that there is a *principled* distinction to be drawn between the two domains—one that depends on something other than the will or administrative capacity of the state itself (what it "shall think most convenient")—is peculiar to, and is indeed a defining feature of, liberal polities. In other words, in a liberal state certain activities that might in principle be of interest to the state, and that could in principle be placed under its control, are nevertheless left in the hands of private actors—and the state's performance of functions that could in principle be performed by private actors comes with certain moral strings attached. Where and how the line between "public" and "private" should be drawn is of course a matter of substantial controversy at any given time and of substantial change over time—to talk about privatization is necessarily to talk about cases—but the idea that it should be drawn *somewhere*, and for something more than pragmatic reasons, is, again, a defining feature of liberal polities.

What criteria should we use to decide whether the performance of a particular social function or the provision of a particular social good is properly "public" or not—or, more precisely, to decide how the balance between public and private considerations should be struck in a given case? The value that liberals have traditionally appealed to in answering this question is freedom or liberty, from which the word "liberal" itself is of course derived. For liberals (unlike for Hobbes), a commitment to the value of freedom entails the acceptance of certain substantive limits on public authority and the way in which it can be exercised. The appeal to freedom may seem to raise more questions than it answers, since the question of what freedom means, or should mean, is famously fraught both among liberals and between liberals and non-liberals. In this essay, I will argue that much of this confusion arises from the fact that the liberal understanding of freedom is internally complex. In particular, I will argue that by attributing or extending liberal freedom to individuals we are in effect doing two things: on the one hand, defining and creating the conditions under which they can properly be held responsible for what they do, and on the other hand, carving out a social space within which the demands of responsible agency are relaxed or absent (section II).[5] As we will see, the distinction between these two dimensions of liberal freedom—which for the sake of convenience I will call *republican* and *market* freedom, respectively—maps rather neatly onto the distinction between the "public" and "private" domains in a liberal polity (section III).[6]

Once we see that the question of whether a given public function should be privatized—or a given domain of private conduct publicized—is a question about the proper allocation of responsibility for social outcomes, it becomes possible to draw three conceptual distinctions that should inform any discussion of privatization: first, a distinction between the *abdication* and the *delegation* of public responsibility; second, a distinction between the de jure and de facto existence of private non-responsibility; and third, a distinction between the *first-order* and *second-order* considerations that bear on the decision whether or not to delegate public responsibilities to private actors in a given case (section IV). As we will see (section V), in addition to helping to remove certain kinds of conceptual confusion, a focus on the internal complexity of liberal freedom also helps to remove a specific kind of ideological bias that infects debates about privatization. Freedom is of course an ideologically powerful word in our political culture, and in debates about privatization the language of freedom is typically deployed rather one-sidedly on the "privatizing" side of the ledger: through appeals to the value of limited government, free enterprise, market competition, and so on.[7] Once we recognize that market freedom is only one aspect of liberal freedom (albeit a crucial one), and that republican and market freedom each entail the imposition of a kind of social authority, we are able to move beyond the rather abstract and sterile debate about the proper relationship between freedom and public authority, and to focus instead on the question of how responsibility should be assigned in different domains.

## II. Two Concepts of Liberty

When we ask whether someone is free to do something—or whether, having done it, they did it freely—we may be asking two different and seemingly contradictory things. To begin with, we may be asking whether it would be appropriate to hold them responsible for what they have done, or whether they can properly take responsibility (for example, in the form of credit or blame) for having done it.[8] In other words, we may want to know whether they are properly subject to what P. F. Strawson calls the "reactive attitudes" on which our practices of holding responsible depend.[9] This way of thinking raises two broad and difficult sets of questions. One set of questions has to do with the agent him- or herself: whether they are capable of making responsible choices in general (are they a child, an addict, or mentally deficient in some way?), whether they were in full possession of their faculties when they made a particular choice (were they intoxicated, sleepwalking, or hypnotized?), whether they were aware of the consequences of the choices that they made (were they ignorant, manipulated, or deceived?), and so on. In short, when we ask whether someone did something freely, or whether they were free to do something, one thing that we could be asking is whether they are (or were) a responsible agent, however we define that term. It follows that one thing that we could be saying when we say that we want to *make* someone free (or more free) is that we want to help them to become a (more) responsible agent: to ensure that they are mentally sound, properly informed, not subject to manipulation, and so on.

A second and equally difficult set of questions raised by the idea of freedom as responsible choice has to do with the social context in which the agent acts. Most if not all of our decisions are shaped, explicitly or implicitly, by the expected costs and benefits of acting in one way rather than another. Do we act freely—can we properly be held responsible for our choices—insofar as our behavior is influenced by these kinds of considerations? Do I act freely when I pay my taxes, take a detour to avoid a traffic jam, use "proper" table manners, or call my sister on her birthday? What about when I pay off an extortionist, take a detour to avoid an unsafe neighborhood, observe "proper" gender norms, or refrain from expressing an unpopular opinion? In order to answer any of these questions in the affirmative we have to tell some kind of story about the relationship that we stand in with respect to the constraints in question, in particular one that establishes that we are in some sense responsible for their existence: because we played a role, or could have played a role, in creating them, because we endorse their content, or would do so on reflection, because we are able to contest them when we disagree, and so on. In other words, we are free in this sense if and to the extent that we are *self-governing* in one of the many possible senses of that term.

For the sake of convenience, and following much precedent, I will call this first kind of freedom *republican freedom,* because it is concerned with the question of how we govern ourselves and thereby make ourselves into agents who can properly be held responsible for what they do. As Philip Pettit, the leading contemporary philosopher of republicanism, puts it, "There is an *a priori* connection" between freedom and responsibility: "someone who did not see why that connection had to obtain would fail to understand what freedom was or what holding someone responsible was."[10] Pettit emphasizes that freedom so understood "has a social as well as a psychological aspect" which "takes us beyond the realm of free will, traditionally conceived, and into politically relevant matters": "From the point of view of those of us in any such [republican] collectivity, the things that the social integrate judges and intends are things that *we* judge and intend; they are not matters of merely impersonal record."[11] Thomas Nagel argues along similar lines that autonomy requires "the extension of ethics into politics," and in particular that we "find ourselves faced with the choices we want to be faced with, in a world that we can want to live in."[12] The converse is true in cases when we do not intend and cannot control or predict the social constraints that we face: all things being equal, we are less likely to think that it would be proper to hold someone responsible for the consequences of their actions if they are obeying the (possibly implicit) wishes of the secret police under a repressive regime than if they are acting within a well-designed and properly enforced system of law which they played (or could have played) a role in making.

Of course responsible agency and republican government do not necessarily entail one another. As the examples mentioned above suggest, some of the conditions that can diminish responsibility, such as the presence of mental illness, are agent-specific. Others are the product of factors such as upbringing, environment, and personal experience that it may not be feasible or desirable for a republican government to regulate. Many people will fail to take advantage of the conditions for responsible agency even when they are present—and again it may not be feasible or desirable for a republican government to compel them to do so. It would therefore be more accurate to say that republican government is a necessary but not a sufficient condition for personal responsibility. The converse is also true, which is why questions about the necessary abilities, education, and conduct of free citizens—often discussed collectively under the heading of "civic virtue"—have always played a central role in republican political thought.[13] The devil is in the details: what it means to be free in this sense will depend on the kind of story that we tell about how the conditions of self-government should be met, and not all such stories will be equally attractive or plausible. Indeed, as my use of the word *story* may suggest, any particular claim that a person or people is self-governing, in the sense of being responsible for (some of) the constraints that it faces, will be contestable in principle and almost certainly contested in fact. Trying to get this right is one of the main things that a liberal politics is about. But as we will now see, the claim that freedom consists in the *absence* of such constraints is equally open to dispute—and poses an equally daunting problem of institutional design.

As I have pointed out, it is rarely if ever the case that we act in the absence of constraints, even if we only consider constraints that are imposed directly or indirectly by other people, as most theories of freedom do.[14] For example, I may be free to choose how to spend my money, but what I can afford to buy is constrained by the choices of all of the other buyers (including the buyers or potential buyers of my own labor and other resources), which add up to an overall pattern of prices that I do not control. I may be free to choose what route to take when I drive to work, but how long it takes me to get there will be constrained by the choices of all of the other drivers, which add up to an overall pattern of traffic that I do not control. I may be free to choose whom to associate with and how to act in a variety of social contexts, but I do not control how other people will react, for better or worse, to the company that I keep or the things that I do. In such cases I am free in the sense that I am the one who decides what to do given what everyone else is doing, or given what I expect them to do; I decide how to respond to the pattern of potential costs and benefits that is created by other people's choices. But I am not free in the sense that I control the pattern itself; indeed, when (or to the extent that) people enjoy this kind of freedom in roughly equal measure, the result is that a pattern of outcomes—with a corresponding pattern of potential costs and benefits—is realized that *no one* can predict or control, and often that no one intended. There is no story to be told here about self-government even in principle.

The flip side of this line of argument is that my decisions affect other people in ways that they do not control: when I choose what to spend money on, which way to drive to work, whom to associate with, or how to act, my choices have a marginal effect on the overall pattern of prices, traffic, association, and behavior—and, again, often an effect that I did not intend. The distinguishing feature of this kind of freedom is thus not the absence of constraint *on* choice: my choices are constrained, as I have pointed out, by everyone else's choices. Nor is it the exercise of control *over* choice: I can act recklessly, compulsively, ignorantly, or out of sheer habit and still act "freely" in this sense. Freedom consists here rather in the absence of responsibility *for* choice: one is free in this sense if and to the extent that one is not accountable to anyone else for what one does, except by choice. To put the point in slightly more technical terms, one is free in this sense if one is allowed to impose costs on other people without being answerable to them for doing so. I decide what price I am willing to sell my house for, and if I lower my neighbors' property values or raise their property taxes in doing so then that is my business. I decide which way to drive to work, and if I waste gas or contribute to a traffic jam in doing so then that is my business. I decide how to respond to the various social pressures that I face—whom to associate with, whose approval to seek, and whose disapproval to ignore—and if I offend some people or encourage what some people regard as bad behavior in doing so then that is my business.

For the sake of convenience, and again following much precedent, I will call this kind of freedom *market freedom*, because it is concerned with allowing people to decide for themselves how to respond to the pattern of potential costs and benefits that they face. As we have seen, the word *market* in this sense can be used to refer to a wide range of social spaces that have little if anything to do with the exchange of commodities—it is similar in this respect to Friedrich Hayek's similarly expansive use of the term "catallaxy."[15] From the standpoint of the individual actor, a market is, again, any domain of conduct in which one can decide for oneself how to respond to the various opportunities and hazards that social life presents, thereby imposing costs on other people without being answerable to them for doing so. (The "individual actor" in question may of course be a corporate entity rather than a "natural" individual; for example a firm or a voluntary association. As we will see, this fact is often crucial in the context of debates about privatization.) From the standpoint of society as a whole, a market is any domain of conduct in which the unsupervised, unregulated, and uncoordinated behavior of individual actors gives rise to an overall pattern of outcomes that no one can predict, control, or take responsibility for; one that is, as Adam Ferguson famously put it, "the result of human action, but not the execution of any human design."[16] Every decision that we make in a "market" has a marginal effect on the overall pattern, but we enjoy market freedom not because we are (in some sense) responsible for that pattern, but rather precisely because we are not: the effects of our choices, and sometimes even the choices themselves, are morally—and often literally—invisible to other people.

### III. Public and Private

Liberalism as I understand it—and, I think, as it was understood by the most admirable and influential liberals of the past—is the political ideology that holds republican and market freedom together in a single political vision, defines their respective limits, and seeks to maintain a fruitful tension between them. As I have suggested, it is this internal complexity of liberal freedom that gives rise to the distinction between "public" and "private" in liberal political thought and practice: liberal freedom depends on the existence of a social space within which citizens can properly be held responsible *for* their actions (the "public" realm), and of a social space within which they are nevertheless not responsible *to* anyone else for what they do, except by choice (the "private" realm). It follows that liberal freedom, like liberal society itself, has two distinct and complementary dimensions, which give rise to two distinct and complementary moral projects: on the one hand, to create the social conditions that make responsible agency possible, and on the other hand to carve out a social space within which the demands of responsible agency are relaxed or absent.

Liberal thinkers, and thinkers who have been inspired by liberal ideals, have sometimes tried to collapse the tension between these two projects in one direction or the other—to treat either responsibility or non-responsibility as being not only a necessary but a sufficient condition for the enjoyment of freedom. I want to argue, however, that there is no way to resolve the tension without stepping outside the non-utopian bounds of a liberal politics. Our aim in theorizing about freedom should therefore not be to determine which of these conceptions is the correct or superior one, but rather to determine what their proper spheres of application might be. Liberal politics consists, in short, of an ongoing debate about the proper boundary between public and private; about what we should hold each other responsible for and how, and thus (conversely) about what the extent of market freedom should be.

We should be careful not to reify these ideal-typical categories; responsibility is a continuous, not a binary, variable, and so we must talk about the *extent* to which a given domain of conduct is "public" or "private" in this sense. It should be clear to begin with that the enjoyment of market freedom depends on a prior guarantee of republican freedom; that is, on the existence of a set of well-enforced rules that make orderly social life possible. It should also be clear (though here the details are more controversial) that the domain of market freedom can appropriately be limited in a variety of ways for the sake of republican freedom. The public and private realms are in this sense interpenetrating: commercial markets depend for their proper functioning on the existence of well-defined property rights and of publicly enforced guarantees against theft, force, and fraud, and all polities regulate or otherwise limit the costs that market actors can impose on other people, for example through minimum wage and maximum hours laws, workplace and product safety laws, anti-discrimination laws, environmental protection laws, and so on. The same is true, *mutatis mutandis*, of markets in the broader sense that I have described: our ability to participate effectively in any "unregulated" social space requires that we have certain guarantees regarding (at a minimum) our personal safety and the reliability of our potential partners. We have therefore decided as a society (not without controversy and struggle) that people should be held responsible— that we will hold each other collectively responsible—for imposing certain kinds of costs on others. I am free to decide what to spend my money on, but I am not allowed to buy something that is not recognized as a legal commodity, such as a person, narcotics, or leaded gasoline. I am free to decide what route to take to work, but I have to stay on public thoroughfares and obey the relevant traffic laws. I am free to decide whom to associate with and which social norms to observe, but I am not allowed to join (what society has defined as) a subversive organization, or to engage in (what society has defined as) obscene or indecent behavior.

Why shouldn't we *always* hold people responsible for their choices, at least in principle, if those choices impose costs on other people without their consent? Why should we allow people to consume wastefully, say hurtful things, neglect their health, or spoil their children? There are a number of reasons that we might have for "privatizing" a function that is currently performed by the state—or for leaving a function that could in principle be performed by the state in private hands—only a few of which are rooted in the neoclassical economic theory that typically provides the rationale for privatization efforts:

(1) *Indifference*. A given domain of conduct is thought to be too insignificant to be worth regulating.

(2) *Tradition*: There is a longstanding practice of letting people make their own decisions in a given domain, and we are unwilling to disrupt those habits of private decision-making, or it simply does not occur to us to do so.

(3) *Conservatism*: We defer as a matter of principle to existing habits of private decision-making, with the thought that there must be a good reason why they exist even if we cannot articulate what it is.

(4) *Infeasibility*: The necessary administrative or coercive capacity to regulate a given domain of conduct does not exist, or it would be unacceptably costly to develop and exercise such a capacity.

(5) *Epistemic modesty*: We do not believe that we would be able to make a good rule if we set out to regulate a given domain of conduct, because we lack the necessary knowledge or judgment.

(6) *Stability*: We disagree so deeply about what the rule should

be that any effort to regulate a given domain would create an unacceptable level of social conflict.

(7) *Prudence:* Imposing a rule in a given domain would give the regulating authority too much power, or set a dangerous precedent for future cases.

(8) *Dispersal of power:* Allowing people to make their own decisions in a given domain would end or undermine a monopoly on certain goods by a dominant class or faction.

(9) *Diversity:* Allowing people to make their own decisions in a given domain allows for a wider range of outcomes than a centralized or "one size fits all" approach.

(10) *Serendipity:* Allowing people to make their own decisions in a given domain would lead to outcomes that cannot be foreseen and that might be deemed beneficial.

(11) *Efficiency:* Allowing people to make their own decisions in a given domain would tend to bring about an optimal distribution of scarce resources (cognitive, material, or otherwise).

(12) *Experimentalism:* Allowing people to make their own decisions in a given domain would make it possible to test alternatives and identify best practices, thereby improving the quality of decision-making over time.

(13) *Perfectionism:* Allowing people to make their own decisions in a given domain would teach them a valuable lesson in self-discipline or self-reliance.

(14) *Anti-paternalism:* People should be allowed to make their own decisions in a given domain because they know their own interests best.

(15) *Sovereignty:* People have a right to make their own decisions in a given domain.

Needless to say the force of each of these reasons, and of whatever other reasons we might invoke, will vary substantially across domains and over time; again, to talk about privatization is necessarily to talk about cases. Which decisions seem insignificant; which traditions seem worth respecting; what it is feasible or prudent to regulate; what we are willing to fight about; how important we think diversity, efficiency, and self-reliance are; how well we think people know their own interests; even what rights we think people have: we disagree about each of these issues now, and our views about them have changed significantly over time and are likely to continue to change going forward. This is not to deny that we have relatively fixed views on certain questions. There are domains of action in which we can agree that it would be illiberal to hold people publicly responsible for their actions—for example, with regard to their religious beliefs and practices (within certain limits)—just as there are domains of action in which we can agree that it would be illiberal not to do so—for example, with regard to their treatment of other people's property (again, within certain limits). Religion is a private matter and property is private property; these are, for the time being, matters of settled judgment in liberal thought. But the caveat is crucial: judgment is settled through experience, and the lessons of experience are subject to revision through further experience over time. It would require a gross reification of terms to suggest that the property rights and religious freedoms that the citizens of liberal societies enjoy today are the same rights and freedoms, practically speaking, as the ones that were defended by the "classical" liberal thinkers of the seventeenth, eighteenth, and nineteenth centuries, and even the most nostalgic liberal today would probably not be willing on reflection to trade today's bundle of rights and freedoms for that of 1690, 1790, or 1890.

## IV. PRIVATIZATION IN PRACTICE: THREE DISTINCTIONS

According to the theoretical framework that I have outlined, to expand the domain of market freedom by "privatizing" a given domain of conduct is to transfer decision-making power from a domain in which society holds itself collectively responsible, at least in principle, for the social outcomes that are realized to a domain in which this kind of responsibility does not exist. More precisely, since responsibility is never perfectly enforced and non-responsibility is never complete, to "privatize" is to shift the balance of considerations from greater public responsibility toward greater private non-responsibility. One kind of freedom is lost in such a shift—republican freedom, the freedom not to be subject to irresponsible or arbitrary power—and another kind of freedom is gained—market freedom, the freedom to make choices without being answerable to others for the choices that one makes. As we have seen, and as any citizen of a liberal society knows, liberals do not agree about how exactly the tradeoffs between these two kinds of freedom should be made—that is what a liberal politics is about—but they do agree that republican freedom should have priority in the procedural sense that the tradeoffs should be made in publicly visible and contestable ways and for publicly avowable reasons. In other words, not only is republican freedom a necessary condition for the enjoyment of market freedom, but a liberal society is one in which the rules that guarantee and limit market behavior are created and enforced in a way that is consistent with the demands of self-government, however those are defined.[17]

As I suggested at the outset, this analysis of liberal freedom allows us to draw three conceptual distinctions that should inform any discussion of privatization. The first distinction is between the *abdication* and the *delegation* of public responsibility. By "abdication" I have in mind cases in which a given domain of conduct is genuinely privatized—deemed no longer to be a matter of public concern—and by "delegation" cases in which there is a shift from the direct to the indirect imposition of public responsibility; that is, from the performance of a given set of functions by the state itself to the performance of those functions by "private" actors working under state supervision. Examples of abdication include traditional liberal policies such as the disestablishment of religion, the relaxation of rules governing sexual mores and behavior, and the elimination of price and wage controls. Again it is important to emphasize that even in these paradigmatic cases the abdication of public responsibility is not complete: religious practices are in fact restricted or prohibited when they conflict with public purposes; for example, with regard to the ceremonial use of certain intoxicants, or the wearing of traditional religious clothing or the display of religious symbols in certain contexts. Sexual behavior is regulated in a variety of ways; for example, through the regulation or prohibition of prostitution and the legal incentivization of marriage. And of course "market" prices are shaped (some would say distorted) by minimum wage laws, the taxation of "vice," and a variety of other mechanisms. Nevertheless, in each of these cases domains of conduct that were once seen as being (perhaps self-evidently) matters of public concern have instead been left largely to the discretion of private actors, and the domain of market freedom has correspondingly increased. The overall pattern of religious, sexual, and economic behavior is therefore and to that extent something for which no one in particular can be held responsible. It is an interesting exercise to consider which of the reasons for privatization listed in section III were decisive in each case.

Some of the cases that are commonly discussed in the scholarly literature on privatization fall squarely into the "abdication" category, most notably the privatization of state-owned enterprises when this entails a genuine transfer of control from state to market. However, many cases are better described as involving the delegation rather than the abdication of public responsibility, and in such cases "outsourcing" seems to me to be a better (because less misleading) term to use than "privatization."[18] Consider for example the distinction between a public educational system that is staffed by state employees and administered (at least formally) by elected officials who are accountable to the public, and a private educational system in which each school has the freedom to choose its own means of meeting a set of state-defined educational standards, and elected officials are in turn accountable to the public for determining what those standards should be and how much leeway "private" schools should have in meeting them. Or consider the distinction between a mail delivery system that is directly administered by the state, like the U.S. Postal Service or the U.K. Royal Mail before 2011, and a system, like the Royal Mail after 2011, that is "privately" administered but legally required to charge uniform rates, guarantee universal delivery, and so on.[19] In each case the state continues to take responsibility for ensuring that a certain pattern of outcomes is reached, and insofar as this pattern is successfully realized in a way that is consistent with the demands of self-government, republican freedom is not lost or compromised. Indeed, the state may be *better* able to monitor and control the behavior of a "privately" administered educational or postal system than of a sprawling public bureaucracy; this, at least, is the hope of many privatizers.

Delegation can of course take a variety of forms depending on the nature of the case and of the public purpose(s) in question. We can distinguish, for example, between state regulation of domains of conduct that could in principle function more like markets—as is arguably the case with respect to education and mail delivery—and state regulation of "natural monopolies," such as electric and water service, where a well-functioning market arguably could not exist even in principle, and where the discretion of the "private" actors in question is therefore typically more limited. We can distinguish further between regulatory schemes that are directly administered by the state, privately administered regulatory schemes whose existence is tacitly approved or at least tolerated by the state (for example, the film ratings that are issued by the Motion Picture Association of America [MPAA]), and regulatory schemes that operate more or less outside the jurisdiction of any state, but on which states and their citizens nevertheless rely (for example, the product standards that are issued by the International Organization for Standardization [ISO]). Despite the considerable variation among these cases, the underlying normative question is the same: whether a public purpose is being pursued in a way that is consistent with the demands of republican freedom.

In addition to taking a variety of possible forms, the delegation of public responsibility can of course also go awry in a variety of ways. This brings us to the second distinction that should be kept in view in debates about privatization: the distinction between cases in which a public decision has been made to create or permit a domain of non-responsible behavior—when there has been a publicly authorized abdication of public responsibility—and cases in which a de facto condition of non-responsibility exists despite a de jure commitment to public responsibility. Whereas the first outcome is perfectly acceptable from a liberal point of view, the second is not. There are two basic ways in which such a situation can arise. The first and more obvious is when the state itself is non-responsible or non-transparent to the public, or to other parts of itself; when, for example, a public bureaucracy successfully ignores or subverts the will of the elected officials to which it is nominally responsible—or when elected officials ignore or subvert the will of the public to which *they* are nominally responsible. This is often portrayed as a problem with republican government—it is arguably *the* problem with republican government—to which privatization offers a possible solution. However, the delegation of state functions to private actors can itself undermine, and can indeed be intended to undermine, republican government. It may be convenient, for example, for the state to allow certain public functions to be performed by agents who are "off the books" politically speaking, as is arguably the case with the extensive and increasing use of private contractors by the United States military. This can allow the footprint of a given military operation to seem smaller than it actually is, and to make casualties and costs seem correspondingly lower, thereby insulating the state (and thus, *a fortiori*, elected officials) from responsibility for any mistakes or wrongdoing.[20]

Moreover, the private actors to whom public functions are delegated may be just as capable of subverting the will of the elected officials to whom they are nominally responsible as a public bureaucracy would be. This brings us to the second way in which formally responsible actors may fail to be so in practice: via regulatory capture, when a system of regulation whose purpose is to induce "private" actors to serve the public interest is instead manipulated to serve the interests of the private actors themselves. Such capture is made especially likely, of course, by the fact that the private actors in question have a direct and focused interest in how the regulatory regime is administered, whereas the public interest that they are supposed to serve is typically indirect and diffuse.[21] It is beyond the scope of the paper to consider how this problem might be solved or mitigated, except to say (unhelpfully) that the answer will vary substantially across cases. However, the possibility of regulatory capture shows why it is so important to keep the conceptual distinction between the abdication and the delegation of public responsibility clearly in view. In cases of actual or potential regulatory capture, the question is not whether the function in question is a "private" one; by hypothesis it is still regarded as properly public, which is of course why the regulatory regime exists in the first place. Rather, the question is how the public interest would best be served. Framing the issue as a matter of "privatization" *tout court* muddies the waters by making it possible for the private actors in question to make the ideologically powerful but normatively inappropriate appeal to market freedom, and thus to non-responsibility: to argue, for example, that a given regulatory regime is too burdensome or intrusive.[22]

This brings us to the third and most fundamental distinction that should be kept in view in debates about privatization:

the distinction between the second-order question of whether a given domain of conduct is, properly speaking, a matter of public concern—and thus whether the relevant actors should be held publicly responsible for the outcomes that are reached—and the first-order question of whether responsibility for pursuing that end should be placed in "public" or "private" hands. The view that all packages and addresses should be treated the same is in effect a claim that citizens should be treated equally along a certain dimension, that mail delivery is to that extent a public purpose, and that whoever delivers the mail should be held responsible for performing it in the right way. The same is true, *mutatis mutandis*, of schools and armies, which have their own distinct public purposes. As we have seen, the observation that a public purpose is being pursued is perfectly consistent with the claim that responsibility for performing it should be delegated to private (i.e., non-state) actors. The question is what further public purpose(s) would be served by doing so. The most common argument in favor of privatization is that it provides an opportunity to realize efficiencies or (what may amount to the same thing) to cut costs. This is of course a legitimate and important public purpose *ceteris paribus*, although we should keep in mind that the costs in question are usually labor costs, and that the privatization of state functions often has the predictable (and intended) effect of lowering wages and weakening public sector labor unions. Insofar as high wages and the existence of strong unions are themselves legitimate and important public purposes (which is of course a matter of debate), the question is not simply a matter of striking the right balance between public and private authority, but rather of adjudicating between competing public purposes.

A deeper worry arises in cases when there is a conflict between the public purposes that a given function is meant to serve and the foreseeable consequences of delegating responsibility for performing it. I have already pointed out that the outsourcing of military functions to private contractors can undermine republican government by reducing transparency and accountability. A more egregious example of such a conflict exists with regard to the privatization of prisons and prison services. The economic incentives of the private prison industry are of course to fill as many beds as possible at the lowest possible cost. The rehabilitation of prisoners, the prevention of recidivism, and indeed the reduction of crime and incarceration more generally—all quite uncontroversial public purposes *ceteris paribus*—are from this point of view simply bad for business. Moreover, experience has shown that the effort to cut costs often leads to inhumane living conditions within prisons—an outcome which, it must be said, is not always politically unpopular—and thus to avoidable suffering and even death among inmates. Finally, the prison industry has an economic incentive to shift costs onto the inmates themselves whenever possible, an example of the more general tendency in privatization efforts to shift costs from taxpayers to "consumers." The difference in the case of prisons, of course, is that the relevant population is not only disproportionately poor, but is quite literally a captive audience. The existence of monopoly power leads to predictably inflated prices, and the resulting inequities break down along equally predictable lines of race and class. On the whole it is hard to think of a case in which the kind of behavior that would be considered blameless among profit-seeking market actors is more obviously in conflict with the purposes that the performance of a given public function is meant to serve.[23]

## V. FREEDOM AND RESPONSIBILITY

I hope to have shown that by focusing on the internal complexity of liberal freedom, and in particular on the balance between public responsibility and private non-responsibility in which it consists, we can dispel some of the conceptual confusion that surrounds debates about privatization. In particular, by placing the focus on the question of whether an actor is responsible for performing a public function, rather than on the question of whether that actor happens to be employed by the state or not—by distinguishing, in other words, between the *abdication* and the *delegation* of public responsibility—we make it possible to ask two further questions about how "privatization" works, or might work, in practice. The first question is whether a de facto condition of non-responsibility exists despite a de jure commitment on the part of "private" actors to assume responsibility for performing a given public function; whether we are dealing, for example, with a case of (objectionable) non-transparency or of regulatory capture. The second and more fundamental question is whether there is a mismatch between the public purposes in question and the incentives that the private actors who are responsible for performing it can reasonably be expected to have; whether, for example, the imposition of "market discipline" can be expected to lead to perverse policy outcomes.

I am of course far from being the first person to point out that the privatization of public functions can lead to a breach of the public trust. What the present analysis helps us to see, I hope, is that from a liberal point of view these breaches result in a loss of (republican) freedom. We have decided as a society that we have a collective interest in how children are educated, how wars are prosecuted, and how criminals are punished, even if we are not parents, soldiers, or victims of crime ourselves. When these functions are performed by "private" actors who we do not control, and in pursuit of ends that we have not approved, we cannot properly be held responsible for the consequences that result, and are in that straightforward sense unfree. It follows that the transfer of authority from state to market does not result in an increase in freedom as such, but in the conversion of one kind of freedom into another. By expanding the domain in which we are not publicly responsible for the consequences of our choices, we do not gain the freedom to act in the absence of constraint—a freedom that rarely if ever exists in modern society. Rather, we gain the freedom to decide for ourselves how to respond to the constraints that we face—constraints that are in large part generated by the choices that everyone else makes, and for which no one in particular can be held responsible. Conversely, by expanding the domain in which we are publicly responsible for the consequences of our choices, we declare a certain domain of conduct to be of sufficient public concern that we take collective responsibility for the outcomes that are reached and the constraints that are thereby generated. As we have seen, strictly speaking, every domain of social conduct is of public concern in at least the limited sense that the state is ultimately responsible for guaranteeing the safety of those who are engaged in it. Beyond that point, it is a matter of political debate in which cases and to what extent individuals should be allowed to impose costs on others without their consent.

I began this essay by invoking Max Weber, who provided an early and influential analysis of how the differentiation of the public and private functions came about. I will conclude by invoking Weber again, this time in an ethical rather than a sociological key. Weber's most important contribution to normative political thought is probably his distinction between the "ethic of responsibility" [*Verantwortungsethik*], which demands that we try to ensure that the foreseeable consequences of our actions are as good as possible, and the "ethic of conviction" [*Gesinnungsethik*], which demands that we adhere to certain principles of action whatever the consequences.[24] Discussion of the ethic of responsibility typically focuses on the problem of "dirty hands" that it raises; the fact that, as Weber puts it, "the attainment of 'good' ends is bound to the fact that one must be willing to pay the price of using morally dubious means"—most notably violence. However, Weber does not begin his discussion of the two ethics by talking about violence, but rather by calling attention to the "sense of proportion" that responsible political action requires, and to the fact that "the final result of political action often . . . stands in completely inadequate and often even paradoxical relation to its original meaning."[25] This emphasis on judgment, fallibilism, and tragic choices is very much in the spirit of the argument that I have offered here. Debates about privatization are too often fought on the field of Weberian conviction: reducing the sphere of governmental authority—or preserving the governmental status quo—is treated as an end in itself, whatever the consequences might be. Once we see that the problem of drawing the proper boundaries between public and private is a matter of striking a balance between two complementary values—two conceptions of freedom—we are in a far better position to do justice to the normative complexities of the issue, and to the liberal tradition from which the debate itself springs.

## NOTES

1 This is of course Weber's definition of what a state is: see for example Max Weber, "Politics as a Vocation" (1918) in *From Max Weber: Essays in Sociology*, trans. and ed. H. H. Gerth and C. Wright Mills (New York: Oxford University Press, 1946): 78.

2 Weber was one of the first and finest students of how this differentiation of public and private functions came about; see in particular the discussion of the transition from patrimonial/patriarchal to legal/bureaucratic authority in his *Economy and Society: An Outline of Interpretive Sociology*, ed. Guenther Roth and Claus Wittich (Berkeley, CA: University of California Press, 1968), part 2, chapters 10–14, and cf. part 1, chapter 3.

3 For example, the growing use of investor-state dispute settlement (ISDS) clauses in bilateral investment treaties, which has led to a substantial erosion of the sovereign authority of states to manage their own economic affairs, is driven by the credible threat on the part of international corporations to exit (or to refrain from entering) a given state's territory—and, of course, by the desire of those states to attract foreign direct investment. For further discussion and citations, see Henry Farrell's contribution to this volume.

4 Thomas Hobbes, *Leviathan*, ed. Richard Tuck (New York: Cambridge University Press, 1996 [1651]): 152 (chapter 21).

5 Despite first appearances, these two categories do not make up an exhaustive typology of human action: the slave—the paradigmatically unfree person—cannot properly be held responsible for his actions because he is (at least in principle) a mere instrument of his master's will. Nor, of course, does the slave enjoy a domain of conduct in which he is *not* held responsible for his actions, because there is no part of a slave's life that is not (in principle) subject to his master's will.

6 I am working on a book, with the working title *Liberal Freedom*, in which I explore these issues in more detail. Much of the material in sections II and III is drawn from the book manuscript.

7 The most influential proponent of this usage is probably Milton Friedman; see in particular his seminal book *Capitalism and Freedom* (Chicago: University of Chicago Press, 1962), which provides both a theoretical rationale and a policymaking template for the privatization movements of the 1970s and 1980s.

8 This position should not be confused with the claim that an agent can only be made *unfree* by constraints for which *other* agents can be held morally responsible: see especially David Miller, "Constraints on Freedom," *Ethics* 94, no. 1 (1983): 66–86, and S. I. Benn and W. L. Weinstein, "Being Free to Act, and Being a Free Man," *Mind* 80, no. 218 (1971): 194–211.

9 P. F. Strawson, "Freedom and Resentment," *Proceedings of the British Academy* 48 (1962): 1–25.

10 Philip Pettit, *A Theory of Freedom: From the Psychology to the Politics of Agency* (New York: Oxford University Press, 2001): 18. Pettit's republican-

ism is described and defended at greater length in his *Republicanism: A Theory of Freedom and Government*, 2nd ed. (New York: Oxford University Press, 1999 [1997]), and more recently in *On the People's Terms: A Republican Theory and Model of Democracy* (New York: Cambridge University Press, 2012). For my own understanding of republican freedom, which is largely consonant with Pettit's, see Eric MacGilvray, *The Invention of Market Freedom* (New York: Cambridge University Press, 2011), esp. chapter 1.

11 Pettit, *A Theory of Freedom*, 4, 118 (emphasis added).

12 Thomas Nagel, *The View from Nowhere* (New York: Oxford University Press, 1986): 135–6. Nagel takes a Kantian position on the meaning of and necessary conditions for autonomy, but as I point out below, a republican need not be committed to such a view.

13 On the reciprocal relationship—or the many possible reciprocal relationships—between the practice of civic virtue and the control of arbitrary power, see MacGilvray, *The Invention of Market Freedom*, chapter 1 and *passim*.

14 The great exception is Hobbes, who argues that "LIBERTY, or FREEDOME, signifieth (properly) the absence of Opposition," that is, of "externall Impediments of motion," and that this definition "may be applyed no lesse to Irrationall, and Inanimate creatures, than to Rationall" (*Leviathan*, 145 [chapter 21]).

15 See for example Friedrich A. Hayek, *Law, Legislation and Liberty*, vol. 2: *The Mirage of Social Justice* (Chicago: University of Chicago Press, 1976): chapter 10.

16 Adam Ferguson, *An Essay on the History of Civil Society* (1767), ed. Fania Oz-Salzberger (New York: Cambridge University Press, 1995): 119 (part 3, section 2); cf. Hayek, *Law, Legislation and Liberty*, vol. 1: *Rules and Order* (Chicago: University of Chicago Press, 1976): 20, and Edna Ullmann-Margalit, "Invisible Hand Explanations," *Synthese* 39, no. 2 (1978): 263–91.

17 I do not mean to suggest that it is not important how these demands are defined, just that defining them lies beyond the scope of this essay.

18 In addition to being analytically more precise, this way of putting the point also allows debates about privatization (in the sense of delegation) to draw upon the extensive literature in business and economics on the pros and cons of "outsourcing" and the ways in which it is best deployed.

19 Analogous conditions have sometimes been imposed when state-owned airlines and railways were "privatized."

20 For further discussion and citations, see Laura Dickinson's contribution to this volume. The state can of course be justifiably non-transparent with regard to certain details of military strategy and tactics,

and with regard to certain matters of national security, but this kind of non-responsibility is usually temporally bounded.

21 The *locus classicus* is George Stigler's "The Theory of Economic Regulation," *Bell Journal of Economics and Management Science* 2, no. 1 (1971): 3–21; see also Mancur Olson's seminal *The Logic of Collective Action: Public Goods and the Theory of Groups* (Cambridge, MA: Harvard University Press, 1965).

22 A regulatory regime *would* count as objectionably burdensome if it hindered or prevented the relevant public purpose from being pursued. This is not, however, typically the form that the objection takes.

23 For a useful discussion of the ethics of prison privatization, and of incarceration more generally, see Sharon Dolovich, "State Punishment and Private Prisons," *Duke Law Journal* 55, no. 3 (2005): 437–546.

24 Weber, "Politics as a Vocation," 115ff.

25 Ibid., 121, 115, 117.

# 10

## IS RULE OF LAW AN EQUILIBRIUM WITHOUT (SOME) PRIVATE ENFORCEMENT?

### GILLIAN K. HADFIELD AND BARRY R. WEINGAST

### I. INTRODUCTION

Almost all theorizing about law begins with government. Ellickson sets out the conventional dividing line between social norms and law: law is the subset of norms that are created and enforced by governments.[1] Positive political theory takes the idea that law is the province of government for granted and focuses on the processes and principles by which the substance of law is determined.[2] Economic analysis of law focuses on the behavioral incentives created by public sanctions—fines, damages, imprisonment; the relational contracting literature, for example, distinguishes between formal contracting, meaning contracts enforced by the state, and informal contracting, meaning contracts enforced by reputation and repeat play.[3] Dixit explores the role of non-governmental mechanisms to enforce contracts and property rights, describing this as the study of "lawlessness and economics."[4]

The idea that law is fundamentally about government is at the core too of both theoretical and pragmatic work on the rule of law.[5] The rule of law is widely defined in terms of the control of government. Hayek defined the rule of law as "government . . . bound by rules fixed and announced beforehand."[6] The World Bank, like other international agencies, defines the rule of law as obtaining when "government itself is bound by the law,"[7] and access to justice is routinely defined in international debates as access to the resources needed to obtain the protections of, and protection from, the centralized enforcement agencies of government.

The widespread presumption that law is quintessentially the product of government makes law both a surprising and an ideal candidate for analysis through the lens of privatization. The concept of privatization is, at its core, paradoxical—it is defined as the transfer of government functions to the private sector, and yet it puts into play precisely the question of what is a government function. Privatization, both politically and as a matter of theory, grows out of a challenge to orthodoxy about what governments can, or should, do. It sends us back to first principles, to derive rather than assume the proper allocation of functions between public and private sector.

In a series of papers beginning with Hadfield and Weingast (2012), we have engaged this challenge in law.[8] We develop the what-is-law framework for analyzing law that begins not with government but with the question of how equilibrium social orders, in which behavior in a community is reliably patterned on shared rules, can be generated and sustained.

We take as our starting point the idea that the key feature that distinguishes legal order from other normative social orders, such as systems based on cultural norms, is that the rules can be authoritatively clarified and changed. This authoritative system distinguishes legal from other social orders of interest from an analytical point of view: in organic social orders, change is emergent; if law is established, there is an entity capable of changing rules and thereby shaping collective behavior to achieve some public (or private) end. By starting with this premise about the distinctive—and interesting—characteristics about law, we derive rather than presume what must be supplied by a centralized institution like a government. And we show that an equilibrium in which rules articulated by a centralized institution are effective—meaning people observe them—does not require a centralized enforcement authority. So long as the institution that articulates the rules displays a set of features that coordinate and incentivize ordinary individuals to bear the cost of punishing transgressions, enforcement can be left to private actors rather than a public agency.

We use the term *legal attributes* to identify those features that support an equilibrium in which enforcement is exclusively supplied by individual decisions to voluntarily help enforce the rules announced by a centralized institution. These attributes include features routinely understood in the legal philosophical literature as characteristic of the rule of law: general rules that are published, clear, and stable, applied in processes that are open and unbiased, and which produce results that are consistent with the rules as announced. But unlike the legal philosophical literature, the legal attributes we identify do not arise from normative claims about what features a regime properly called "legal" should possess.[9] Nor do they arise from a reliance on intuition to unpack the concept of "law" as it is used in ordinary, or even professional, language.[10] Rather, they arise from our positive analysis of how a community sustains an equilibrium based on centralized classification of conduct (distinguishing punishable from non-punishable actions) when enforcement requires the voluntary participation of ordinary citizens.

In our what-is-law approach, the legal attributes are necessary to secure coordination and incentive compatibility in a regime of fully decentralized enforcement. Without them, the effort to sustain an equilibrium based on centralized classification fails. A regime characterized by rule of law is the only equilibrium, we argue, when enforcement of public classifications relies exclusively on private enforcement. A failure to observe the rule of law destroys the equilibrium by destroying the incentives of individuals to enforce and their ability to coordinate.

Specifically, we ask, is there an equilibrium characterized by rule of law in a regime in which enforcement is fully centralized, that is, without any role for private ordering? Most political and economic theories of law take this form of enforcement for granted. But we think the taken-for-granted assumption—the normal assumption about government—is highly problematic. Indeed, we argue that the answer to our question is: no. With the power to authoritatively articulate and change the rules, any centralized classification institution faces an obvious and well-known moral hazard problem: namely, the persistent temptation to announce classifications that benefit those in charge. This is the basic premise of the economic model of behavior and the challenge of government: those granted the authority to govern face an incentive to turn that authority to their benefit.

Adam Smith illustrates this point in his *Wealth of Nations*. Smith explains that when the executive also serves as judge, he is unlikely to take an impartial view of cases in which he has a direct interest:

> When the judicial is united to the executive power, it is scarce possible that justice should not frequently be sacrificed to, what is vulgarly called, politics. The persons entrusted with the great interests of the state may, even without any corrupt views, sometimes imagine it necessary to sacrifice to those interests the rights of a private man. But upon the impartial administration of justice depends the liberty of every individual, the sense which he has of his own security. In order to make every individual feel himself perfectly secure in the possession of every right which belongs to him, it is not only necessary that the judicial should be separated from the executive power, but that it should be rendered as much as possible independent of that power.[11]

Our framework shows that, when those with control over classification entirely depend on voluntary private enforcement, an equilibrium in which classifications are implemented (rules are followed) is achieved only if those in charge of classification honor the rule of law. But if those in charge of classification also wield a monopoly over the legitimate use of force and are capable of securing compliance for *any* rule they announce—which is the presumption of centralized enforcement models of law—then there is no strategic reason for them to observe the rule of law. When the incentive arises, as it predictably will, to announce classifications at odds with announced rules or to engage in closed procedures or to announce a result driven not by impersonal reasoning but by personal favor or ambition, rulers can act on those incentives without sacrificing compliance. There will be an equilibrium in which individuals follow the rules, but it will not be characterized by the rule of law because the ruler can do better: secure compliance *and* take advantage of any private benefits available.

We build our argument as follows. In section II, we recap the what-is-law model of Hadfield and Weingast (2012), which demonstrates that the presence of the legal attributes that most legal theory has merely asserted are characteristic of legal orders, such as generality, clarity, and neutrality, can be derived from a minimal normative premise about what constitutes law in a setting where all enforcement is decentralized and private. That premise is that anything we want to productively define as law must, at a minimum, have the capacity deliberately to adapt the content of the rules without disrupting equilibrium. In section III, we turn to the question of our title, whether rule of law is an equilibrium in the absence of private ordering. We begin this section with a more careful treatment of the definition of the rule of law and what we mean by a rule of law equilibrium. We then consider whether a regime that has the capacity deliberately to adapt the content of rules but is not dependent on private enforcement must implement the rule of law in order to secure equilibrium. We argue that it does not. Section IV concludes our discussion with observations about the implications of this analysis for the project of building rule of law in the poor and developing countries around the world that lack productive legal order.

## II. PUTTING THE PRIVATE AT THE CENTER: THE WHAT-IS-LAW MODEL

All human societies are characterized by normative social order. This form of order identifies rules of conduct that partition acceptable conduct from unacceptable. Even the simplest human societies are chock-a-block with rules, about what can be eaten, worn, said, or done.[12]

In the simplest human societies, there is no public apparatus to enforce these rules; all rule enforcement is what we call private, carried out by ordinary individuals who make a voluntary choice about whether to participate in punishing rule violations or not. Private enforcement in these settings includes collective criticism, mocking, exclusion from benefits, ostracism and, sometimes, physical punishment.[13]

With the development of the state and its centralized and official enforcement apparatus,[14] much enforcement of law passes from the realm of the private to the public. But even in modern states, with elaborate centralized enforcement systems (police and prisons), much private enforcement of law takes place. Individuals who break the law (or who fail to comply with legal obligations such as those in contract) are sanctioned in the modern state in much the same way as early humans were sanctioned for violating social norms: by disapproval, criticism, and exclusion. Individuals who violate the law are turned down for jobs, excluded from private associations and networks, and are forced out of public offices; those who break contracts lose existing business relationships and earn a reputation that damages their prospects for new ones. Companies and other organizations that violate the law lose employees and customers and public contracts. For many, the risk of private sanction for rule violation is arguably as important in inducing compliance as the risk of public sanction.[15]

Even when enforcement is private, however, the transgressions that are punished can be fundamentally public, the product of social processes for determining what is acceptable and what is not. These processes distinguish the violation of a social norm from conduct that one individual simply objects to in another. An individual may personally object to a man wearing a skirt because he or she thinks it makes men look weak or not serious. But this objection is based on a social norm only if the individual's community collectively shares the view that men should not wear conventionally female clothing and, further, people of this community are willing to undertake costly actions to help police this norm.

In human societies before the development of sophisticated social and governance structures, the normative *classification* of conduct as wrongful (warranting punishment) is emergent, a result of repeated interactions of many members of a community. In a stable organic social order, we can identify what is punishable and what is not, but we cannot identify any formal or institutionalized source of classification. Classification occurs through informal group discussions or simply as a matter of practice.[16] Thus, the normative social order is not the product of directed enforcement action by public officials.

Normative classification in an organic social order can change in response to changing circumstances or knowledge, but change is itself organic. It emerges, or not, from shifts in informal discussions and changes in practice, often in the face of various forms of shocks (changes in exogenous variables). Given the radical egalitarianism that characterizes much of early human society,[17] no leaders exist who are capable of both announcing new classifications and inducing people to shift their enforcement activities from the old to the new. Classification is for this reason likely to be relatively slow to change and hard to channel. The people of Papua New Guinea, for example, have had for time out of mind a rule that only men can plant and harvest yams; only women plant and harvest sweet potatoes. A woman who plants yams may be beaten. A man who plants sweet potatoes will be ridiculed and shunned.[18] Even if his family is starving because the yam crop has failed, he will go perhaps a long time before touching the sweet potatoes. And even if the group moves to an area where yams are difficult to grow, it may take generations before the norm changes to accept routine male participation in the production of sweet potatoes.

Both Hart[19] and Fuller[20] attribute the development of formal legal systems to the need for a more deliberate means of adapting normative classification to changing or complex circumstances. They both imagine the possibility that a simple and stable society of homogeneous participants could exist based solely on what Hart calls primary rules of behavior; that is, the rules regulating behavior in a given society. But both scholars propose that such a society would be slow to adapt to changes in the environment or circumstances or population. It is then, they say, that Hart's *secondary rules* are likely to emerge. These are the meta-rules that establish the validity of primary rules, often in the face of dispute— resolving ambiguity and disagreement about which rules are valid ones, how a rule is validly changed, and how it is to be applied in concrete, sometimes novel, circumstances. In a society with a stable legal order in Hart's sense, the secondary rules are effective: when the legal institutions that determine validity announce a change in rules or their interpretation, enforcement shifts from the old to the new.

In our what-is-law approach to the phenomenon of legal order,[21] we focus on the problem of enforcement and in particular what it takes for enforcement to follow an institution that is capable of changing the rules. We build a formal model based on the idea that, as societies move beyond simple stages, the demand grows for more efficient and timely adaptation through some form of official *classification institution* to resolve ambiguity about what is and what is not punishable conduct.

The model we develop adds the classification institutions without any shift in the private enforcement mechanisms of organic social order. Our model identifies legal order as a normative social order in which classification of behavior is supplied by a centralized classification institution that has the capacity to supply deliberate content to classifications. Importantly, we do not assume that law necessitates a shift to public centralized enforcement authority; transgressions continue to be punished by decentralized collective punishment—the same sanctions that support organic social order. We examine the conditions under which a candidate classification institution is capable of sustaining an equilibrium in which there is exclusively decentralized collective enforcement of the behavioral rules it articulates.

Our approach frames the analysis in terms of the need to coordinate and incentivize individuals—whom we model as ordinary economic agents with standard preferences (that is, not pro-social preferences)—to engage in the costly activity of third-party punishment.[22] In particular, individuals have to be willing to orient their punishment behavior around the classifications announced (and potentially changed from time to time) by the classification institution.

Meeting the constraints of coordination and incentive compatibility, we show, requires that the classification institution possess several features. The overall classification scheme has to be sufficiently convergent with the classifications preferred by the (often, many) individuals who are required for enforcement. That is, potential enforcers have to conclude that life for them in an equilibrium coordinated by the classification institution is at least as good as life in the alternative.[23] We call this convergent feature *qualified universality.*[24] In the absence of qualified universality, a classification institution fails to sustain equilibrium because enforcers won't enforce. Other features of the content of classifications and their application that we argue are necessary to induce enforcers to enforce and hence sustain equilibrium are: *publicity; clarity, non-contradiction, and uniqueness; stability; prospectivity and congruence* (between classifications as announced and classifications as enforced); *generality; impersonal, neutral, and independent reasoning;* and *openness* (to new arguments about how conduct should be classified).[25]

We call these features *legal attributes.*

In a recent paper, we use a thought experiment in the context of the legal system in ancient Athens to demonstrate the relationship between decentralized, private enforcement by ordinary individuals and the legal attributes.[26] During the classical period (508–322 BCE), Athens possessed a centralized classification institution consisting of a legislative assembly, written laws, unwritten customs, and popular courts. Citizens—native Athenian males—could bring suit if they felt they had been the victim of wrongdoing or if they sought to prosecute for a wrongdoing that caused harm to others or the public at large.

To bring a suit, Athenians had to identify written laws that were allegedly violated. The case was heard by a jury—ranging in size from 201 to 6,000—of randomly selected citizens who voted on a verdict in a secret ballot, without discussion, after hearing each party make his case. These procedures took place in public and in particular were matters of common knowledge—spectacles in the agora.

Enforcement of a verdict—an order for a defendant to pay damages or a fine, for example—was decentralized and collective, a form of private ordering. Although all citizens were authorized to assist in enforcement—and hence could be deemed to be acting in an "official" capacity—Athens did not maintain a centralized enforcement agency. No officials had both the responsibility and the means to execute a judgment under the direction and control of a central agency. The plaintiff who secured the verdict was responsible for carrying out the judgment—going to collect the money owed or seize sufficient property to satisfy the order. To collect was a collective act, we argue, because a successful plaintiff likely needed the support of other ordinary individuals to take what was (now) his. At a minimum, he needed others to voluntarily acquiesce in his efforts—not to interfere if he was required to use force to get what he was owed. For some—notably the friends and supporters of the losing defendant—acquiescence may have been costly. Indeed, we emphasize that the Athenians were aware that encouraging people to condition their judgments and efforts to help or hinder collection efforts on the jury verdict required them to ignore personal assessments and affinities, to choose to act neither on the basis of enmity nor favor but rather on the basis of the law alone—the jurors' oath said as much.[27]

To achieve effective private collective enforcement of jury verdicts required both coordination and incentive compatibility.

Coordination is necessary because we presume that an individual will only participate in helping to enforce legal rules if others are also going to help. This coordination may have been a consequence of the nature of the necessary enforcement efforts: taking the property of a robust owner, for example, probably required a little ganging up. But more generally, enforcement required confidence that even unilateral enforcement efforts would not themselves be deemed to be violations of the law (against theft, for example). This coordination required that a punisher have confidence that fellow citizens would use the same classification scheme as he was. Coordination was achieved by the existence of a unique, formal, common knowledge system with clear judgments—conditions that the Athenian verdicts clearly satisfied.

The subtler issue is incentive compatibility. Our thought experiment seeks to illuminate the problem of incentive compatibility by asking, what would you do? Suppose you are a friend of the successful plaintiff. Will you help him to collect, taking the risk that the defendant will fight back or retaliate? Suppose you are a friend of the losing defendant. Will you aid your friend even if doing so entails interfering with the successful plaintiff who asks no more of the losing party than that he honor the court's judgment?

We don't have direct evidence about what people in fact did in ancient Athens. But we have good reason to believe that, systematically, people helped successful plaintiffs to carry out the judgments they secured from the jury. We infer this from two things. First, the Athenians frequently litigated—some estimates suggest Athenian courts heard between 2,000 and 8,000 cases a year, which is a litigation rate for a population of 250,000 (of whom only 30,000 were citizens with direct access to courts) comparable to modern-day Germany, France, and England.[28] A high rate of litigation doesn't prove that litigation was routinely effective in securing redress, but it is hard to understand why the Athenians continued to make use of this costly institution if it was all theater that failed to produce redress.

Second, the Athenians enjoyed extraordinary levels of prosperity and stability in the ancient world. A basic premise of the economic analysis of growth and development is that a successful economy requires a reasonably reliable mechanism for enforcing contracts and property rights,[29] and it is a basic premise of political theory that a stable political regime requires confidence that the structures of governance and norms of behavior are reasonably well observed. For these reasons, we think that the Athenian system routinely provided redress, and that Athenians must have been willing to bear the costs and risks of helping to enforce jury verdicts.

Using the model of Hadfield and Weingast (2012) as a guide, we argue that ordinary Athenians were willing to participate in the private enforcement of jury verdicts based on public classification of wrongdoing by the jury because they looked to the equilibrium order secured by their classification institution (the laws, the assembly, the jury, the procedures all followed) and saw in that order a better life for themselves than the alternatives. These alternatives included the chaos and bloodshed of the previous several hundred years, a history of tyrants, warring factions, and elite rule. If ordinary citizens were not willing to help enforce the laws, the equilibrium they enjoyed would fail.[30]

This point was not lost on the Athenians. The great Athenian orator, Demosthenes, urged the point upon the juries he addressed:

> And what is the power of the laws? Is it that, if any of you is attacked and gives a shout, they'll come running to your aid? No, they are just inscribed letters and have no ability to do that. What then is their motive power? You are, if you secure them and make them authoritative whenever anyone asks for aid. So the laws are powerful through you and you through the laws. You must therefore stand up for them in just the same way as any individual would stand up for himself if attacked; you must take the view that offenses against the law are common concerns.[31]

We argue that stability did not arise from blind absorption of this call to help with enforcing the democratic legal order. Individual Athenians had to believe that the order would provide benefits for themselves. The need to secure confidence that order will be achieved and beneficial generates the constraints on the classification institution that we identify as legal attributes.

Consider, for example, a feature of the Athenian system that puzzles classical scholars and leads them to question the extent to which the Athenians achieved the rule of law: the openness of the rules of argument. Unlike modern courts in the Western tradition, Athenian legal procedures placed no limits on the evidence or arguments that could be marshaled to convince a jury to convict or not. Although a specific written law had to be identified to get the matter before a jury—violation of the rule against lying to a trading partner in the agora, for example—once you were there you could ask the jury to find in your favor for reasons completely irrelevant to the written charge: the defendant was a prostitute in his youth, he doesn't take care of his aging parents, he doesn't contribute to public festivals.[32] Classical scholars such as Lanni argue that the jury system as a result did not reliably enforce "the law," although the law did serve to buttress enforcement of social norms (against promiscuity or neglect of one's family, for example).[33]

We argue, however, that openness to these arguments was an important part of securing the participation of ordinary citizens in enforcing jury verdicts. Openness reassured Athenians that the system they supported was responsive to a wide variety of community norms they cared about. The written laws might have been the product of initially novel procedures—emerging from large-scale assemblies in which thousands of ordinary citizens participated—but those laws did not displace the rules they had long come to treat as relevant in deciding who to punish and who to forgive.

For similar reasons, it was important for the Athenians to have the confidence that the verdicts that emerged from the jury could not be corrupted by elite influence or alliances between factions. Otherwise, the jury system would be no better than the elite rule and factional conflict they were trying to replace. For this reason, we argue, the classification institution needed to display neutrality and independence.

To achieve neutrality and independence, the Athenians employed several devices. The ballots for assessing verdicts and punishments were cast in secret, helping to reduce social pressure and make bribery difficult. The large scale of juries also made bribery difficult. The random selection of jurors using a mechanism that ensured that juries were representative of the diversity of Athenian citizens helped to minimize the risk that a jury came to the case aligned with one of the litigants. The lack of deliberation among the jurors reduced the likelihood that influential voices could sway the jurors or exercise subtle control over the case. Even the absence of professional lawyers (litigants could hire speech-writers but they had to deliver their speeches on their own) can be understood as a feature that helped to secure confidence in the neutrality and independence of the system: rich and poor, educated and not were largely on equal footing before the court.

Last, although the Athenian system did not reflect modern norms of equality—women and slaves and foreigners lacked complete, direct access to courts and, especially, the institutional system of governance—the Athenian rules put in place had to display the kind of qualified universality that Hadfield and Weingast (2012) predicts—that is, it was beneficial to those whose *voluntary* participation was required for stability.[34] We can see this in the general form in which rules were composed—rights and duties attached to the status of citizen and not individual identity.[35] We also opine that the Athenian rules achieved universality among citizens because of the broad-based participation in lawmaking in the Assembly, as well as in the jury's ultimate determination of the content of the legal rules.

The what-is-law approach thus relies on a positive model to derive the normatively attractive features that legal philosophers identify as characteristic of law/the rule of law—generality, clarity, independence, neutrality, and so on. The positive model shows that these legal attributes emerge as part of the incentives necessary to coordinate participation in private enforcement of the classifications of conduct reached by a public institution by ordinary self-interested individuals.

### III. Is Rule of Law an Equilibrium Without Private Enforcement?

We have so far focused on the question of what constitutes law in a regime with fully decentralized enforcement—the type of enforcement we find in organic social orders. Our answer is that law emerges when there is a shift from organic classification to formal classification by an institution capable of articulating and adapting the content of classifications. We then derive the normatively attractive legal attributes from the positive imperative to coordinate and incentivize voluntary participation in decentralized enforcement.

The question we now confront is this: if the legal attributes ordinarily associated with the rule of law and principles of legality are attributable in a regime with fully decentralized enforcement to the need to coordinate and incentivize private actors to participate in enforcement, what, if anything, secures legal attributes in a regime with fully centralized enforcement? We suggest that the answer is simple: nothing. That is, fully centralized enforcement is incapable of sustaining an equilibrium characterized by rule of law.

To see the logic of this claim, we first provide a more formal definition of the rule of law and how our usage compares with the literature in legal philosophy. We then consider the characteristics of the equilibria that can be achieved in a regime in which enforcement is fully centralized.

## What Is Rule of Law?

The effort to define the concepts of law and the rule of law have long preoccupied legal theory. According to legal positivists, the existence of law depends on facts about the system of governance in place. Austin asserts that law exists where a sovereign issues and enforces commands.[36] Hart claims that law exists where, as a matter of social fact, there exists a set of secondary rules that officials treat as obligatory (whether they actually follow them or not) to determine what is a valid primary rule of behavior.[37] Raz follows Hart, but draws a more careful distinction between the existence of law—which is a matter of fact—and the ideal of the rule of law.[38] For Raz, law exists when there is an institutionalized normative system that claims to be both comprehensive and supreme with respect to other systems of norms and which, at a minimum, consists of norm-applying institutions such as courts that are obligated to follow secondary rules in adjudicating particular cases. The ideal of the rule of law exists in a legal system, according to Raz, when people are obligated to use, and are capable of using, legal rules to guide their behavior. Raz argues that, for practical reasons, to achieve the rule of law a legal system must be characterized by the normatively attractive features we associate with the rule of law: publicity, stability, neutrality, generality, etc. If law is not characterized by these features, people cannot look to it as a guide to behavior and hence cannot fulfill their obligation to obey it. This, he emphasizes, does not mean that law does not exist, only that not all legal systems are characterized by the rule of law.

Raz's primary target is Fuller, who argues that it makes sense only to identify as a legal system a regime in which people can, in fact, follow the law.[39] For Fuller also, achieving such a regime implies practical constraints on how government carries out its legal function. In Fuller's view, a legal order only exists when governance is sufficiently characterized by normatively attractive legal attributes, which he identified as the following list: publicity, generality, clarity, stability, prospectivity, non-contradiction, feasibility, and congruence (between rules as announced and rules as applied.)

We recognize that a central project for these philosophers is to investigate the relationship between law and morality and the nature of the obligation to obey the law; the program among legal philosophers differs from ours. But the philosophers do claim to be saying something about real-world legal systems and how they behave, without paying careful attention to the behavioral elements of those claims.

As social scientists and not legal philosophers, we confess to finding the appeal to "social facts" and behavioral claims in legal positivism a bit muddled. Hart as elaborated by Raz suggests that law can exist as a matter of social fact—there are secondary rules that officials are supposed to use to assess the validity of primary rules when they are applying rules, even if the law is so secretive and volatile that no one can, in actuality, use the law as a guide to behavior. This seems like positing the existence of a social "fact" in concept that does not exist in practice. And to a social scientist, the much-maligned Fuller seems to be conducting the same type of casual behavioral analysis as Raz: assessing what is necessary, in a practical sense, for people to use the law to guide their behavior. The principal difference appears to be that Fuller calls this "law" while Raz calls this "rule of law."

Our approach is organized by more formal attention to the positive analysis of what it takes to sustain an equilibrium in behavior. We use the terms "law" and "rule of law" to mean the same thing as "legal order," which we define in terms of equilibrium as follows:

A *normative social order* is an equilibrium characterized by conduct in a relevant community that is systematically patterned on community-based normative classifications of behavior. A *legal order* is a normative social order in which behavioral classifications are articulated and subject to modification by a centralized classification institution that possesses legal attributes.

We thus say that a regime is characterized by the rule of law when it is in equilibrium, with behavior systematically patterned on the classifications established and applied by a centralized classification institution, but only if the content and processes of that classification institution display legal attributes: universality; publicity; clarity, non-contradiction, and uniqueness; stability; prospectivity and congruence; generality; impersonal, neutral, and independent reasoning; and openness. Equilibrium with rule of law requires both that individuals have an incentive to pattern their behavior in accordance with the classifications announced by the classification institution and that those who control the classification institution have an incentive to operate the institution in a manner consistent with the legal attributes.

In our approach, then, a classification institution that makes rules in secret, applies them in a biased, personalized, or contradictory fashion, or ignores them altogether, does not generate rule of law.

A few observations about the relationship between our definition and those found in the legal philosophical literature. First, we use the concept of "classification" where the legal philosophical literature uses "rules." Classification in our model refers only to the normative evaluation of whether a particular behavior is, within a normative system, on the "positive" (right, valid, desired, permissible, not punishable) side of a binary partition or the "negative" (wrong, invalid, undesirable, impermissible, punishable.) The concept of "rules" goes beyond normative classification, to describe a way in which classifications might be used. A rule implies classification—the rule requires the positive action and punishes or invalidates the negative.

Our approach reveals why the use of "rules" as a primary category is problematic. If we define law as a system of governance by rules (as all legal philosophers do), then we are led to say "law" must have the attributes of "rules," by definition. Fuller struggles, then, to avoid circularity in explaining why "generality" is a necessary feature of a legal system: "the first desideratum of a system for subjecting human conduct to the governance of rules is an obvious one: there must be rules. This may be stated as the requirement of generality."[40] We avoid this problem with the concept of classification.

Raz similarly seems brought up short by the concept of rules. Although he rejects Fuller's claim that principles of legality such as generality, prospectivity, clarity, and so on are necessary for a system to properly be called legal, he does concede that

> it is, of course, true that most of the principles . . . cannot be violated altogether by any legal system. Legal systems are based on judicial institutions. There cannot be institutions of any kind unless there are general rules setting them up . . . Similarly, retroactive laws can exist only because there are institutions enforcing them. This entails that there must be prospective laws instructing those institutions to apply the retroactive laws if the retroactive laws are to be valid.[41]

Second, note that our list of legal attributes includes those that Fuller and Raz propose are necessary as a practical matter for people to use law to guide their behavior. The equilibrium in our model requires that those living under a law are able to guide their behavior on the basis of the law, and hence the equilibrium also requires some of these features for that purpose. But the core of our analysis looks not at what people need in order to comply with the law but, more fundamentally, what they require in order to decide, voluntarily, to participate in helping to enforce the law. As we explain more fully in Hadfield and Weingast (2012), this is a demanding requirement. It requires, for example, stability over a much longer time horizon than does a model that looks only at what it takes for people, as a practical matter, to be able to comply with the law. Moreover, our model produces a more drastic consequence for failures to achieve legal attributes than the legal philosophers anticipate. In our approach, legality can collapse entirely, perhaps rapidly, if people begin to worry that no one else is willing to help enforce. Even small deviations could trigger that result, given the coordination aspect of private ordering enforcement. In the legal philosophical approach, marginal—even substantial—failure to achieve generality or prospectivity, for example, could interfere with the effort by individuals to comply, injecting noise into the translation of rules into conduct. But a regime—and this is Raz's principal point—could continue to operate as a stable legal system even in the presence of gross failures of legality.[42]

Last, note that our list of legal attributes goes beyond what Fuller and Raz say is necessary from a practical point of view if the basic idea of governance by rules is to make sense. It also includes some of the overtly normative features that Waldron urges should also be a part of our understanding of the concept of law.[43] Our concept of universality is comparable to Waldron's idea that law should have an orientation to the public good. Openness, in our sense of openness to evidence and argument from parties, captures his idea that there must be opportunities for fair hearing for both sides to a dispute.

### Are Equilibria Supported by Fully Centralized Enforcement Characterized by Rule of Law?

Hadfield and Weingast (2012) shows that if a centralized institution is dependent entirely on private, decentralized enforcement to induce people to behave in accordance with its classifications, then if it achieves equilibrium, it must be that those operating the institution choose to abide by legal attributes. We now turn to ask whether the same is true when the centralized classification institution also has full control of a centralized enforcement authority.

To approach this question, we need to pay explicit attention to the incentives of those who control the classification institution. This is something we do not yet model in our work to date. Although we do not develop a formal model here, we can provide a more careful informal treatment in order to explain the logic of our claim that rule of law is not an equilibrium with fully centralized enforcement authority.

We call the person or group of people who control the classification institution the authoritative steward; this is the unique entity capable of articulating classifications that the community of enforcers, as a matter of common knowledge, treats as authoritative. What are the incentives of this steward? We do not fully characterize the utility function of the steward, but we make the following assumption: the steward has some private interests that can diverge from public interest. We think this assumption is an empirically grounded one and consistent with the animating assumption in most political theory, beginning with Locke, Montesquieu, Smith, and Madison[44] and continuing in the modern literature with Acemoglu and Robinson, Besley, Ferejohn, and Persson and Tabellini.[45] Moral hazard in the executive frames the challenge of governance: how to achieve alignment between the decisions of the central authority and the interests of citizens. As Madison puts it, "Possible abuses must be incident to every power or trust, of which a beneficial use can be made."[46]

Now define a rule-of-law equilibrium. We have two (groups of) actors in our model: the authoritative steward and ordinary individuals. The steward chooses what classifications to announce and, relatedly, the procedures that will be followed in reaching those classifications. (In the parlance of conventional legal systems, the steward decides the content of laws and adjudicates results in particular cases.) Ordinary individuals choose whether to take actions that are classified as punishable (whether to break the rules) and, if the regime depends on decentralized punishment, whether to participate in collective punishment of those who do violate the rules.

In a rule-of-law equilibrium, ordinary individuals choose to comply with the classification scheme announced by the central authority, and the central authority announces classifications in a manner that is consistent with the legal attributes. Moreover, as in any equilibrium, all actors must be making choices that maximize their utility, given the equilibrium choices made by other actors. This means that ordinary individuals cannot do better, if the authoritative steward is observing legal attributes, by deviating and choosing to violate the rules, and that the authoritative steward cannot do better by deviating to a classification scheme that violates one or more of the legal attributes (announcing a law or deciding a case in order to reap private benefits and in doing so violating the requirements of prospectivity or publicity or impartial reasoning, for example.)

The gist of the result in Hadfield and Weingast (2012) is that in equilibrium the authoritative steward has no incentive to deviate from classifications (and procedures) that are consistent with the rule of law because deviations by the steward will be met with deviations by ordinary individuals in their *punishment* behavior: without assurance that the classification institution is observing the rule of law, individuals do not expect their contributions to punishment today to pay off tomorrow, because they either cannot predict or do not trust what the regime will allow and what it will deter in the future. Compliance with the announced classification scheme then collapses because the punishment threat is no longer credible. As long as the utility benefits to the steward depend on continuation of the enforcement system, the steward has the incentives to maintain the characteristics necessary to support voluntary enforcement; namely, the legal attributes.

This equilibrium logic fails if we now assume that the authoritative steward controls not only the classification institution but also a centralized enforcement apparatus. If that apparatus is fully capable, as standard accounts of law assume, of inducing compliance with *any* classification (rule) that it announces, then the authoritative steward can, whenever the opportunity arises, deviate from the rule of law to announce classifications that secure private benefits for the steward *without* disrupting the incentive of ordinary individuals to continue to comply with the law. Equilibrium reasoning then says that observance of the rule of law is not an equilibrium: because, given equilibrium behavior by the individuals subject to the rules (compliance), the authoritative steward can do better by deviating from the rule of law.

Our point is this: if a classification institution capable of providing deliberate content to rules is established and if it is supported exclusively by centralized enforcement, then behavior will be patterned, as much as possible, on the basis of the announced classifications, regardless of whether the institution displays legal attributes or not. A ruler with control over a fully effective enforcement apparatus can put that apparatus to work for any reason. Nothing compels the ruler to produce classifications characterized by legal attributes. Classification in the form of legislation can be issued in secret. Classification in the form of adjudication can be based on rules that are retroactive or vague or applied in biased fashion; indeed, results may be completely incongruent with the announced classifications.[47] Finally, the regime can use the violence potential of the state to target specific individuals—typically perceived as opponents of the regime. The ruler's decision to exercise force in a particular way is presumably informed by the prediction that it will change behavior in ways that the ruler wants. Behavior will be patterned on the classifications—even if ex post—announced by the classification institution. But it will not necessarily be based on rules that are public, prospective, coherently applied, and so on. The system overseen by a centralized institution with complete control over both classification and enforcement may produce some form of order, but not legal order. It might produce a stable equilibrium—the world does not lack for examples of long-lived dictatorial regimes—but the equilibrium will not be characterized by the rule of law. Put differently, rule of law is not among the equilibria we can expect to emerge under the standard definition of government: a single body with the power to both make and enforce the law.[48]

Are there other constraints arising from the need to preserve enforcement that might generate incentives for the authoritative steward to observe the rule of law? To answer that question, we need to explore the question of how a fully centralized enforcement regime induces officials to act in accordance with the central institution's classifications. How is Weber's "staff" of enforcers motivated?[49]

One mechanism is monetary incentives: enforcement officials are paid a wage above their next best alternative by the central institution and keep their jobs if and only if they enforce appropriately. A less (financially) expensive mechanism would be to rely on threats of violence directed to enforcement officials who fail to enforce as directed.[50] Threats of violence, in fact, could be used to "deputize" the entire citizenry, requiring them to participate in punishments as directed by the center.[51]

Both of these mechanisms impose constraints on what the central institution can achieve. Financial incentives may be very expensive, indeed exponentially so, since official incentives must be implemented by another layer of enforcement officials, who also must be appropriately incentivized, implying yet a further layer of enforcement, and so on. And so a poorer country—the kind, in fact, that still routinely lacks reliable legal systems—may be unable to implement fully centralized enforcement that is not thoroughly undermined by poor training, corruption, or other failures among officials. Using violence to induce officials, and perhaps ordinary citizens, to carry out punishment of transgressions as classified by the central institution may also be expensive.[52] It also requires a means of controlling the organization of violence.[53] The more critical violence is to maintaining centralized enforcement of law, the more powerful it must be, but also, the more difficult to prevent subunits from attempting coups.

Violence therefore imposes both financial and moral costs. A central government seeking to improve the welfare of its people through better rules may well conclude that its welfare-improving effort would be a failure on net if it required outrageous punishment visited upon enforcers who fail to enforce.

So the constraints imposed by the need to activate an enforcement apparatus through monetary incentives or threats of violence are likely to compromise the efficacy with which the central institution translates its classifications into actual behavior. But—and this is our key observation—those constraints do not induce a classification institution to produce rules and processes characterized by legal attributes. If enforcement officials are motivated only by money or fear, it does not matter to them whether the rules they are asked to enforce are promulgated prospectively, in public and general terms, coherently applied in adjudication, implemented in neutral and open processes, and so on.

To be clear, we are not claiming that rule of law requires *exclusive* dedication of the enforcement function to private actors. We have no doubt that centralized enforcement is both a necessary and an efficient component of legal enforcement in societies of substantial scale. Our point is that under standard assumptions about the risk of moral hazard for those wielding power, it is only if the central authority is dependent on voluntary participation in the enforcement of its rules (perhaps in addition to other forms of enforcement) that rule of law is an equilibrium.

## IV. CONCLUSION

Virtually all discussions of the rule of law assume that rule of law is a product of government. Governments are defined as the entities that both make and enforce the rules in a country. Although there is ample recognition of the presence of pockets of private ordering within regimes operating under the rule of law, private ordering is presumed to be governed by the regime's overarching framework of publicly enforced laws.

Against this background, we make a stark claim. A legal system cannot achieve rule of law, we argue, unless there is an essential role for private, decentralized enforcement of law. We emphasize that private enforcement does not mean private security forces or mafia goons; it does not mean spontaneous and undisciplined mob violence. Decentralized enforcement of law, like the decentralized enforcement of social norms, generally involves social sanctions such as criticism (generating bad reputations) and exclusion (from valuable relationships and opportunities). When it does involve the private use of force, it is disciplined force, limited to the type and extent of force authorized by law. Private individuals also participate in enforcement when they cooperate with, or at least do not interfere with, those (whether private individuals or officials) who are authorized to enforce law.

In making this claim, we draw from the legal philosophy literature's approach to the rule of law, especially the characterization of rule of law as embodying a series of normatively attractive legal attributes. Yet our approach differs from the literature in that we go beyond normative considerations of the rule of law that focus on what is desirable in a governance regime. In addition, we ask the positive question typically ignored by legal philosophers; namely, "how is the rule of law sustained?" Put another way, what are the characteristics that lead a community to produce and sustain law? We begin with the idea that law does not necessarily involve centralized coercion. We next ask what conditions are necessary for a legal system to emerge. To participate in enforcement, most individuals have to believe they are better off under the legal system. Thus, if one group gains valuable privileges, then those outside the group have little incentive to participate in enforcement. In contrast, when the rules are characterized by generality and universality, then citizens know that the law protects them as well. Generality and universality therefore contribute to the standard enforcement mechanisms of repeat play: I'll participate in today's enforcement that benefits you because I know that I can rely on your participation in punishment that benefits me tomorrow. More broadly, our framework demonstrates how these normatively attractive legal attributes emerge as part of an equilibrium of decentralized enforcement of law. In so doing, our approach provides a positive model about how normative principles can be sustained in practice.

Our claim is not of merely theoretical interest. It is widely recognized that economic and political development require stable legal systems that reliably implement basic rules of property and contract, regulate markets to overcome externalities and market failures, and protect basic human rights, autonomy, and dignity. Thus the project of building rule of law in the many countries around the globe that lack legal order is one of the major challenges of our time. But as we emphasize elsewhere, most rule-of-law building projects have failed miserably, despite billions of dollars spent to promote this goal.[54] We believe this failure is in part a result of the theoretically poorly informed and exclusive focus on reproducing the visible institutions of our highly stable and successful advanced Western legal systems. Poor and developing countries are encouraged (sometimes required, for WTO membership, for example) to adopt the legislation and regulatory regimes of wealthy nations. The focus in the international community then shifts to achieving effective public enforcement of the resulting laws and regulations—equipping and training police and security forces, educating judges and regulators, weeding out corruption—and then attempting to force governments to observe limits on their use of their enforcement tools.

Our analysis suggests that the aid community's approach misses an important piece of the story, namely the need to fashion a regime that is dependent to some significant extent on private ordering and then to coordinate and incentivize the participation of ordinary individuals in enforcement efforts. We have no doubt that this too is an enormous challenge. But our work suggests that it is one that scholars and policymakers should be taking on.

## NOTES

1 Robert C. Ellickson, *Order Without Law: How Neighbors Settle Disputes* (Cambridge, MA: Harvard University Press, 1991).

2 McNollgast, "Political Economy of Law," in *Law and Economics Handbook*, vol. 2, eds. A. Mitchell Polinsky and Stephen Shavel (Amsterdam: North-Holland, 2007).

3 Gillian K. Hadfield and Iva Bozovic, "Scaffolding: Using Formal Contracts to Support Informal Relations," *Wisconsin Law Review* 2016, no. 5 (2016): 981–1032.

4 Avinash Dixit, *Lawlessness and Economics, Alternative Modes of Governance* (Princeton, NJ: Princeton University Press, 2004). See also Elinor Ostrom, *Governing the Commons: The Evolution of Institutions for Collective Action* (Cambridge: Cambridge University Press, 1990); David Skarbek, *The Social Order of the Underworld: How Prison Gangs Govern the American Penal System* (Oxford: Oxford University Press, 2015); and Peter Leeson, *Anarchy Unbound: Why Self-Governance Works Better Than You Think* (Cambridge: Cambridge University Press, 2014).

5 Gillian K. Hadfield and Barry R. Weingast, "Microfoundations of the Rule of Law," *Annual Review of Political Science* 17 (2015): 21–42.

6 F. A. Hayek, *The Road to Serfdom* (Chicago: University of Chicago Press, 1944[2007]): 48.

7 World Bank, *Legal and Judicial Reform: Strategic Directions* (Washington, DC: The World Bank, 2003).

8 Gillian K. Hadfield and Barry R. Weingast, "What is Law? A Coordination Model of the Characteristics of Legal Order," *Journal of Legal Analysis* 4, no. 2 (2012): 471–514.

9 Lon L. Fuller, *The Morality of Law* (New Haven: Yale University Press, 1969); Jeremy Waldron, "The Concept and the Rule of Law," *Georgia Law Review* 43, no. 1 (2008): 1–61; Jeremy Waldron, "The Rule of Law and the Importance of Procedure," *NOMOS L: Getting to the Rule of Law* (New York: NYU Press, 2011): 3–31.

10 "It is a criterion of adequacy of a legal theory that it is true of all the intuitively clear instances of municipal legal systems" (Joseph Raz, *The Authority of Law: Essays on Law and Morality*, 2nd ed. (Oxford: Oxford University Press, 2009): 104.

11 Adam Smith, *An Inquiry into the Nature and Causes of the Wealth of Nations* (London: Alex. Murray & Co., 1776[1872]): 570.

12 See, e.g., E. Adamson Hoebel, *The Law of Primitive Man: A Study in Comparative Legal Dynamics*, 2nd ed. (Cambridge, MA: Harvard University Press, 1954[2006]).

13 See, e.g., Polly Wiessner, "Norm Enforcement among the Ju/'hoansi Bushmen: A Case of Strong Reciprocity?," *Human Nature* 16, no. 2 (2005): 115–45. Compare this idea of social sanction with Hart's account of the internal aspect of rules: "What is necessary is that there should be a critical reflective attitude to certain patterns of behavior as a common standard, and that this should display itself in criticism (including self-criticism), demands for conformity, and in acknowledgments that such criticism and demands are justified, all of which find their characteristic expression in

the normative terminology of 'ought', 'must', and 'should', 'right' and 'wrong'" (H. L. A. Hart, *The Concept of Law*, 3rd ed. (Oxford: Oxford University Press, 1961[2012]): 57).

14 For Weber, law is distinguished by its enforcement "by physical or psychic sanctions aimed to compel conformity or punish disobedience, and applied by a group of men especially empowered to carry out this function" (Max Weber, *Economy and Society: An Outline of Interpretive Sociology*, trans. Guenther Roth and Claus Wittich (Berkeley, CA: University of California Press, 1956[1978]): 129).

15 Based on interviews with businesses engaged in relationships that are critical for innovation, where the prospect of effective public enforcement is remote, Hadfield and Bozovic ("Scaffolding") found that companies rely on private sanctions for contract breach to support contractual commitments. These private sanctions include the termination of a valuable business relationship or damage to business reputation that hinders future contracting. Bernstein shows similar results for a sample of supply contracts in manufacturing (Lisa Bernstein, "Beyond Relational Contracts: Social Capital and Network Governance in Procurement Contracts," *Journal of Legal Analysis* 7, no. 2 [2015]: 561–621).

16 Wiessner, "Norm Enforcement among the Ju/'hoansi Bushmen."

17 Christopher Boehm, "Egalitarian Behavior and Reverse Dominance Hierarchy," *Current Anthropology* 34, no. 3 (1993): 227–54; Christopher Boehm, *Moral Origins: The Evolution of Virtue, Altruism, and Shame* (New York: Basic Books, 2012).

18 Paul Sillitoe, "The Gender of Crops in the Papua New Guinea Highlands," *Ethnology* 20, no. 1 (1981): 1–14.

19 Hart, *Concept of Law*, 92–93.

20 Fuller, *Morality of Law*, 55.

21 Hadfield and Weingast, "What is Law?"

22 We make this assumption for methodological reasons, not because we think it is the most accurate account of the psychology of actual human beings. Building models based on this minimal assumption about human motivation increases the robustness of our approach and allows us to avoid limiting ourselves to explaining law in settings in which humans possess the pro-social preferences that obviate any need to discipline their behavior to achieve pro-social goals. See Hadfield and Weingast, "Microfoundations of the Rule of Law," for a discussion of the limitations we perceive in models based on pro-social preferences.

23 The alternative could be disorder or it could be some other form of normative social order.

24 We describe a set of rules as "universal" if they address the needs and interests of everyone in society. Our model predicts that universality

will be qualified, in the sense of not necessarily extending to everyone in society; in particular, we expect that only the needs and interests of those people who are needed for effective collective punishment will be reflected in the rules.

25 Note that these features do not include many of the values of democratic systems; rule of law is not the only desirable feature of a legal political regime. We emphasize in particular that generality refers only to the form of a rule—it is based on categories rather than personal identity, but categories could be narrowly, and discriminatorily, drawn. Impersonal reasoning refers only to the fact that ex post classifications of specific events and behaviors are derived from ex ante rules and principles that can in principle be replicated by any individual; classification is not a function of the identity of the classifier. It does not mean that all persons are treated equally by the law.

26 Federica Carugati, Gillian K. Hadfield, and Barry R. Weingast, "Building Legal Order in Ancient Athens," *Journal of Legal Analysis* 7, no. 2 (2015): 291–324; see also Federica Carugati, *In Law We Trust (Each Other): Legal Institutions, Democratic Stability and Economic Development in Classical Athens* (2015) (unpublished Ph.D. dissertation, Department of Classics, Stanford University). For other historical examples of legal orders without fully centralized enforcement, see Gillian K. Hadfield and Barry R. Weingast, "Law without the State: Legal Attributes and the Coordination of Decentralized Collective Punishment," *Journal of Law & Courts* 1, no. 1 (2013): 3–34.

27 Edward M. Harris, "The Rule of Law in Athenian Democracy: Reflections on the Judicial Oath," *Dike* 9 (2006): 157–81.

28 Rates in these modern-day settings vary between five and nine per 100 persons (Gillian K. Hadfield and Jamie Heine, "Life in the Law-Thick World: The Legal Resource Landscape for Ordinary Americans," in *Beyond Elite Law: Access to Civil Justice in America*, eds. Samuel Estreicher and Joy Radice [Cambridge: Cambridge University Press, 2016]). In Athens the rate was between seven and twenty-seven per 100 citizens and between one and three per 100 persons (including women, slaves, and foreigners who had no direct access to regular courts—claims on their behalf had to be brought by citizens).

29 Douglass C. North, *Structure and Change in Economic History* (New York: Norton, 1981).

30 There is a free-rider challenge in this equilibrium, which we do not address here. In Hadfield and Weingast, "What is Law?," the challenge is overcome in a small punishment group because participation in punishment in equilibrium is a signal of the ongoing acceptability of the classification institution to an individual necessary for the stability of equilib-

rium. In larger populations, we conjecture, punishment groups are often small (the small subset who are on hand at collection time, for example). As Demosthenes's statement quoted in the text also shows, there were sustained efforts to inculcate the belief that failing to help out with democratic institutions would render them ineffective.

31 Demosthenes, *Against Meidias*, 21.224–5.

32 Carugati, *In Law We Trust.*

33 Adriaan Lanni, "Social Norms in the Courts of Ancient Athens," *Journal of Legal Analysis* 1, no. 2 (2009): 691–736.

34 We emphasize, as do most legal philosophers, that even systems that are oppressive, intrusive, and which discriminate against even large segments of the population can follow the rule of law. Although the concept of the rule of law is often used in the literature to mean democratic values such as equality and personal freedom, we restrict the term to mean only that the classification institution possesses the legal attributes of clarity, generality, impersonal reasoning, and so on. See Hadfield and Weingast, "Microfoundations of the Rule of Law," for further discussion.

35 As an example: "And if anyone give away an alien woman in marriage to an Athenian man, as if she were related to him, let him be disenfranchised, and let his property be forfeited to the state, and let a third part of it belong to the successful prosecutor" (Douglas M. MacDowell, *The Law in Classical Athens* [Ithaca: Cornell University Press, 1978]: 56 [quoting Demosthenes 59.52]).

36 John Austin, *Lectures on Jurisprudence or The Philosophy of Positive Law*, vol. 1 (London: John Murray, 1885).

37 Hart, *Concept of Law.*

38 Raz, *Authority of Law.*

39 Fuller, *Morality of Law.*

40 Ibid., 46.

41 Raz, *Authority of Law*, 223.

42 "I have been treating the rule of law as an ideal, as a standard to which the law ought to conform but which it can and sometimes does violate most radically and systematically" (Raz, *Authority of Law*, 223).

43 Waldron, "The Concept and the Rule of Law" and "The Rule of Law and the Importance of Procedure."

44 John Locke, *Second Treatise of Government*, ed. C. B. Macpherson (Indianapolis, IN: Hackett Publishing Co., 1689[1980]); Charles de Secondat Montesquieu, *Spirit of the Laws* (Cambridge: Cambridge University Press, 1748[1989]); Adam Smith, *Lectures on Jurisprudence*, eds. R. L. Meek., D. D. Raphael, and P. G. Stein (Indianapolis, IN: LibertyFund, 1762–63, 1763–64, 1767[1981]); and Alexander Hamilton, James Madison, and John Jay,

*The Federalist Papers*, ed. Clinton Rossiter (Harmondsworth, UK: Mentor, 1961).

45 Daron Acemoglu and James Robinson, "Economic Backwardness in Political Perspective," *American Political Science Review* 100, no. 1 (2006): 115–31; Timothy Besley, *Principled Agents? The Political Economy of Good Government* (Oxford: Oxford University Press, 2006); John A. Ferejohn, "Incumbent Performance and Electoral Control," *Public Choice* 50, no. 1 (1986): 5–25; and Torsten Persson and Guido Tabellini, *The Economic Effects of Constitutions* (Cambridge, MA: M.I.T. Press, 2003).

46 Hamilton, Madison, and Jay, *The Federalist Papers*, 251.

47 An interesting question, a topic for further work in our project, is why authoritarian regimes bother with the trappings of legislation and adjudication—that is, formal adjudication—if they are only going to manipulate classification. Why bother aligning classification, generating secret or retroactive legislation, and conducting show trials with the exercise of force at all? We suspect it is because such regimes depend to some extent on decentralized enforcement efforts among citizens and so need to at least appear to be implementing legal attributes.

48 The case of a classification institution supported in part by centralized enforcement but which relies for efficacy on decentralized participation in enforcement follows the logic of the fully decentralized case. The need to induce decentralized participation in enforcement requires legal attributes.

49 In distinguishing law from convention, Weber proposes that "the concept of *law* will be made to turn on the presence of a staff engaged in enforcement" (Weber, *Economy and Society*, 34).

50 Threats of violence of this type have a famous pedigree, often called the "right of rebellion." This mechanism for policing public officials was made famous by Locke in his *Second Treatise of Government*, Montesquieu in his *Spirit of the Laws*, and in the American founding (e.g., in the third paragraph of the Declaration of Independence; and in various Federalist Papers, such as F26 and F46). Most successful constitutions rely in part on the right of rebellion, whether explicit or not (Sonia Mittal and Barry R. Weingast, "Self-enforcing Constitutions: With an Application to America's First Century, *Journal of Law, Economics, and Organization* 29, no. 2 (2012): 278–302).

51 We would characterize a system in which individual citizens are required, on threat of punishment from the center, to participate in punishment "centralized." This is in contrast to a regime of decentralized enforcement in which individual citizens are motivated to participate in punishment, or not, on the basis of a comparison between the value of

the equilibrium coordinated by the central classification institution and the alternative.

52 Although the more violent the threats, the less intensively the center has to monitor enforcers. This makes the mechanism less expensive for the center (although it also implies increasingly grotesque methods).

53 Douglass C. North, John Joseph Wallis, and Barry R. Weingast, *Violence and Social Orders: A Conceptual Framework for Interpreting Recorded Human History* (Cambridge: Cambridge University Press, 2009).

54 Hadfield and Weingast, "Microfoundations of the Rule of Law."

# 11

## WHAT IS POLITICS WITHOUT THE STATE?

## A REPLY TO HADFIELD AND WEINGAST

### ALEX GOUREVITCH

The promise of the modern state has been that citizens, freed from the need to police each other by a reliably enforced system of law, might enjoy the liberty to pursue their particular conceptions of the good life. The rule of law, alongside a centralized coercive apparatus impartially enforcing that law, is a necessary part of the broad architecture of individual liberty. That, anyhow, is what many political philosophers have thought. But Gillian Hadfield and Barry Weingast (hereafter "H-W") have thrown down the gauntlet. A legal order based on centralized enforcement is the *least* likely to bear the characteristics of the rule of law and therefore is the most inimical to a liberal society. Only when enforcement is (mostly) decentralized will we expect to see the legal order conform to those normatively desirable attributes known as "rule of law." Perhaps we ought to seek ways of privatizing norm enforcement.

But here is a puzzle. In the history of political thinking, decentralized punishment is associated with both the most beautiful, utopian regimes and with the most nightmarish, dystopian regimes. For instance, Lenin described the withering away of the state in the following way:

> Only communism makes the state absolutely unnecessary, for there is *nobody* to be suppressed—"nobody" in the sense of a *class*, of a systematic struggle against a definite section of the population. We are

not utopians, and do not in the least deny the possibility and inevitability of excesses on the part of *individual persons,* or the need to stop *such* excesses. In the first place, however, no special machine, no special apparatus of suppression, is needed for this; *this will be done by the armed people themselves, as simply and as readily as any crowd of civilized people, even in modern society, interferes to put a stop to a scuffle or to prevent a woman from being assaulted.* And, secondly, we know that the fundamental social cause of excesses, which consist in the violation of the rules of social intercourse, is the exploitation of the people, their want and their poverty. With the removal of this chief cause, excesses will inevitably begin to "*wither away*" . . . With their withering away the state will also *wither away.*[1]

Such descriptions of stateless utopias can be traced backwards through Marx and Owen to Thomas More and even to Plato's *Republic* (before the guardians show up in Book II). Yet, on the other hand, we have the corrosive and oppressive conditions of East Germany and Communist Russia, in which ordinary citizens spied on each other and denounced them publicly; of Maoist China, in which children turned on parents, students on teachers, voluntarily going well beyond anything the public rules required. In the United States, there was, in the somewhat distant past, the informal policing by slave patrols in the pre-bellum American South, as well as the Pinkerton assassins and employer blacklists of the post-bellum North and West.[2] There are the twentieth century's Red Scares, in which university administrations and private employers fired gays, political activists, and lefties of various stripes, and former friends named names.[3] Hannah Arendt thought it a defining feature of a totalitarian regime that not just the formal security apparatus but everyone was a participant in law enforcement. We catch a whiff of that problem today when we see signs on the New York subway that read, "If You See Something, Say Something."

For all of the above historical cases, it turns out to be possible to incentivize a vast amount of decentralized enforcement without particularly strong rule of law. That is to say, the legal order does not need to display very many of the attributes associated with the normatively desirable rule of law for us to find numerous private actors willing to participate in enforcing that legal order. Indeed, we might wonder whether it is correct for H-W to argue that "the

case of a classification institution supported in part by centralized enforcement but which relies for efficacy on decentralized
participation in enforcement follows the logic of the fully decentralized case. The need to induce decentralized participation in
enforcement requires legal attributes."[4] There is little doubt that
the aforementioned regimes, whether dictatorial or more liberal,
"relied for efficacy" on these private activities. So it looks like a vast
amount of decentralized enforcement can be incentivized without
strong legal attributes.

These historical experiences are precisely what have made political philosophers so nervous about private law enforcement. For,
in modern history, private enforcement has often looked either
like vigilante justice or as a way of buttressing oppressive regimes
and policies. Perhaps, given abundant historical evidence, the
ideal of a stateless society, based entirely on private law enforcement, should remain just that: an ideal that should be confused
with no actual or feasible regime. It is an attractive picture but
not an aspiration towards which we strive. On the other hand, our
present, ongoing experience with the extreme injustices of centralized enforcement—starting with racial oppression and mass incarceration in the United States—is reason to continue to hope that
there is a better way of enforcing social norms. Perhaps we ought
all to be Leninists in spirit and hope not only that the state wither
away, but that, as H-W might put it, the stateless society is a stable
equilibrium of exclusively private enforcement. We are, at the very
least, on the horns of a dilemma: knowing neither whether to try
to bring the state closer to the idea of the rule of law or whether to
aspire to the ideal of a stateless society.

Against this background, how is a political theorist to respond
to H-W's positive "what-is-law" theory of the rule of law? What
should we think about results that say legal attributes are necessary
to induce decentralized participation or about the complementary
results, found in the paper for this volume, that fully centralized
enforcement is unlikely to generate rule of law attributes in a legal
order? There are at least three things to say, each a response to a
different question:

- First, what does "private" mean in the phrase "private enforcement"?

- Second, what can a model demonstrate on its own, independent of historical evidence?
- Third, what is this model's relationship to historical evidence such that we could know whether the facts support or don't support the model?

Allow me to state briefly my responses to each question, and then elaborate on them below.

1. With respect to "what does private mean," there are very important differences, analytically and normatively, between "private," "decentralized," and "official." The H-W approach elides these distinctions in ways that matter both to positive and normative theorists. This is of particular concern for a volume on privatization.

2. With respect to "what does the model demonstrates on its own, independent of experience" we are in unexpected terrain. H-W provide the first positive theory of utopia I know of in the history of political thought. Their results suggest that we do not need a state in the sense of a centralized coercive apparatus. This might even be Leninist game theory! That is an exciting prospect. Yet the reason to withhold judgment is that their model is based on strategic interaction among private actors, not actors motivated by respect for the authority of the law nor out of any sense of being *public* agents. So if it is Leninist game theory, it might not actually have captured the irreducibly public aspect of the rule of law and, as such, might not even be a positive theory of the "rule of law."

3. However, when we turn to historical evidence we discover the inverse problem. We have less a positive theory of utopia than we do of dystopia or, possibly of greater concern, a model whose predictions conflict with some central facts. Either (3a) H-W's is a positive theory of dystopia when we consider the one empirical example in the paper of private enforcement with legal attributes—a slave society (Athens). It looks like the model predicts a high degree of rule of law coupled with extreme economic exploitation and group exclusion. Or (3b) it is a positive theory in conflict with historical evidence when we consider the great development of modern politics: the rise of the modern state, whose centralized *enforcement* apparatus was at least partially a product of voluntary decisions of private enforcers to give up their enforcement powers

to an independent, permanent police force, and where the rule of law was demanded *in response to and as an attempt to control* this centralized enforcement, rather than as a way of consolidating private enforcement. So private enforcement looks like an unstable, not stable, equilibrium easily tipped into the dynamics of state development when faced with the modern economy as H-W themselves describe it. Those are the concerns briefly stated—let us look at them in greater detail.

## I. WHAT DOES PRIVATE MEAN?

The first concern is that H-W are imagining a society of private law enforcers but it is unclear what private means. Since privatization is the volume's central theme, it is worth us thinking through how difficult it is to define the concept, and why this matters both for normative as well as positive theory. In political philosophy, it is customary to distinguish between "private/public" status, "centralized/decentralized" institutions, and "standing/informal" authority. I am not sure where H-W stand on these distinctions, which affects any attempt to evaluate the scientific status of the model.

In their various papers, private is most commonly defined as the opposite of "official."

> "By decentralized enforcement, we mean that the imposition of penalties results from individual decisionmaking among *ordinary agents acting independently,* not the decisionmaking of official legal actors."[5]
> ". . . those (*whether private individuals or officials*) who are authorized to enforce law."[6]
> "In the simplest human societies, there is no public apparatus to enforce these rules; all rule enforcement is what we call *private, carried out by ordinary individuals* who make a voluntary choice about whether to participate in punishing rule violations or not."[7]
> "Although all citizens were authorized to assist in enforcement—and hence could be deemed to be acting in *an 'official' capacity*—Athens did not maintain a centralized enforcement agency."[8]

Note that, in their view, decentralized and private are synonymous, but only because decentralized really means "not official."

The problem is that "acting in an official capacity" is perfectly compatible with highly decentralized enforcement, even though that enforcement is not "private."

To see the ambiguities here, consider an example that the authors use: ancient Athens. In Athens, we have "private" enforcement *only* in the sense that there was no standing, centralized police force.[9] But it is more appropriate to call this decentralized *public* enforcement. That is because, whenever Athenians enforced judgments by the institution, they did so as "official" agents with formal legal standing. They were classified, *by the public classification system*, as citizens, whose citizen-status included the official authority to enforce law. Such, in fact, has been the case in many slave societies, including classical Rome and the American South.[10] In Athens, the fully "private" individuals were those who had little or no standing in law: slaves, women, and (somewhat) metics. (Indeed, even citizens were considered private only as "despotes," when acting as rulers of the household over non-citizens, or as "idiotes," those consigned to private life, but not when interacting with other citizens). The central distinction separating public from private was the one separating free citizens from everyone else. This separation structured the entire legal order. When citizens brought a case or enforced it, they did so as agents acting in an "official capacity," namely *as citizens*.

Further, from that standpoint, it looks like Athenian society had fairly *centralized* enforcement: only a minority of the overall population could legitimately bring a case, let alone enforce a ruling. So even if enforcement was in some sense private, it was still highly centralized. That was not an incidental feature of the legal order, since the stability of the legal regime, to the degree that there was stability, depended significantly on the legal power of citizens over non-citizens.[11]

So the public/private distinction in Athens, and therefore any claims about "private ordering," do not map straightforwardly onto "centralized" and "decentralized" nor "official" and "unofficial." You can have decentralized enforcement by official public agents, which was Athens. Or you can have centralized enforcement by official agents, which is another possible view of Athens. You can even have centralized enforcement by private agents—the Athenians had slaves, the Scythian archers, as part of a small police force that appears to have engaged in the discipline and arrest of citizens.[12]

One response to this might be for H-W to replace the term "private" with "decentralized." But it might be that the most important distinction is between a standing force and an informal or ad hoc one. And, further, we might instead be interested in the legally distributed permission to use force. After all, as the Athens example again attests, depending on the *scope* of the relevant population, enforcement might look very centralized even if it is private or informal in the sense of not involving a standing police force. If a relatively small share of the population has the legal or social permission to use force, relative to the population that could be coerced, then that is quite reasonably characterized as centralized enforcement even when none of the enforcers is officially employed as an enforcer.

The general point is that, while H-W use "private" to contrast with the modern, centralized enforcement apparatus of the state, their concept applies to too many heterogeneous social alternatives and enforcement activities for us to know what is being analyzed in the case of "private enforcement." A standing force, a decentralized organization, and acting in an official capacity are different enough that subsuming them under the single concept "private" is confusing.

The reason these conceptual issues matter is, for one, that they speak to the puzzle about dystopian and utopian regimes from the opening of this essay. For instance, H-W associate dictatorial regimes with centralized, e.g., non-private, enforcement. But it seems like one of the great historical worries has been around the intrusion of what should remain a specialized and centralized policing function into the private lives of individuals. By intrusion I don't mean violation of private civil liberties—wiretapping, illegal search and seizure, arbitrary detention, etc.—but rather the deputization of civilians into law enforcement: if you see something, say something. It was that pervasive sense that anyone and everyone might take personal action against you, impose various penalties, or report you to the authorities, for some real or imagined infraction that made the famous twentieth-century authoritarian regimes so oppressive.

So, conceptually, it is unclear why H-W want to claim that dictatorial regimes are somehow *specially* centralized, since a core aspect of their regime characteristic was the breakdown of these distinctions between public and private, centralized and decentralized. The oppressiveness of dictatorial regimes was felt both in the fact that citizens had less of a private life *and* no real public existence. At the very least, it is not clear how H-W's concept of "centralized enforcement" helps us understand this absolutely crucial feature of dictatorial regimes, despite the fact that a judgment running through their series of papers is that dictatorial regimes are especially "centralized" while rule of law is characteristic of legal orders relying more on "decentralized" enforcement.

Furthermore, as a matter of knowing what kind of society H-W are modeling, and therefore knowing what kind of evidence we would need to test the model, these distinctions matter. Have they modeled a non-existent utopia? Or have they given us an explanation of some of the features of known dystopias? Again, we cannot answer these questions without greater care and precision in the use of the term "private." Is it the opposite of "public"? of "standing"? of "centralized"? And what would count as concrete historical examples of each?

## II. A Positive Theory of Utopia?: The Model Independent of Historical Evidence

Now one might respond to this first set of concerns by saying that we do not need examples, at least in the first instance, because H-W provide us with a model. More than that, it is a positive theory of utopia in the literal sense of modeling a regime with which we have no experience: it is nowhere and all good, "utopia" and "eutopia." After all, H-W say theirs is a model of a regime in which everyone subject to the law and capable of understanding it can also be the law's enforcers. As they put it: "A regime characterized by rule of law is the only equilibrium, we argue, when enforcement of public classifications relies *exclusively* on private enforcement."[13] Exclusive private enforcement of public classifications (rules) must mean no publicly employed policemen, sheriffs, or gendarmes. In that society, with which we have no modern experience, we would have rules with the attributes that philosophers describe as rule of law. This sounds like a positive theory of why we do not need a modern state, in the sense of special bodies of armed men with authority to coerce everyone else into obeying the law. In fact, the less we have of that, and the more we have of private enforcement, the more that a legal order will come to look like the kind of regime we want.

It is important to remember here that a central motivation for H-W's work on this subject is to highlight the degree to which *normative* theories of law include under-theorized *positive* theses about how legal subjects will *actually* behave. They are right to emphasize this issue and to note that their positive theory is a corrective to and relevant for normative and analytic theory. So perhaps the role for their what-is-law approach is not to make predictions testable against actual experience, but rather to provide more robust behavioral foundations for ideal theory: the ideal of a society governed by public norms that are in the interest of all. This is Leninist withering-away-of-the-state as game theory. In a radically different society in which all enforce the law, the law will be in the interest of all, and, in a virtuous circle, enforcement will preserve those laws.

This is an exciting possibility, but I worry it draws H-W away from their stated aims. They say their intention is to complement and improve legal philosophy by showing that the behavioral or positive basis of the rule of law is most likely achieved not in the modern state, with its monopoly of coercive authority, but rather with privately organized enforcement. However, for many theories of the rule of law, and for much political philosophy, H-W's model is missing a crucial *behavioral* or *positive* component. In those legal and political theories, what matters is not just *that* people behave in certain law-obeying and law-enforcing ways but, further, that they do so *for the right reasons.* That is the full *behavioral* component of these theories. For complete rule of law, those subject to the law must follow the law at least in part because they acknowledge its authority.[14] That is one reason they emphasize the difference between a legal as opposed to a purely coercive command: the police and the robber each have guns, but only in one case are we supposed to accept the authority of the gun-holder whereas in the other we act purely out of fear. A positive theory of the rule of law is going to have to include those kinds of reasons for acting *as outcomes in the model*; otherwise, it is modeling something else. This should be worrying for theorists intending to add the behavioral or positive component that legal theory is missing.

It is true that H-W say that the individuals in their model have no "pro-social" preferences, which sounds like it excludes making any claims about the motivations or interests of actors. But that is only a half-response. The good half is that it means utopia is feasible. Self-interested actors, on H-W's model, will enforce norms if there is a clear legal order bearing the attributes of the rule of law because it is in their interest. We can have Leninist outcomes with Kantian crooked timber. The stateless utopia is within reach even assuming a bunch of self-interested actors. Calculations of personal advantage are enough to arrive at a stable equilibrium in which each is willing to enforce disinterested public norms even when a particular instance of norm enforcement might appear to be personally costly. However, the bad half is that H-W's model requires assuming that the actors are *always and everywhere* acting strategically, out of self-interest. That means these actors do not recognize the authority of the law as something that requires they act in a certain way independent of their personal calculations. By methodological construction, there is no room in the model for motivation based on respect for the law itself. There is therefore no room in the model for actors who believe in the rule of law.

Here, I think, is the strongest sense in which H-W are talking about private action: actors are modeled as individuals who have no conception of themselves as public beings, citizens producing and enforcing a public life together as legal and political subjects, living under common authority. True, there is common knowledge of the rules, but only in the same way there is common knowledge of the laws of gravity. That common knowledge is different from incorporating into one's identity and preferences the awareness of living in a public world, having an existence as an agent *because* one lives in a legally constituted community of political actors. Life as a political agent responsible for the laws is not permitted as itself a value included in the individual's preferences, nor is any sense of the authority that public agencies enjoy.

Such values and preferences are not the same as "pro-social" attitudes, in which we care about the wellbeing of other individuals. To be clear, I am not criticizing H-W for excluding "pro-social" attitudes generally. My criticism is internal to their own project of modeling the rule of law. It is hard to understand quite what "acting for the right reasons" or "obeying authority" could even mean in the model. If that is the case, then we have an incomplete positive theory of the rule of law. We have only a theory of behavioral compliance with a legal order. In other words, I am not criticizing the model for being unrealistic because people tend to have some pro-social attitudes. That kind of criticism might be fair, but it is irrelevant. Rather I am pointing out a deep inconsistency based on the terms that H-W have themselves accepted: the behavioral assumptions of rule of law theory. The very concept of a public authority requires modeling these individuals as required to acknowledge the legitimacy of that authority. Their public selfhood, as we might call it, is what explains why they are supposed to recognize the authority of the law in the first place.

Nor is H-W's model evolutionary. It does not predict that actors will come to see the rule of law as legitimate, or act on the basis of the authority of the law. Strategically interacting individuals make calculations about their own interests, they enforce law for the sake of assuring others, but they never ask or come to ask whether the rule of law attributes are themselves reasons for obeying and enforcing the law. In this model, there are only ever men and women, not citizens. That is why H-W's game-theoretic approach excludes rather than models behavioral considerations required for a full, positive theory of the rule of law.[15] This is probably going to be a problem for any game-theoretic model of the rule of law, since even an evolutionary or "iterated game" approach has to assume a capacity for normative motivation or for strong identification with shared norms.

For these reasons, then, no matter how exciting it is to think that we have the first example of Leninist game theory, this paper is not a positive theory of utopia, and might not even be a positive theory of the rule of law. Again, that is because on theories of the rule of law to which H-W refer, the central behavioral or "positive" question is not just how those subject to the law behave, but why. This criticism matters because the rule of law is in part attractive, at least in political philosophy, because of the way it constitutes us as citizens and induces us to behave *as* citizens. It gives us new reasons for acting. That, for instance, is what Rousseau meant when he spoke of trading natural liberty for a civil and political equality. Moreover, there is a non-trivial irony in the fact that, although H-W present their theory as the opposite of the dictatorial approach to legal order, it is only in dictatorial regimes that legal subjects are assumed to be indifferent to the sources of law and to the legal order's authority. In those regimes, we have private actors who are forced to relate strategically to a legal order that is in an important sense not their own and where force and fear tend to replace normative modes of authority.

### III. From Utopia to Dystopia: The Rule of Law in History

Perhaps, however, H-W are unconcerned with some of these criticisms because their intention lies elsewhere. The model is a heuristic for understanding the real features of actual legal regimes, not the potential features of ideal regimes. Their model therefore makes empirical, testable predictions. This brings use to the third general set of concerns. For if it is the case that this is a testable theory, it looks like a positive theory of dystopia, one that either predicts why some will be denied the authority to enforce public norms, or one that stands in some tension with historical experience.

*A Positive Theory of Dystopia:* Consider, again, that the one concrete example H-W refer to is the example of a slave society. If democratic Athens is proof of the model, it sounds now like a nightmarish positive theory, one whose primary purpose is to show us how the most likely equilibria is not that everyone subject to the law will also be its enforcers but, rather, why the most likely equilibrium is one in which the laws will be shaped in a way to generate enforcement from a powerful minority of those subject to those laws. There might be some rule of law internal to the enforcers, but only on condition that they share an agreement to exploit the wider class of private individuals. As H-W themselves argue, in a clarifying footnote, "our model predicts that universality will be qualified, in the sense of not necessarily extending to everyone in society; in particular, we expect that only the needs and interests of those people who are needed for effective collective punishment will be reflected in the rules."[16] What H-W call "qualified universality" has a more accurate name: class rule. In saying that we will get legal attributes that "incentivize and coordinate" punishment, what they are predicting is not just that some will be authorized to make and enforce laws, but further that there is strong reason to think there will be systematic *denials of* the private capacity to change or enforce laws, and that these norms will be enforced by those whose interests are represented in the law.

In this case, Athens stands as a very disturbing, rather than supportive, example. After all, what is doing the work here in stabilizing the equilibrium characteristic of the Athenian juridical system is not just the formal characteristics of the legal regime, but also its substantive class character. Athenian oligarchs and poor residents could live together as legal equals at least in part because the wealthy turned to an alternative source of dependent labor: slaves. Enslavement took the form of social and legal death— condemnation to a purely private existence. As scholars of Athens observe, the Solonian and Cleisthenic legal reforms establishing citizenship for all male Athenians, including some of the iconic features of the legal order—like isegoria (free public speech), isonomia (equality before the law), and abolition of debt-bondage— emerged out of the class compromises among wealthy and poor Athenians, compromises that in turn relied on the turn to slave labor.[17]

We can translate this point at least somewhat back into the language of H-W: there was a legal order with public classification and private enforcement so long as that private enforcement was carefully circumscribed—even centralized—to secure dominant interests. As crucial to the private enforcement of the law was the prohibition on private enforcement of it by others—e.g., slaves and women.[18] However exactly we phrase it, we have to say that, as a model that aims to explain actual regimes, this looks more like a positive theory of dystopia, of why we will get rule of law features only in extremely exploitative regimes, where large groups are banished from full legal status or private enforcement capacity. To call this "qualified universality" underplays its significance.

Moreover, recognizing the class character of "qualified universality" requires admitting back into a positive theory of legal development some kind of historical sociology of law. At the very least, we want to know whether H-W think their model is primarily predictive of these severely dystopian regimes, in which strong internal rule of law among the primary enforcers is predicated on the systematic denial of legal powers and enforcement capacities from a large body of adults. Importantly, the same points could be made by reference to the antebellum slave-holding South and other modern regimes. It could even be made about contemporary debates about law enforcement, gun control, and gun rights.[19] So it is no answer to say that the example of Athens is poorly chosen. After all, the deeper point is that if we want to explain legal attributes, it looks like we must do so by reference to the political sociology of a regime. The question of who enforces looks, itself, to be a political question that is determined by those powerful, organized groups who can shape both the law and its enforcement in their interests. That again seems to be a prediction of the model, which is why it looks like a positive theory of dystopia.

*A Positive Theory Falsified by Evidence?* Finally, if we move to other parts of the historical record, we find a set of facts that raise questions about just what H-W intend their model to explain. H-W note that the historical trend is towards centralized *enforcement*, not just classification. Importantly, this trend has occurred at least in part by groups *voluntarily giving up* some private control over enforcement for the sake of creating a centralized, public enforcement agency. That is to say, under conditions of private enforcement, instead of getting a "demand" for a legal order with rule of law characteristics, we have instead seen a "demand" from at least some private enforcers for *more centralized* law enforcement by official agents. It is unclear to me just how this fits with H-W's claim that their results are equilibrium results. Here again, the stakes are high, because if we even want to grasp where the utopia of a decentralized enforcement regime comes from, we first have to grasp the rise of the modern state to which that utopia is a reaction.

To take the example I know best, consider the origins of the modern police force in America, particular its emergence as a centralized, professional, militarized apparatus. As Sam Mitrani observes, in his excellent history of the Chicago Police Department, "the police are now so ubiquitous that it is hard to imagine a time before they existed." Yet, as Mitrani further reminds us, "the police evolved relatively late in U.S. history."[20] The expansion in legal powers, military capacity, and sheer size of the formal security apparatus began in the mid- to late nineteenth century, which is also when we got many of the major rule of law changes. For instance, in mid-nineteenth-century Chicago, the major and minor employers of labor had, for a long time, resisted paying taxes to fund a properly paid and trained police force, instead preferring to hire their own private security guards to protect their property. During this time, police did little in the way of protecting property or arresting murderers and rapists; rather, they mostly arrested drunks and prostitutes.[21] The protection of person and property was largely a private or communal affair, managed through informal or ad hoc groups.

With the rise of major strikes in the late nineteenth century, which private guards were unable to quell, Chicago's leading figures agreed to pay the taxes to create a public, centralized, permanent police force operated by the state. They even used private funds to buy weapons, uniforms, and build military structures to supply the police. This was a pattern followed in many major and minor cities, and it went hand in hand with these same leading figures paying more taxes, and donating personal wealth, to other centralized enforcement agencies like the National Guard.[22] For decades upon decades, this centralization occurred in order to improve the enforcement of legal norms. In numerous instances, as documented by the federal military itself, national soldiers were used to preserve domestic order. As one author puts it, for many decades in the late nineteenth and early twentieth centuries, "the U.S. Army came close to being a national police force."[23] While various kinds of private enforcement activities continued (from blacklisting and private security forces to reporting individuals to public authorities), we have here a state-building, legal development story about how centralized enforcement arose out of more informal, decentralized enforcement. So the historical record suggests that the main driver behind public classification that H-W identify—"the increased ambiguity about what counts as right and wrong that accompanies the increased economic specialization and social differentiation that growth, mobility, and economic integration generate"[24]—also promotes centralized enforcement.

The American story is not so unique. With national variations, we find the same basic story repeated in all developed countries. Decentralized enforcement develops into centralized enforcement, often with the cooperation of those who had controlled those more decentralized modes of enforcement. This looks problematic for one of the central predictions of the H-W model. After all, the point here is not just the generalized ambiguity about norms that arises from specialization and differentiation, which would only require centralized classification. Rather, centralization of enforcement emerges from the failure of private modes of enforcement to contain class conflict. This particular kind of class conflict is itself the product of the "increased economic specialization and social differentiation" of the modern economy—which concentrates, urbanizes, and expands the class of workers in a way not seen under earlier societies. Such developments dramatically change the conditions under which it is possible to enforce a normative order. So it appears that the same factor that H-W identify as driving the transformation from an organic to a legal order—increasing social complexity and differentiation—is also what changes the conditions of enforcement. Private enforcement of certain contested legal norms around property, contract, and labor law becomes impossible. In the face of that kind of conflict, only a powerful, centralized coercive apparatus can preserve law and order.

We might find a response to this concern in H-W's argument that the legal order will be structured to incentivize the law enforcers' participation in enforcement. But it is unclear how we are therefore to measure that prediction against the history of centralized enforcement. If the wealthy tend to find their interests reflected in the structure of law as well as in its enforcement, which is presumably why they end up supporting the creation of the police, it is unclear why the H-W model would predict that fact. After all, the wealthy are those who have *given up* large shares of control over private enforcement to create public enforcement. Perhaps we can make sense of this by adding in the fact that the wealthy *do* shoulder the burdens of norm enforcement, not directly by engaging in policing, but by paying taxes that finance the police. We might also hypothesize that they have ways of controlling policing through their disproportionate influence on policy and administration. However, that seems to be outside the model. It once again suggests that modeling the form of legal order and enforcement by reference to anonymous, self-interested individuals rather than groups or some other political sociology seems to miss a great deal. In any case, whether we can or cannot accommodate the growth of the modern police to the model is less the issue than just how we are supposed to relate actual historical evidence to possible predictions from the model. If the political bargains leading to the creation of an official, centralized police force are not a falsification of the model, what would be? Or if this model does predict the rise of a police force primarily protecting the interests of the wealthy, then that looks once again like a positive theory of dystopia. It might even require H-W to call the modern, centralized enforcement of law in the United States and elsewhere quasi-dictatorial, since it contains so many features similar to those that H-W call purely dictatorial.

One further twist. H-W say that in their model, the rule of law is something "demanded" by private enforcers, to incentivize and coordinate that enforcement. Yet it should be noted that the demand for the rule of law has, historically speaking, been a response not from private enforcers of the law but, rather, from those seeking to discipline and control the use of force by already centralized enforcement powers. That is to say, the flip side of the story about centralizing enforcement that I just sketched is that the social demand for rule of law has arisen *as a response to* the exercise of that power, rather than as a demand from private enforcers. Both revolutionary movements by private individuals, such as the democratic revolutions in Europe during the nineteenth century, which attempted to constitutionalize state power, as well as evolutionary and reformatory movements, such as, say, the civil rights movement in the United States, demanded the rule of law *not* because it incentivized their private enforcement but rather because they sought to make the centralized enforcement of power less arbitrary and more consistent with their interests.

It is true that we might see revolutions themselves as a form of private, "unofficial" norm enforcement. Perhaps what incentivizes that kind of revolutionary private enforcement of basic constitutional norms is the *promise* of a legal order that possesses more of the attributes of the rule of law than previously. So perhaps a further implication or even prediction of H-W's model is that non–rule of law legal orders will produce revolutionary responses by private agents who attempt to transform the legal order into something that is more in line with their agents. We can thereby see revolutions as acts of private norm enforcement. But this again seems like a bending of the game-theoretic model. Moreover, it cannot answer why the usual demand for rule of law has taken the form not for more private enforcement of legal norms but for more professionalized police forces enforcing better laws (however conceived).

To recap, at the theoretical level, it is still unclear how we are to think about what the H-W model predicts and whether historical evidence is in conflict with it. It looks very much like a positive theory of dystopia, which predicts strong internal rule of law among enforcers, but on condition that there is an exploitable, legally subordinate group. Yet it also appears that the history of centralized enforcement and popular demands that the state conform to rule of law conflict with the model's predictions. And at a deeper level, this raises the worry that a game-theoretic model of the development of legal order is bound to remain at a level of such abstraction as to be of little use in explaining actual legal regimes. At least, that appears to be the case for models that strip out any political sociology from their explanations or predictions of equilibrium legal orders.

## IV. Conclusion

Although I have been critical of their efforts, I believe Hadfield and Weingast ask one of the most foundational and pressing questions in political science. Wouldn't it be better for the laws to be universally and privately enforced? It is a strange fact about our profession that so few political scientists and economists—though not legal scholars—show interest in law enforcement when it is such a major feature of our political life.[25] As I edited this essay, news footage appeared of a Baton Rouge police officer shooting a black man named Alton Sterling at point-blank range while Sterling was pinned to the ground by another police officer.[26] A day later, a woman named Diamond Reynolds filmed her husband, Philando Castile, dying in their car when a police officer shot him during a routine traffic stop.[27] Within days, policemen in Dallas and Baton Rouge then found themselves on the receiving end of murderous violence.[28] In the United States, these are the most immediate images we have of centralized law enforcement. The images are not mere visual anec-data. The best data suggests that poor minorities are disproportionately likely to be killed by the police than other people and that these same groups make up a massively disproportionate share of those who have coercive encounters with the police or are incarcerated.[29] The best studies show that this cannot be explained by the fact that these minorities are more likely to commit crimes.[30] They are targeted for who they are, not what they did. On top of which, the age of mass incarceration appears to be the era in which the United States has decided to deal with poverty by throwing the poor in jail. As the numbers show, the racial disparity in incarceration rates has remained constant since the 1970s, but the class disparity has massively increased.[31] In fact, though the United States is one of the worst, many countries have turned to more repressive strategies for dealing with social disorder, and global incarceration rates have increased.[32]

More than in most industrial democracies, Americans are faced with the question of whether we ought to subject the police and justice system generally to more rigorous rule of law principles or whether we ought to hope that we can disband that system. But what does "disband" mean? Is it the elimination of all specialized, official security personnel? Do we mean private coercive enforcement with publicly managed prisons? Do we mean the abolition of the prison system itself? There is something utopian and deeply desirable about the abolition of all but the most temporary coercive enforcement of public norms. The elimination of crime, and therefore the need to punish crime, has been one of the longest-standing dreams of modern political thought. It is the original germ of what became the socialist critique of poverty. Eliminate the social conditions that create crime and we will not need a state.[33] This is not just a world of privately enforced norms but also a world in which enforcement of any sort is much less needed.

That social vision is compelling. It is of a world with a richer public *and* private life. There would be fewer, if any, individuals with impoverished private lives and, not accidentally, most people would have a stronger attachment to the public norms that bind the community as a whole. There would be less coercion, whether by private or public forces. This might very well be utopian, at least as far as any of us can see today, which admittedly is not very far. But if we are to grasp what makes the vision utopian, either as a picture of human relations or as a model with certain assumptions about human motivation, we need to think not just about who enforces norms but why the norms are what they are and why there is crime in the first place. We could do worse than return to the questions of an earlier era, when social theorists dared to ask whether the need to enforce norms itself could be, if not eliminated, then drastically reduced. The answer to that question returns us to the question of the relationship between private and public life, or what political theorists once called the relationship between man and citizen. Whatever that answer looks like in its details, it cannot be one in which one side of that relationship disappears or becomes instrumental to the other. If we see citizenship, our participation in collective life, merely as a means by which our own private interests are secured, then we have a poor theory even of what private interests are. For we conceive our interests as utterly separate from the kinds of social relations we have with others, and we strip away those motivations that might stabilize our willingness to be a part of society in the first place. Moreover, as we have seen with Hadfield and Weingast's model, this way of deriving rule of law from private interests predicts a society in which public rules and their enforcement are shaped to exploit some for the benefit of others. That is a society that creates crime and then represses it in the name of law and order. Better to call that ideology, not justice.

## NOTES

1 V. I. Lenin, *The State and Revolution* (London: Junius, 1994): 87–88. Emphasis added.

2 On slave patrols as informal policing, see Philip Reichel, "Southern Slave Patrols as Transitional Police Type," *American Journal of Police* 7, no. 2 (1988): 51–77.

3 On the persecution of homosexuals, under the auspices of anti-communism, see the discussion in Corey Robin, *The Reactionary Mind* (Oxford: Oxford University Press, 2011): 201–16.

4 Hadfield and Weingast, this volume, endnote 48.

5 Gillian Hadfield and Barry Weingast, "What is Law? A Coordination Model of the Characteristics of Legal Order," *Journal of Legal Analysis* 4, no. 2, (2012): 473.

6  Hadfield and Weingast, this volume. Emphasis added.

7  Ibid. Emphasis added.

8  Ibid. Emphasis added.

9  That is not entirely true, given the existence of the 300 Scythian archers—usually understood as a public police force. For now we will accept the description of Athens as entirely private since the function of the Scythian archers is not very clear. See endnote 12.

10  On the bundles of rights and privileges bound up with the Roman status of "civis," see Chaim Wirszubski, *Libertas as a Political Idea at Rome During the Late Republic and Early Principate* (Cambridge: Cambridge University Press, 1968), chapter 1, and Claude Nicolet, *The World of the Citizen in Republican Rome,* trans. P. S. Falla (Berkeley, CA: University of California Press, 1980), esp. chapters 1 and 8. On the private policing of slaves in Rome by citizens, see K. R. Bradley, *Society and Slavery at Rome* (Cambridge: Cambridge University Press, 1994). For the American case, see the important discussion of informal policing in Reichel, "Southern Slave Patrols."

11  For discussions of this point, see Josiah Ober, *Mass and Elite in Democratic Athens: Rhetoric, Ideology, and the Power of the People* (Princeton, NJ: Princeton University Press, 1990): 60–64; Keith Hopkins, *Conquerors and Slaves* (Cambridge: Cambridge University Press, 1991): 114; Moses Finley, *Ancient Slavery and Modern Ideology* (New York: Penguin Books, 1992): 82–84; Orlando Patterson, *Freedom Vol. 1: Freedom in the Making of the Modern World* (New York: Basic Books, 1991): 64–81.

12  The evidence for the role of Scythian archers is slim beyond the fact that they appear to have been a small police force owned publicly, by the Athenians as a whole. For a discussion of their role, see Mogens Herman Hansen, *The Athenian Democracy in the Age of Demosthenes,* trans. J. A. Crook (Norman, OK: University of Oklahoma Press, 1999): 123–24.

13  Hadfield and Weingast, this volume. Emphasis added.

14  The degree to which normative theories of the rule of law require that kind of motivational foundation is contested, but just about every theory of the rule of law requires at least some actors to be motivated by the authority of the law. H-W, however, do not, and, as I argue in the next paragraphs, *cannot* allow for that motivation in their theory.

15  Lurking in the background might be a concern about the limits of game-theoretic modeling of norms. After all, from the perspective of normative theory, people follow norms because those norms have authority and that authority is relatively independent from calculations of self-interest. So to model actors as purely self-interested is just to fail to model normative action and, at some point, to say those norms do not exist *qua norms.* On the question of normative authority, especially with respect to

the context of the law, see Joseph Raz, *The Morality of Freedom* (Oxford: Oxford University Press, 1986): 23–64.

16 Hadfield and Weingast, this volume, endnote 24.

17 See Wirszubski, *Libertas as a Political Idea*; Nicolet, *The World of the Citizen*; and Bradley, *Society and Slavery at Rome*.

18 It has to be added, moreover, that this was not a particular stable legal regime, since even among Athenians the "private enforcement" tipped over into revolution and counter-revolutionary tyranny multiple times. It is for this reason that early modern political philosophers, when looking to the ancients, tended to see Sparta, not Athens, as the paradigm of a stable regime, at equilibrium, ruled under law, rather than "democracy." Rousseau, for instance, spoke much more favorably of Sparta than Athens on just these grounds.

19 See for instance my article on gun control. Alex Gourevitch, "Gun Control's Racist Reality: The Liberal Argument against Giving Police More Power," *Salon.com*, June 25, 2015, www.salon.com.

20 Sam Mitrani, *The Rise of the Chicago Police Department* (Urbana, IL: University of Illinois Press, 2013): 217.

21 Ibid., 54, 136; Keith Harring, *Policing a Class Society: The Experience of American Cities, 1865–1915* (New Brunswick, NJ: Rutgers University Press, 1983): 149–223.

22 On Chicago, see Mitrani, *The Rise of the Chicago Police Department*. For the broader story, see Harring's *Policing a Class Society*, as well as my review essay, Alex Gourevitch, "Police Work: The Centrality of Labor Repression in American Political History," *Perspectives on Politics* 13, no. 3 (2015): 762–73.

23 Barton Hacker, "The United States Army as a National Police Force: The Federal Policing of Labor Disputes, 1877–1898," *Military Affairs* 33, no. 1 (1969): 261.

24 Hadfield and Weingast, this volume.

25 On the relative silence of American political science on the question of policing, see the excellent review essay by Joe Soss and Vesla Weaver, "Learning from Ferguson: Policing, Race, and Class in American Politics" *Annual Review of Political Science* 20 (forthcoming).

26 Wesley Lowery, Travis M. Andrews, and Michael Miller, "Outrage After Video Captures White Baton Rouge Police Officer Fatally Shooting A Black Man," *Washington Post*, July 6, 2016, www.washingtonpost.com.

27 Mitch Smith, "Philando Castile's Last Night: Tacos and Laughs, Then a Drive," *New York Times*, July 12, 2016, www.nytimes.com.

28 F. Brinley Bruton, Alexander Smith, Elizabeth Chuck, and Phil Helsel, "Dallas Police 'Ambush': 12 Officers Shot, 5 Killed During Protest," *NBC News*, July 8, 2016, www.nbcnews.com.

298    ALEX GOUREVITCH

29 Cody T. Ross, "A Multi-Level Bayesian Analysis of Racial Bias in Police Shootings at the County-Level in the United States, 2011–2014," *PlosOne* 10, no.11, doi:10.1371/journal.pone.0141854; Sandhya Somashekar, Wesley Lowery, Keith L. Alexander, Kimberly Kindy, and Julie Tate, "Black and Unarmed," *Washington Post*, August 8, 2015, www.washingtonpost.com; Ryan Gabrielson, Ryann Grochowski Jones, and Eric Sagara, "Deadly Force, in Black and White," *ProPublica*, October 10, 2014, www.propublica.org.

There are numerous books and articles on this subject. The best review article is Soss and Weaver, "Learning from Ferguson." Useful overview books are Bruce Western, *Punishment and Inequality in America* (New York: Russell Sage Foundation, 2007) and Marie Gottschalk, *Caught: The Prison State and the Lockdown of American Politics* (Princeton, NJ: Princeton University Press, 2015). On the origins of racial disparities in incarceration, showing that they date back to the Northern policing strategies around the Great Migration in the 1920s, see the very important work by Christopher Muller, "Northward Migration and the Rise of Racial Disparity in American Incarceration, 1880–1950," *American Journal of Sociology* 118, no. 2 (2012): 281–326.

30 See especially Soss and Weaver, "Learning from Ferguson," fn21.

31 Muller, "Northward Migration," and Western, *Punishment and Inequality in America.*

32 Roy Walmsley, *World Prison Population List* (London: Institute for Criminal Policy Research, 2015).

33 For example, one of the first modern socialist plans, in the sense of a practical plan of social reform, not just idealized but separate community, was the "College of Industry" proposed by the Quaker John Bellers in 1696. One of Bellers's main arguments for the creation of a community of workers, populated by the unemployed and the working poor, which would guarantee all members an income in exchange for their work service, was that it would eliminate crime. That became a standard argument among socialists for decades and Robert Owen found Bellers's proposal so attractive that he reprinted it in 1818 with Owen's own foundational socialist text *New View of Society*. That is, I think, the origin of what, passing through nineteenth-century social theory, became the Leninist ideal of the stateless society. I provide here the citation for Bellers's original publication, followed by that for Owen's republication. John Bellers, *Proposals for Raising a College of Industry* (London: T. Sowle, 1696), reprinted in Robert Owen, *New View of Society* (London: Longman, Hurst, et al., 1818).

# 12

# PRIVATIZING WAR

## CÉCILE FABRE

### I. Introduction

Privatization is commonly defined as the outsourcing to non-state actors of the financing and/or provision of services and goods which are, or have hitherto been, normally regarded as within the remit of state action—such as garbage collections, telecommunications, health care, school provision, energy and transports, law enforcement, and war.[1] It is common to assume that a state privatizes the financing or provision of a good/service when and in so far as it explicitly and deliberately outsources either or both to for-profit organizations. Strictly speaking, however, this need not be the case. For example, within the context of a welfare state, a decision to entrust a charity with the task of providing food for the needy is an act of privatization; likewise, a state which is committed to capital punishment for murder engages in privatization when it knowingly lets non-state agents such as Mafia gangs engage in the punitive killing of murderers. As those examples suggest, beneficiaries of privatization can be non-profit actors, and privatization itself can proceed either by an act of explicit conferral of rights to the beneficiary, or in virtue of the fact that the state does not perform its functions and thus creates space for other agents to do it.

In this paper, I focus on the privatization of war as a means to enforce morally justified norms. Although war is traditionally seen as a means to protect the rights of state or individuals, it has more recently been conceptualized as a means to enforce international law.[2] Hence my question here: may war construed as a form of policing be privatized? By privatization, I mean not the outsourcing of war to for-profit actors such as private military corporations but, rather, its outsourcing to non-state actors in general, whether individuals or organizations, and whether they act for profit or not.[3]

Friends and foes of the privatization of norm enforcement share a commitment to the rule of law. Its moderate friends believe that norm enforcement can comply with the rule of law even if it is carried out by private actors. Its radical friends hold that the rule of law obtains only if private actors are given an essential role in the enforcement of norms. Contrastingly, enemies of privatization object to it on the grounds that private actors are simply unable to properly enforce norms in compliance with the rule of law.

I argue in favor of the moderate view, in the specific context of war. To do so, after setting the stage in section II, I adapt to the case of war Gillian K. Hadfield and Barry R. Weingast's defense of the radical view. In section III, I argue that whatever its merit as an account of private enforcement in the municipal realm, Hadfield and Weingast's argument does not translate well to the enforcement of international norms by means of war. In section IV, I reject one of the most plausible arguments against all forms of privatized norm enforcement—recently developed by Alon Harel. Drawing on my criticisms of those two views, in section V, I provide an argument for the moderate privatization of war as a means to enforce international moral norms. Section VI concludes.

## II. SETTING THE STAGE

### The Violent Enforcement of Moral Norms

By focusing on the use of violence to enforce morally justified norms, I exclude from my inquiry the enforcement of egregiously unjust practices such as slavery in the antebellum American South. I also exclude the enforcement of norms which, though morally justified, nevertheless ought not to be enforced, such as the duty to keep promises. The moral norms I have in mind are norms which ought in principle to be turned into legal norms, whether or not they are, as a matter of fact, currently enforced. With this claim in hand, I ask whether the state may justifiably, indeed must, allow private actors to decide whether or not to enforce international moral norms by means of war.[4]

To answer that question, we must have a working account of the justified violent enforcement of moral norms. Descriptively, I posit that to enforce a norm violently is to threaten putative wrongdoers with physical and/or psychological harm as a means to deter breaches of the norm, or to harm active wrongdoers as a means either to stop them from breaching the norms or, ex post, as a means to punish them for such breaches. Enforcement, in other words, can be defensive or punitive. In this paper, in so far as my concern is with war, and as punishment is not an adequate justification for war, I focus on defensive enforcement.[5]

Now, in this paper, I posit that the enforcement of moral norms by means of war is morally justified only if it meets two sets of conditions. First, it must meet the requirements of justified war in general. More precisely, war must enforce a morally justified legal norm (the just cause requirement); the harms resulting from it must not be out of proportion to the goods it brings about; it is a necessary means to the end of defending the norm/punishing breaches thereof; it has a reasonable chance of success; combatants must not deliberately target the innocent.

Second, violent enforcement, in this context, is the violent enforcement of moral norms which ought to be turned into legal norms, it is justified only if it complies with the rule of law broadly construed—so long as conditions are propitious for the establishment of, and compliance with, the rule of law (I shall return to this proviso in section V). The rule of law is a contested notion. Still, I will adopt the following, relatively uncontroversial, definition. The rule of law obtains only when (a) relations between individuals are regulated and constrained by enforceable moral norms which are publicly available, prospective, predictable, and determinate; (b) the enforcement of those norms is itself constrained and regulated by rules which are publicly available, prospective, predictable, and determinate; (c) those norms apply equally to all and are enforced by agents who act impartially in the light of the rules of enforcement, rather than on the basis of their own personal preferences.[6]

Although the rule of law is not a particularly controversial ideal in the context of municipal law enforcement, not all scholars accept that there is an *international* rule of law—even though there is such a thing as a body of international law in general, and a body of international public law (of which the laws of war are a subset) in particular.[7] One of the main objections to the idea of an international rule of law is that there is no overarching arbiter and enforcer of international enforceable moral norms, at the cost of predictability and transparency. As many legal theorists have countered, however, the charge is somewhat overstated. After all, there are many international non-judicial and judicial institutions, each with the ultimate authority to interpret norms and adjudicate conflicts in their own areas of competence (viz. the UN Security Council, the ICC, the ICJ, to name but a few), and it makes sense therefore to hold that their decisions should comply with and reflect the core ideals of the rule of law. Moreover, to the extent that states incorporate those international norms in their municipal legal system, they too can plausibly be held to those ideals when so acting. Generally put, states' decisions have a far-reaching impact on the lives of millions of individuals within *and* outside their borders; so do decisions taken by supranational organizations. It is thus a requirement of governance in the international sphere that it should be characterized by the aforementioned features of the rule of law.[8]

## Privatization

On my reading of their works, proponents and foes of privatization whose arguments I shall review in sections III and IV would (I believe) agree with the foregoing points. The question, thus, is whether the nature of the enforcers, as state agents or private agents, makes a difference to the justifiability of the enforcement of norms by means of war (henceforth, *per bellum* enforcement.) To answer that question, we need to have a firm handle on what is meant by the privatization of war. Generally, when one talks of the privatization of a service, one might have in mind the act by which the state entrusts a private actor with the task of deciding whether or not to provide that service, or the mere fact that the state lets a private actor provide that service without explicitly authorizing her to do so. Or we might mean the act by which the state, having decided that the service will be provided in general, entrusts a private actor with the task of actually providing it, or simply lets private actors provide it without explicit authorization. To illustrate:

the state might decide that the norm against insulting other heads of state is not one that it will itself enforce through war, yet leave it to non-state actors to decide whether the norm will be enforced. Or it may decide that the norm against unwarranted military aggression does warrant enforcement in principle by way of a military response, and leave subsequent decisions (whether actually to enforce that norm in a given case, and if so how to enforce it) to non-state actors such as private military corporations and/or private individuals acting in their own capacity. Or it may decide that the moral norm against non-aggression does warrant enforcement and reserve itself the right to decide in a given case whether to respond in kind, yet entrust the task of fighting that war to non-state actors.

In the remainder of this paper, in so far as I am concerned with enforceable moral norms, I take it for granted that the state, and the state alone, either on its own or in partnership with other states, decides to turn a moral norm into a legal norm. The question is whether the task of enforcing that legal norm must be performed solely by non-state actors, may be carried out solely by private actors, or may/must be carried out by both—where enforcement denotes (as the case may be) either the act of determining that a breach has occurred, or the act of inflicting violence in response to the breach, or both. For lack of space, I shall restrict my remarks to cases where the state explicitly authorizes private actors to wage or fight in war and set aside cases of passive acquiescence.

### III. PRIVATE WAR AND THE RULE OF LAW: AGAINST RADICAL PRIVATIZATION

Consider the moral norm against unjustified military aggression— one of the least controversial that there is. It has been turned into a legal norm by the international community of states via a number of international documents such as Chapter VI of the UN Charter, violations of which expose wrongdoers to defensive military responses and to punishment ex post by relevant international courts. Suppose, then, that state A (Aggressor) unwarrantedly invades state D (Defender), in violation of the legal norm against aggression. Enforcing the norm, in this scenario, takes the form of a military response aimed at repelling Aggressor's troops.[9]

To what extent does such a decision comply with the rule of law? In section II, I averred that an enforcer complies with the rule of law only if her actions are constrained and regulated by rules which are publicly available, predictable, prospective, and determinate, and if she acts in the light of those norms rather than on the basis of her own personal preferences. Accordingly, Defender complies with the rule of law by resorting to a war of self-defense against Aggressor only if its decision to do so is constrained and regulated by publicly available, predictable, prospective, and determinate legal rules that enshrine the conditions under which war is morally justified. Those norms are necessity, proportionality, and the prohibition on targeting the innocent—in other words, something like international humanitarian law and its instantiation in municipal law.[10] When deciding to repel Aggressor's invasion by force, and in so doing to authorize the deliberate killing of Aggressor's soldiers and the likely collateral killing of some of its innocent civilians, Defender—or, rather, its leaders and citizens—must act in the light of those norms and not on the basis of their individual preferences. This requires of Defender, first, that it should be able to determine, fairly, impartially, and beyond reasonable doubt, that Aggressor is indeed acting in breach of the legal norm against aggression; second, that once it has so determined and decided to enforce that norm by violent means (*per bellum*), the resulting war should be constrained by the law of armed conflict.

Suppose that Aggressor *has* been found to breach the norm against military aggression. Who can enforce that norm? In other words, who can go to war in defense of Defender? To many, the answer is obvious: well, Defender itself and, indeed, any other state willing to step in, since in the world as we know it, there simply is no overarching, international army to interpose itself in between the two parties.

Note, though, that this response would not on its own satisfy friends of the rule of law: after all, they might rejoin that entrusting to Defender and anyone willing to do it the task of defending that particular norm because there is no overarching enforcer gives us no reason to trust that they will comply with the rule of law when going to war.

But perhaps this would be too hasty a response. Perhaps the absence of an overarching enforcer *is* guarantee of compliance with the rule of law. Or so Gillian K. Hadfield and Barry R. Weingast would argue. In a number of recent articles, including their contribution to this volume, they claim that compliance with the rule of law requires that private, decentralized actors be given an essential role in norm enforcement.[11] Two features of their account are worth highlighting here. First, they are not concerned with privatization understood as outsourcing to *for-profit* actors. Rather, they seek to defend the outsourcing of enforcement to non-state actors in general—whom they sometimes call private actors, sometimes decentralized actors. Second, theirs is a descriptive, social-scientific account of what a legal system is *qua* legal system—namely, a system of rules characterized by the rule of law. Contrastingly, my concern in this paper is to assess the normative case for and against privatization. Nonetheless, in so far as justifiably enforcing international moral norms requires adherence to the rule of law, if Hadfield and Weingast are right, justifiably enforcing those norms by means of war does require that an essential role be given to private actors.

Their argument for radical privatization goes like this. Each and every one of us is a self-interested maximizer, with competing understandings of the rules under which we can best live. It is in the interest of each and every one of us to live under a system that classifies those understandings into norms that warrant coercive enforcement and norms that do not warrant it. At the same time, in so far as specific enforcement decisions might go against our individual interests, we need incentives to comply with those decisions. Enter the rule of law. The rule of law obtains when rules and processes of norm-shaping (what they call classification), together with the enforcement of those norms, display the attributes of publicity, clarity, stability, and generality. It is important for two reasons. First, it is in our interest to live under the rule of law, in so far as those features of the legal system make it easier to pursue our own interests. Second, the fact that the legal system abides by the rule of law gives us a strong incentive to respect its pronouncements.

Herein lies the rub. Centralized classification institutions—for short, the state—with full control over enforcement processes in general and the use of violence in particular need not act transparently, impartially, and predictably when enforcing norms. This is because they have monopoly over the use of violence and can thus ensure compliance from transgressors and induce third parties to cooperate by threatening, coercing, and terrorizing those who are subject to their directives. By contrast, decentralized, private actors have no choice but to provide other private agents with incentives to cooperate with them when they enforce those norms—precisely because they lack such monopoly. The best way for them to do so is precisely to comply with the rule of law: if I know that private enforcer $E$ does not so comply, I will have no incentive to abide by and cooperate with its decisions—and every incentive to abide by and cooperate with the decisions of rule of law–compliant private enforcer $E^*$.

From the point of view of per bellum enforcement, Hadfield and Weingast's account is particularly interesting. Admittedly, they do not explicitly construe their argument as an argument about the international legal system, the international rule of law, and the enforcement of international moral norms through war. However, the international system can be aptly described as a system of states all of which are, in some important sense, self-interested maximizers. Moreover, there is no overarching norm-enforcer, in the form (for example) of an international army under the auspices of a world state with monopoly over the resort to war. Accordingly, the international system as it is closely resembles the domestic societies to which their argument is primarily intended to apply—and thus provides a natural habitat, as it were, for their model.

And yet, there are reasons to doubt that their model would work well in the case of war.[12] For a start, in so far as it relies on the importance of providing agents with incentives to comply with collective enforcement, and thereby of enforcers having incentives to act in such a way as to maximize compliance, the relevant distinction is not between state and private actors; rather, it is between centralized and decentralized actors. But as Alex Gourevitch notes, equating private—or non-official—actors with decentralized actors and *vice versa* is problematic.[13] In the context of war, in fact, it is *particularly* problematic. If the worry is that a *centralized* state or state-like classification system with monopoly over the use of violence lacks incentives to comply with the rule of law, and as there is no such system currently (the UN does not have monopoly of violence), there are no reasons *not* to entrust the task of enforcing the norm to decentralized *state* actors such as, in this instance, Defender itself under Chapter VI of the UN Charter.

Hadfield and Weingast might be willing to accept that point and be tempted to respond that so long as there are several states willing and able each to enforce international norms in any given case, the rule of law will obtain. To properly respect the rule of law, in this case, would mean that Defender's *state* would not have monopoly of the use of force as a means to defend its members from Aggressor: other states would be able to come to those members' defense, would have an incentive to comply with the rule of law, etc.[14]

I can see the force of this putative reply. It seems to me however that Hadfield and Weingast must commit themselves to understanding privatization not just as decentralization, but as the process by which enforcement decisions and tasks are devolved to, and taken up by, agents who are not acting in an *official* capacity—who are not, in other words, *state actors* of any kind. For if privatization so construed is a requirement of the rule of law in the domestic realm, it seems arbitrary not to think of it as a requirement of the rule of law in the international realm.

If I am right, their account calls for a decentralized *and private* enforcement system along the following lines: Defender, via its membership in the United Nations, has classified the protection of states' territorial integrity and national sovereignty as a norm, transgressions of which warrant defensive enforcement. If Defender has exclusive control over both the processes and institutions by which a putative aggressor is deemed to be in breach of international norms and the armed forces whose deployment will serve to enforce those norms, it has no incentive to comply with the rule of law, since it need not act in such a way as to incentivize third parties to comply with its decisions. By contrast, private actors would have such incentives and thus would maintain the rule of law even if they alone were authorized to decide whether to enforce the norm against aggression, so long as there would be several such enforcers *and* as they would comply with Defender's (and the UN's) authoritative guidance both on the conditions under which Aggressor is justifiably found in breach of the relevant moral norms and on the conditions under which defensive war is justified.

However, this application of the Hadfield-Weingast model to per bellum enforcement is not without problems. First, a decision to wage war exposes a number of agents to harm—not least the harm of reprisals at the hands of the enemy, but also the harms of an unsuccessful, badly conducted war. Although the consent of those agents is not required for enforcement to be justified in situations of extreme emergency (where, for example, a decision has to be made now whether to repel a rapidly advancing aggressor, failing which vast numbers of people will die), it is required in less urgent cases. I shall elaborate on this point in section V, but let me simply note here that this is why, in most countries, the decision to go to war is entrusted to elected representatives of the people.

Second, the Hadfield-Weingast model requires that private enforcers be able and willing to abide by the norms which are constitutive of the rule of law at all stages. It is not clear why, in a world of fully decentralized private enforcers, the latter would comply with the rule of law rather than outgun each other into terrorizing all of us into complying with their enforcement decisions (however haphazard and conflicting those decisions might be.) Moreover, even if private enforcers are able and willing to comply, it is imperative, first, that their decisions be open to appeal and, second, that there be only one ultimate, authoritative arbiter of the validity of those decisions.

Could Hadfield and Weingast object to the last point that such is the role of the state as a *classification* system, not as an *enforcement* system? I doubt it. For if, in a given case, the state finds that a private enforcer's decision to go to war was not in fact made transparently and by appeal to publicly shared norms, respect for the rule of law requires that they be stopped. In so deciding, the state does not merely pronounce on the soundness of that decision: it interferes in the enforcement process itself.[15]

Finally, state officials themselves may well have incentives to comply with the rule of law (as applied to war) when deciding whether to go to war in defense of the norm of aggression. Most clearly, on the international stage, they may well have strong incentives so to comply vis-à-vis other states, whose cooperation is needed in the form of non-interference with collective enforcement. At home, they might also have incentives to comply with the rule of law vis-à-vis their compatriots. In so far as *elected* state officials in the end vote for or against the war, their reelection prospects might well depend on how well they are seen by their constituents to respect the rule of law. Even if they are not elected, their continuing political survival might depend on their willingness to subject their decision to go to war to the rule of law.[16]

Hadfield and Weingast are not convinced by this very last point: as they see it, more enforcers would themselves be needed to sanction state officials, who would themselves have to be induced or threatened to do their job properly, failing which they would have to be sanctioned by yet another layer of enforcers—and so on, endlessly, in an expensive infinite regress.[17] By way of reply: having one set of "secondary enforcers" to control and sanction "primary enforcers" might be enough; if it is not enough, it might be the best that we can do. As has long been responded to those who raise a similar objection to the very idea of binding a sovereign to his own laws, sovereignty need not reside in one unitary actor but can vest in a multiplicity of institutional actors who check and balance one another. This does not solve the problem of regress, but it does somewhat alleviate it.[18] To evaluate Hadfield and Weingast's response, we would need to compare this state of affairs with one in which violent enforcement is devolved to private enforcers. They give us no reason to think that the latter would always do better than the former irrespective of the contingent features of the case.

To recapitulate, I am not persuaded that the Hadfield-Weingast model applies to the *per bellum* enforcement of international moral norms. However, even if I am right, it does not follow that private *per bellum* enforcement is morally objectionable. In fact, I make a qualified case for it in section V. Beforehand, however, it is worth considering an influential and recent argument against privatization.

## IV. Against the Privatization of War: Harel's Argument

The claim that war should not be left to private agents is not new—though it has not always been held.[19] It applies both to the decision to wage war in the first instance and to the decision to entrust the task of fighting the war to this or that agent. As applied to the first decision, it is best expressed by the just war requirement of competent authority, to the effect that the right to wage war vests in a state, coalition of states, a quasi-state such as a national liberation movement, or in a people as a whole rising up against a foreign invader. As applied to the second decision, it is most often couched as a prohibition on the use of private soldiers such as mercenaries, and private armies such as private military corporations. The literature on mercenaries and germane phenomena is vast; the literature on legitimate authority less so.[20] Of the many objections leveled against the privatization of the resort to war and the privatization of armed forces, one in particular recurs which has been powerfully articulated by Alon Harel—to wit, in so far as war is morally justified as a means to defend the state's interests and is thus an essentially public enterprise, it can be conducted only by state agents—failing which it would no longer *be what it is*.[21]

This objection to privatization differs from other, standard objections that advert to the supposed instrumental failures of privatized war (such as the fact, for example, that mercenaries are supposedly less likely than regular soldiers to abide by the laws of war.) Rather, it adverts to the intrinsic feature of war of national defense.[22] As it is somewhat complex, it is worth formalizing as follows:

(1)  A war of national self-defense is by definition waged for the sake of the state's interests and in the name of the state, and every one of its constitutive acts must be carried out in the light of that fact.

(2)  Agents who act in the interests and name of the state must (if they are to succeed in doing so) act out of "fidelity of deference" to the state's judgment in the matter, and not out of "fidelity to [their own] reason."

(3)  Fidelity of deference "requires the existence of a practice which integrates the political and the bureaucratic in the execution of the relevant functions."[23]

(4)  Private agents are not able to fulfill this integrative function. Therefore, (5) the privatization of war cannot deliver the good of national security.[24]

This is an interesting argument, particularly in the light of claims (2) and (3). For the practice that enables agents to defer to the state's judgments has features that closely resemble the rule of law: agents that take part in the practice (here, the practice of war) abide by norms that have been deliberated upon over time, that are predictable, action-guiding, and adopted on the basis of those agents' impartial judgments as to what is in the state's interests, and not on the basis of their own, private, individual preferences. Thus, although Harel would not dissent from Hadfield and Weingast's construal of the rule of law and its importance, he draws the radically different conclusion that private actors ought not to be given *any role* in the enforcement of moral norms in general and international moral norms in particular. His claim applies to the decision to resort to war as well as to the decision to entrust the task of fighting the war to specific agents; it also implies that a state simply ought not passively to let private actors fight in the war (as when paramilitary forces outside state control fight alongside the regular army without authorization to do so.)

Is Harel on surer footing than Hadfield and Weingast? Consider claim (1). It assumes that, in so far as a war of national defense is just, it aims to protect the state's legitimate interests in the political communal goods of territorial integrity and political sovereignty. However, there are reasons to resist his statist construal of wars of national defense. A state *qua* state does not have interests that are not reducible to the interests of its individual members. Thus, to say that the state has a particular interest can only be a shortcut to express the view that individual members of that state jointly have that interest, which they collectively further through state institutions. Second, even if we grant Harel his understanding of the state, it does not follow that a war in defense of those interests *ipso facto* has a just cause. War kills, and as many just war theorists have noted, one can legitimately wonder whether the protection of those interests *alone* justifies killing. Suppose that Aggressor can invade Defender *without shedding a drop of blood*. Would Defender's soldiers be morally entitled to kill Aggressor's? I do not think so. Soldiers, on the battlefield, defend their lives and limbs, and those of their comrades, as much as if not more than the communal values of territorial integrity and state sovereignty. As a matter of principle, for a Defender soldier to kill an Aggressor soldier *merely* on the grounds that the latter is contributing to encroaching on the integrity of Defender's territory and self-governing institutions is wholly out of proportion to his individual, marginal contribution to the resulting harm. What justifies this act of killing, rather, is the fact that the Aggressor soldier will kill the Defender soldier if the latter makes any attempt to resist by force, even non-lethal force, instead of surrendering his legitimate interests in political communal goods.[25]

If I am right, a war of national self-defense should be construed and morally assessed, not as a war in defense of the state's interests in territorial integrity and political sovereignty but, rather, as a war in preemptive defense of its individual members' (soldiers' and civilians' alike) *combined* interests in those communal goods, as well as in their life and bodily integrity. Accordingly, such a war is not waged in the name of the state so much as in the name of its individual members taken singly (in so far as their lives and bodily integrity are at stake) and jointly (in so far as communal political goods are at stake.)

Those remarks point to a crucial difference between Harel's understanding of war and mine. On my account, as I noted in section III *pace* Hadfield and Weingast, there is considerable space for the articulation and expression of collective political judgments regarding the resort to war—precisely because some of the interests at issue, and the norms which protect those interests, are communal and political—whose defense is likely to expose the citizenry as a whole to the harms of war. At the same time, there is also considerable space for the articulation and expression of individual judgments in the matter—precisely because some of the interests are individual interests.

If so (*contra* claim (2)), it is by no means clear that agents who act in defense of all of those interests (who use force, in other words) must always and in every single one of their war-related acts defer to the state's judgments. If my life is under threat from a wrongdoer, as it will be on the battlefield, I may use my own judgment to evaluate the soundness of the orders that I am given. I may not have reason to believe that those order are unlawful and/or immoral. But I may have reason to believe that my commanding officer, though acting in good faith, has made an erroneous judgment call, as a result of which I (and indeed my comrades) may well die needlessly. It is hard to see why I may nevertheless not draw on my judgment to query those orders. The same considerations apply, *a fortiori*, when I have reasons to believe that the orders I am giving are unlawful and/or immoral, and that I might be led to compromise my moral integrity by killing people who ought not, in fact, to be killed. State officials, after all, might and indeed often do get it wrong, and using my own judgment is my ultimate safeguard against being turned into an instrument for wrongful killings.

The claim that there is space for the expression of private judgments in war opens two fruitful lines of inquiry. First, it raises the question of whether and when soldiers rightfully disobey orders. There is a rich literature on this issue, which I will set aside here.[26] Instead, I want to focus on a second, less obvious question, to wit, whether and when agents whose individual fundamental interests in remaining alive, not being aimed, and not being oppressed by Aggressors, may rightfully entrust the task of self-defense to actors other than state officials. I believe that they may—a claim on which I shall expand in the next section. At this juncture, let me highlight a difficulty with Harel's argument. He would resist the claim that individuals have a rightful say in who is best placed to defend them, on the grounds (affirmed by claim (3)) that only Defender's officials are sufficiently meshed into the practices and processes of the state itself to act out of fidelity of deference. By his own admission, his argument against privatization does not apply to other kinds of wars, for example wars of humanitarian intervention against another state. This is because interveners, who by definition are outsiders in relation to that state, are not integrated in the latter's bureaucratic and political war-making institutions; nor are they integrated in the state structures of the intervention's beneficiaries, since those individuals precisely do not have a state to begin with. Now, he seems willing to concede that such wars *can* be just, notwithstanding the fact that they are fought privately (on his own conception of "private.")[27] Let us assume that he is right. Let us also concede that a war of national self-defense, if it is to *count as such* as opposed to a private war, must be waged and fought by public agents acting out of fidelity to deference. Here is the difficulty: why should that *matter*? If wars of intervention can be just though they are by definition private, why must wars of national self-defense be fought by state actors on pain of being unjust? After all, in the end, we want to know whether that war is morally justified all things considered. Whether it is fought in accordance with their nature, as it were, is relevant. If a conflict fought in defense of those national interests by private agents (understood as agents who act out of fidelity to reason and out of fidelity of deference) would in fact succeed at securing those goods, we would have no intrinsic reason to object to it as unjust. For what it is worth, I suspect that Harel would resist the thought that such a war would succeed. But if so, he would have no choice but to rely on precisely the kind of instrumental reasons which he seeks to eschew.[28]

## V. Privatizing War: A Hybrid View

Whereas Hadfield and Weingast claim that the rule of law can obtain only if private enforcers are given an essential role in enforcing moral norms in general and (on my reconstruction of their position) international moral norms in particular, Harel argues that it can obtain only if they are given *no* such role—at least in cases of national defense. In this section, I draw on my objections to both positions to defend a hybrid normative account of the privatization of war.

*Pace* Hadfield and Weingast, the state, or as the case may be state-like institutions, acting on behalf and at the behest of those who are subject to their directives, ought to decide whether or not war should be waged—in most cases. The qualification is crucially important. Recall that on my account, the enforcement of moral norms that ought to be turned into legal norms is justified so long as it complies with the rule of law broadly construed (section II). Sometimes, however, the rule of law proviso cannot be met. Suppose for example that in the face of Aggressor's invasion, Defender's institutions have collapsed, leaving it to Defender's citizens and residents to take matters in their own hands—not *qua* citizens necessarily, but rather *qua* individuals acting in a private capacity. Under those circumstances, in the absence of any institutional oversight, even if the individuals left behind do as much as they can to comply with the norms of war, the acts by which they enforce the norm against aggression do not comply with the rule of law (or at any rate are very unlikely to comply with it.) To conclude that they are not justified in defending themselves is to condemn them to moral ignominy as a result of factors over which they have no control. A proponent of the view that war ought to be construed and justified as an operation of norm enforcement can and should concede, then, that in such cases, compliance with the rule of law is not a necessary condition for just enforcement. Put more generally, and as I argue elsewhere, it is not a necessary condition of a just war of defensive enforcement that it be waged by a legitimate authority such as a state, quasi-state, or coalition thereof: when institutions have collapsed, for example, war can be just even though there is no state-like institution to declare it and authorize its constitutive acts in compliance with the rule of law.[29]

However, in non-emergency cases, matters are somewhat different. An agent, be it individual or collective, who wages war against Aggressor *on behalf of* the latter's victims (his compatriots or, as the case may be, distant strangers) exposes those victims themselves as well as third parties to the harms of war. Unless those individuals are under a duty to allow themselves to be so harmed, their consent is required. This point applies to the case of war the deeper anti-paternalistic principle that I may not be harmed for my own good unless I do not, or would not, consent to it. To be sure, there are huge difficulties in determining what it means for a set of individual agents to consent, or not, to a war: whether they can in a given case be deemed truly to have consented; whether their explicit consent to the war is necessary, or whether their presumptive consent is sufficient.[30] These difficulties are not unique to war, however: they inhere in any and all accounts of democratic decision-making. That being said, decisions that are likely to cause innocent people supererogatory severe hardship albeit for their own good must, if they are to be legitimate, somehow elicit those people's consent, whether presumptive or explicit, whether direct or indirect. If this is right, it must be devolved either to those individuals themselves, or to their properly elected representatives.

On this point, thus, I agree with Harel that not all acts of enforcement can be legitimately carried out by private actors. The crucial question, at this juncture, is whether, once the *decision to wage war* has been made, private actors may be authorized to *fight the war*. I believe that they may. War harms—sometimes grievously so—individuals in their life and limbs—both those who fight and those on whose behalf they fight. It is precisely for that reason that, as I have just noted, they should have a say in the decision to wage in the first instance. But if that is correct, then there is no reason to rule out from the outset, as a matter of principle, the possibility that non-state actors might be in as good a position as—indeed, a better position than—state actors, to fight that war and thereby protect those individuals. Put differently: the imperative of enforcing international moral norms that protect collective interests is itself rooted in the imperative of protecting individuals' fundamental moral rights. That imperative underpins a conclusion that Harel does endorse, namely that only the state can decide whether to go to war in non-emergency cases (though he defends that conclusion on different grounds). However, it *also* underpins the claim that *instrumental* considerations are decisive when working out who may actually fight the war. Suppose that, in a given case, private actors are better able than official actors to protect those norms. For example, Defender's armed forces are not able on their own to thwart Aggressor's unwarranted attack; however, Defender can enlist help from private actors such as for-profit firms, perhaps, and also foreign volunteers, and in so doing successfully defend itself while respecting legally enshrined, morally justified requirements of the just war. Given that, *ex hypothesi,* it thereby succeeds at protecting individuals' fundamental moral rights, it is hard to see why it is morally unjustified in doing so. By that token, note, it is not clear at all that private soldiers *must* be given an *essential* role in fighting wars, as Hadfield and Weingast would have it. For in just the same way as private fighters might in a given case be better than state soldiers at fighting a just war, state soldiers might in another case be better at doing so than private soldiers.

Of course, whether private fighters can help defend Defender's territorial integrity and political sovereignty and thereby its individual members' fundamental human rights while abiding by the rule of law, is contingent on whether or not they act in the light of the rule of law as opposed to their private judgment; it also depends on whether the just war requirements are enshrined in publicly available, transparent, prospective, and predictable rules. If Defender's legal system does display those qualities (for example, through clearly articulated military law), it may be that those private fighters ought to be incorporated into Defender's armed forces, or at any rate be clearly subject to their command—and treated in exactly the same ways as regular combatants. If Defender's legal system does not display those qualities, private fighters can always refer to the international law of armed conflict.

None of this is to deny that, perhaps more often than not, private fighters act contrary to the rule of law—but then again, so do regular combatants. None of this is to deny, either, that incorporating private fighters into regular state armed forces raises serious difficulties—particularly when those fighters are employed by for-profit military corporations. In particular, the latter's involvement in wars might lead politicians who depend on their financial support to start or prolong wars for reasons that have nothing to do with the national interest. Less repugnantly, there is a risk that, under the terms of their employment contract, individual private fighters are accountable primarily to their employer, and not to the state on whose behalf they are in fact supposed to fight. Those are well-documented difficulties, to which greater regulation is an equally well-documented response.[31] *If* regulation fails, and if, therefore, the private *per bellum* enforcement of international norms simply cannot comply with the rule of law, or, less strongly, is less likely to comply with the rule of law than state *per bellum* enforcement, then we ought to rule it out in favor of the latter. That, however, is (to repeat) a contingent point, which does not condemn private enforcement as a matter of principle.

## VI. Conclusion

Let us conclude. Both Hadfield and Weingast on the one hand, and Harel on the other hand, would on my reconstruction endorse the following two claims: (1) the *per bellum* enforcement of international moral norms is morally justified only if it complies with the rule of law; (2) the rule of law obtains when (2a) relations between individuals are regulated and constrained by moral norms which are publicly available, prospective, predictable, and determinate; (2b) the enforcement of those norms is constrained and regulated by publicly available, prospective, predictable, and determinate rules, and (2c) enforcers act impartially in the light of those rules rather than on the basis of their personal preferences. From that premise, Hadfield and Weingast draw the conclusion that a system of enforcement must (if it is to secure individuals' cooperation with enforcement) give an essential role to private actors, indeed that an enforcement system need not give any role to state enforcers so long as the state complies with (2a). This is anathema to Harel, who claims, on the contrary, that functions essentially discharged for the sake of the state's interests can only be properly carried out by state agents. In the case of war, their respective arguments pertain both to the decision to go to war in the first instance and to the decision to authorize private actors to fight (in) the war.

I have argued that those arguments do not support their purported conclusions. Whether or not private enforcers may decide to wage war, or fight in the war, depends on whether the consent of those who are wrongfully harmed by the war must be sought on pain of the war being unjust, and on the extent to which they do as well as, or better than, state soldiers at fighting a just war. However, I have not denied, nor sought to deny, that the Hadfield-Weingast model works for the case of municipal enforcement; nor have I denied, or sought to deny, that Harel's skepticism of private enforcement might well be warranted in the case of punishment. For what it is worth, I suspect that war is no different from municipal enforcement in general and punishment in particular, and that those cases also call for a hybrid account of privatization. That, however, is a task for another paper.

## NOTES

1 An earlier version of this paper was presented at the Oxford Jurisprudence Discussion Group on May 12, 2016, and at an informal discussion group on privatization in June 2016. I am grateful to participants in both groups for very helpful discussions, in particular Hasan Dindjer, Timothy Endicott, John Gardner, Ian Loader, Francesca Menichelli, and Lucia Zedner. Max Harris, Melissa Schwartzberg, and Frederick Wilmot-Smith provided a raft of written comments, for which I also thank them.

2 Iain Atack, *The Ethics of Peace and War: From State Security to World Community* (Edinburgh, UK: Edinburgh University Press, 2005); A. J. Coates, *The Ethics of War* (Manchester, UK: Manchester University Press, 1997): 127; Helen Dexter, "The 'New War' on Terror, Cosmopolitanism and the 'Just War' Revival," *Government and Opposition* 43, no. 1 (2008): 55–78; David Held, "Violence, Law and Justice in a Global Age," (2001), available at www.theglobalsite.ac.uk; Mary Kaldor, *New & Old Wars*, 2nd

ed. (Cambridge: Polity, 2006); David Rodin, *War and Self-Defense* (Oxford: Clarendon Press, 2002); Michael Walzer, *Just and Unjust War: A Moral Argument with Historical Illustrations,* 4th ed. (New York: Basic Books, 2006): 59; Paul W. Kahn, "The Paradox of Riskless Warfare," *Philosophy and Public Policy Quaterly* 22, no. 3 (2002): 1–7.

3 I offer a qualified defense of for-profit privatization of war in Cécile Fabre, "In Defence of Mercenarism," *British Journal of Political Science* 40, no. 3 (2010): 539–59.

4 I am grateful to Hasan Dindjer for helping me circumscribe the paper in this way.

5 I reject punitive wars for the same reasons as adduced by David Luban and Jeff McMahan. (See David Luban, "War as Punishment," *Philosophy & Public Affairs* 39, no. 4 (2011): 299–330; Jeff McMahan, "Aggression and Punishment," in *War-Essays in Political Philosophy,* ed. Larry May (Cambridge: Cambridge University Press, 2008).) Note that the distinction between punitive and defensive force does not make sense if one endorses a defensive conception of punishment, such as Warren Quinn's or Victor Tadros's. I assume that punishment is not the same at all as defense. (See Warren Quinn, "The Right to Threaten and the Right to Punish," *Philosophy & Public Affairs* 14, no. 4 (1985): 327–73; Victor Tadros, *The Ends of Harm: The Moral Foundations of Criminal Law* (Oxford: Oxford University Press, 2011).) I should say at the outset that I am generally skeptical of the view that wars ought to be understood as operations of norm enforcement, but that view is widely held, so I shall take it for granted here. I express my skepticism in Cécile Fabre, "Cosmopolitanism and Wars of Self-Defence," in *The Morality of Defensive War,* eds. Cécile Fabre and Seth Lazar (Oxford: Oxford University Press, 2014).

6 Of the many characterizations of the rule of law, I loosely draw on Jeremy Waldron's. See Jeremy Waldron, "The Concept and the Rule of Law," *Georgia Law Review* 43, no. 1 (2008): 1–61.

7 Or so I assume, though the idea of international law was not by any means uncontroversial fifty years ago. For a recent philosophical account thereof, see Ronald Dworkin, "A New Philosophy for International Law," *Philosophy & Public Affairs* 41, no. 1 (2013): 2–30.

8 See, e.g., James Crawford, "International Law and the Rule of Law," *Adelaide Law Review* 24, no. 1 (2003): 3–12; Jeremy Waldron, "Are Sovereigns Entitled to the Benefit of the International Rule of Law?," *European Journal of International Law* 22, no. 2 (2011): 315–43; Peter Rijpkema, "The Concept of a Global Rule of Law," *Transnational Legal Theory* 4, no. 2 (2013): 167–96; Brian Z. Tamanaha, *On the Rule of Law: History, Politics, Theory* (Cambridge: Cambridge University Press, 2006), ch. 10; Mattias Kumm, "International Law in National Courts: The International Rule of

Law and the Limits of the Internationalist Model," *Virginia Journal of International Law* 44, no. 1 (2003): 19–33.

9 I use the case of a war of self-defense against aggression to illustrate my points, but the latter also apply, *mutatis mutandis*, to wars of humanitarian intervention.

10 I say "something like" international humanitarian law, because there is one sense in which humanitarian law does not adequately reflect the morality of war: it permits the deliberate killing of all combatants, irrespective of the justness of the war for which they fight. Many just war theorists, notably Michael Walzer, hold that humanitarian law has got it right, morally speaking (Michael Walzer, *Just and Unjust War: A Moral Argument with Historical Illustrations*, 5th ed. (New York: Basic Books, 2015). But many others claim, on the contrary, that combatants who fight for a just cause ought not to be killed (Jeff McMahan, *Killing in War* (Oxford: Oxford University Press, 2009); Cécile Fabre, *Cosmopolitan War* (Oxford: Oxford University Press, 2012); C. A. J. Coady, *Morality and Political Violence* (Cambridge: Cambridge University Press, 2008); Helen Frowe, *Defensive Killing* (Oxford: Oxford University Press, 2014); Rodin, *War and Self-Defense*).

11 Gillian K. Hadfield and Barry R. Weingast, "Is Rule of Law an Equilibrium Without (Some) Private Enforcement?," in this volume. See also Gillian K. Hadfield and Barry R. Weingast, "Law without the State: Legal Attributes and the Coordination of Decentralized Collective Punishment," *Journal of Law and Courts* 1, no. 1 (2013): 3–34; Gillian K. Hadfield and Barry R. Weingast, "Microfoundations of the Rule of Law," *Annual Review of Political Science* 17, no. 1 (2014): 21–42; Gillian K. Hadfield and Barry R. Weingast, "What Is Law? A Coordination Model of the Characteristics of Legal Order," *Journal of Legal Analysis* 4, no. 2 (2012): 471–514.

12 This is in addition to doubts raised about the model in general by Alex Gourevitch and Alex Guerrero. See Alex Gourevitch, "What is Politics without the State? A Reply to Hadfield and Weingast," in this volume; Alex A. Guerrero, "Comments on 'Is Rule of Law an Equilibrium Without Private Ordering?,'" presented at original conference.

13 Gourevitch, this volume.

14 I am grateful to Melissa Schwartzberg for suggesting this argumentative move.

15 This point applies to the model in general, and not merely to its application to war.

16 On the question of whether rulers in general, and wicked rulers in particular, have incentives to comply with the rule of law, see the debate between H. L. A. Hart and Lon Fuller, and the debate between Matthew Kramer and Nigel Simmonds. H. L. A. Hart, *The Concept of Law*, 1st ed. (Oxford: Clarendon Press, 1961); Lon Fuller, *The Morality of Law*, 1st ed.

(Yale: Yale University Press, 1964); Matthew H. Kramer, *In Defense of Legal Positivism: Law without Trimmings* (Oxford: Oxford University Press, 1999); Nigel E. Simmonds, *Central Issues in Jurisprudence: Justice, Law and Rights*, 1st ed. (London: Sweet and Maxwell, 1986).

17 Hadfield and Weingast, this volume. Of course, to the extent that they would agree that private enforcers do need to be kept in check by the state, their position also suffers from the problem of infinite regress.

18 The point is well put in Waldron, "Are Sovereigns Entitled," 318.

19 Grotius famously allows that private wars can be morally justified. Hugo Grotius, *The Rights of War and Peace*, ed. Richard Tuck. (Indianapolis, IN: Liberty Fund, 2005[1625]), bk I, ch. 4. For a fascinating history of the process by which Western states gradually restricted the privatization of war (particularly mercenarism), see Sarah Percy, *Mercenaries: The History of a Norm in International Relations* (Oxford: Oxford University Press, 2007).

20 For recent exceptions, see Fabre, *Cosmopolitan War*, ch. 4; Jonathan Parry, "Just War Theory, Legitimate Authority, and Irregular Belligerency," *Philosophia* 43, no. 1 (2015): 175–96; Christopher J. Finlay, "Legitimacy and Non-State Political Violence," *Journal of Political Philosophy* 18, no. 3 (2010): 287–312.

21 Alon Harel, *Why Law Matters* (Oxford: Oxford University Press, 2014), ch. 3. This chapter is based on a paper he co-authored with Avihay Dorfman (Avihay Dorfman and Alon Harel, "The Case against Privatization," *Philosophy & Public Affairs* 41, no. 1 (2013): 67–102.) I refer to the views set out therein as his rather than theirs partly because he has made some changes to the article itself.

22 I reject those and other objections in Fabre, "In Defence of Mercenarism." For other intrinsic objections to privatization in general, see Michael Sandel, *What Money Can't Buy: The Moral Limits of Markets* (London: Penguin Books, 2013); Debra Satz, "Markets, Privatization, and Corruption," *Social Research* 80, no. 4 (2013): 993–1008; Debra Satz, "Some (Largely) Ignored Problems with Privatization," in this volume.

23 Harel, *Why Law Matters*, 89.

24 On Harel's account of a private agent, a state official in fact acts as a private agent just if she acts, not on the basis of the aforementioned features, but rather on the basis of her own reasoned judgment—and this even if she acts in defense of her state's interests. By implication, being in the employ of a non-state actor is not a necessary condition for being a private agent—contrary to my own account of privatization. In line with my account however, it is a sufficient condition, simply because, as per the combination of (3) and (4), only state agents can act out of fidelity to deference.

25 For a fuller argument, see Fabre, "Cosmopolitanism and Wars of Self-Defence." The bloodless invasion problem was first raised by Richard Norman and David Rodin. See Richard J. Norman, *Ethics, Killing, and War* (Cambridge: Cambridge University Press, 1995); David Rodin, *War and Self-Defense*; David Rodin, "The Myth of National Self-Defence," in *The Morality of Defensive War*, eds. Cécile Fabre and Seth Lazar (Oxford: Oxford University Press, 2014). See also Thomas Hurka, "Proportionality in the Morality of War," *Philosophy & Public Affairs* 33, no. 1 (2005): 34–66; Jeff McMahan, "What Rights May be Defended by Means of War," in *The Morality of Defensive War*, eds. Cécile Fabre and Seth Lazar (Oxford: Oxford University Press, 2014).

26 For Harel's view on this, see Harel, *Why Law Matters*, 104–5. See also David Estlund, "On Following Orders in an Unjust War," *Journal of Political Philosophy* 15, no. 2 (2007): 213–34. For a classic defense of the view that soldiers must exercise their own judgment about the moral status of the war they are asked to fight, see McMahan, *Killing in War*.

27 Harel, *Why Law Matters*, 99 fn. 59.

28 For a powerful defense of instrumental objections to privatization, in response to Harel's view, see John Gardner, "The Evil of Privatization," *Social Science Research Network* (2014), available at papers.ssrn.com.

29 See Fabre, *Cosmopolitan War*, ch. 4. I am grateful to Timothy Endicott and Melissa Schwartzberg for helping me clarify my thoughts here. Interestingly, Harel would agree with me on this point. See Harel, *Why Law Matters*, ch. 4.

30 See Fabre, *Cosmopolitan War*, sections 4.3 and 5.5.2.

31 I develop those points at some length elsewhere, specifically in the context of mercenarism. See Fabre, "In Defence of Mercenarism."

# INDEX

237; relative to other values, 148; and
the rule of law, 308
Trudeau, Pierre, 212
Trump, President Donald, 1

UN Charter, Chapter VI of, 303, 307
Underwriters Laboratories (UL), 86
United States Postal Service, 236

Value pluralism, 121, 132, 134–136,
141n25. *See also* Basic structure; Civil
society
Vogel, Steven, 179, 180

Waldron, Jeremy, 263
Wallace, George, and opposition to
integration of the University of
Alabama, 85
Waller, Maureen R., 183
War: and conscription, 168n47; in
defense against an aggressor, 304;
in defense of others, 307, 315;
and humanitarian intervention,

313; and international norms, 300;
the morality of killing in, 166n25,
311–313, 320n10; and paramilitary
participation, 311; political costs of,
38; and punishment, 301; and the
scope of executive power, 40–44;
and the use of mercenaries or private military corporations, 11, 14,
20, 37–46, 152, 153, 166n21, 238,
310, 316, 317
Warner, Mildred, 218
Weber, Max, 223, 242, 243n2, 266,
271n14
Weingast, Barry, 276–278, 280, 282–
293, 295, 300, 305–309, 311, 314, 317
Wellbeing, 148, 149, 163
Wellman, Christopher, 160
Williamson, Oliver, 203
Woods, Ngaire, 180
World Trade Organization (WTO), and
intellectual property rules, 189
World Wildlife Fund, and the Forestry
Stewardship Council, 191